Inside information

British government and the media

EDITED BY

Annabelle May and Kathryn Rowan

CONSTABLE
London

First published in Great Britain 1982
by Constable and Company
10 Orange Street London, WC2H 7EG
Introductory material Copyright © 1982 by
Annabelle May and Kathryn Rowan

Hardback ISBN 0 09 464160 9
Paperback ISBN 0 09 464190 0

Set in Times 10pt by
Rowland Phototypesetting Limited
Bury St Edmunds, Suffolk
Printed in Great Britain by
St Edmundsbury Press

466

In the same series

Journalists at work
Jeremy Tunstall

The making of a TV series
Philip Elliott

The political impact of mass media
Colin Seymour-Ure

The manufacture of news
Stan Cohen and Jock Young (editors)

Children in front of the small screen
Grant Noble

The Fleet Street disaster
Graham Cleverley

The silent watchdog
David Murphy

The media are American
Jeremy Tunstall
(USA: Columbia University Press)

Putting reality together
Philip Schlesinger

The sociology of rock
Simon Frith
(USA: Pantheon)

Newspaper history
George Boyce, James Curran, Pauline Wingate (editors)

Deciding what's news
Herbert J. Gans
(USA: Pantheon)

The international news agencies
Oliver Boyd-Barrett

The bounds of freedom
Brian Lapping (editor)
(not USA)

---

*This book is the fifteenth volume in a series
edited by Jeremy Tunstall and devoted to
explorations of the interrelationships between
society and all forms of communication media.*

Acknowledgments

The publishers would like to thank the following for their kind permission to quote material: Macmillan for Geoffrey Robertson's 'Law for the press' and Philip Elliott's 'All the world's a stage' from J. Curran (ed.) *The British Press*, and Anthony Smith's *Television and political life* (also St Martin's Press); Campbell Thomson & McLaughlin for Anthony King and Anne Sloman's *Westminster and beyond*; Junction Books for David Leigh's *The frontiers of secrecy*; *The Listener* for James Cornford's 'The right to know secrets'; *The Guardian* for Chris Cook and John Stevenson's 'Political hide and seek' and David Leigh's 'Ten years that brought the law into contempt'; the *New Statesman* for Duncan Campbell's 'The D Notice quangette' and Bruce Page's 'The secret constitution: the Cabinet committee system under James Callaghan'; André Deutsch for Keith Middlemas's *Politics in industrial society*; Chatto and Windus for Leslie Chapman's *Your disobedient servant*; Granada Television for John Mackintosh and Angus Maude's *State of the Nation: Parliament*; Pergamon Press for Nevil Johnson's 'The Leviathan at the centre' in *In Search of the constitution*; the BBC for Anthony Jay and Jonathan Lynn's 'Yes Minister'; Hodder & Stoughton for Brian Sedgemore's *The secret constitution*; Jonathan Cape for Joe Haines's *The politics of power*; A. D. Peters for Peter Kellner and Lord Crowther-Hunt's *The civil servants*; Croom Helm for Roger Williams's *The nuclear power decisions*; *Index on censorship* for Peter Taylor's 'Reporting Northern Ireland'; *Political Quarterly* for Keith Middlemas's 'Cabinet secrecy and the Crossman Diaries'; Hutchinson for John P. Mackintosh's *The government and politics of Britain*; Hamish Hamilton and Holt, Rinehart and Winston for Richard Crossman's *Diaries of a Cabinet Minister*; Michael Joseph and Messrs Little Brown for Harold Wilson's *The Labour Government* (U.S. title: *Personal record*); Collins for Douglas Hurd's *Sketch of a government 1970–74*; W. H. Allen for James Margach's *The abuse of power*; Oxford University Press for Colin Seymour-Ure's 'Presidential power, press secretaries and communication'; *New Society* and Ronald Dworkin for 'Open government or closed'; Harper & Row for David Curzon's 'The generic secrets of government decision making' from Itzhak Galnoor's *Government secrecy in democracies*; *The Sunday Times* for Martin Bailey and Charles Medawar's 'How useful are MP's questions?'; H.M.S.O. for extracts from the Franks Report (Cmnd 5104) vols 3 and 4, the Annan Report (Cmnd 6753), Third Report from the Defence Committee (HC 773 Appendix 12 and

6

Leonard Downie's oral evidence given in the above; the Open University for extracts from tapes by the Audio-Visual Research Group (1978) – David McKie, 'The Lobby and other matters', Henry James 'The role of the COI', W. E. H. Whyte 'The F.C.O. and the media'; Mr Tony Benn for 'Manifestos and mandarins'; Hugo Young for 'The Thatcher style of government'; Stuart Dresner for *Open government: Lessons from America*; and Michael Flood and Robin Grove-White for 'The political impact of nuclear security' from *Nuclear prospects*.

Contents

8   *Contents*

PART FOUR: STAGNATION?

Introduction

No British government during the last twenty years, whether Labour or Conservative, has made a genuine attempt to open up the processes of government to public scrutiny. But during this time the power of the state has continued to increase. And the growth of information technology has meant that the state now knows, or can easily find out, far more about the individual than ever before. The citizen, however, has become increasingly excluded from this information explosion. The government allows him little or no opportunity to participate in informed debate about the vital issues which affect his day-to-day life.

Decisions about policy issues of fundamental importance, such as energy or defence, are increasingly removed from the wider political arena. They have become the province of small, élite groups of policy-makers. All too often, these groups appear to have a vested interest in the outcome of their deliberations. Because of the diffusion of power into committees, even members of the Cabinet, the highest political executive, may no longer be aware which decisions have been taken, and why. Decisions taken in this way can lead to policy failure, as we aim to show. And in many cases the political and administrative machinery of British government has not adapted itself to cope successfully with the rapid changes of the twentieth century.

In a period of social, political and economic crisis, informed and open debate of all policy options is more desirable than ever before. Yet the response of successive governments has been to close their doors, and to secure them with an impressive battery of legislative locks and bolts. Britain has no written constitution. So the citizen has no 'right to know'. It is all too easy for the government to retreat into authoritarian and élitist 'we-know-best' attitudes. But ignorance is an outdated, and ultimately ineffective, means of social control – although fears about educating the lower orders do have a respectable pedigree in British political history.

Professor Peter Townsend, in a recent attack on the Thatcher government's plans to cut its statistical services, claims that by this proposal the government is, in fact, restricting democratic rights. In the guise of saving money and cutting manpower, these proposed cuts seek to 'divert, contain and reduce' possible criticisms of government policies. 'By restricting the flow of information,' argues Townsend, 'the government is restricting the right to free and open discussion of the industrial, economic and social conditions of Britain.'[1]

But in present-day Britain, free and open discussion is the prerogative of a privileged few. This book is an attempt to illustrate the theory and the practice of information control within the British system of government. We have used a wide range of source material. The field, of course, is enormous; necessarily, we have had to be selective.

Authoritarian views on information management lie at the heart of many of the values and assumptions which pervade our political culture. In a recent paper, Joan K. Stringer and J. J. Richardson discuss the ability of British government to define policy problems, and to manage the political agenda to their own advantage. Some problems, they claim, can fail to reach the political agenda, or even fail to be defined as problems at all, because of the way in which data on that particular policy area is collected, analysed and presented – or not presented – by the government. The present system, they argue, stifles public discussion. A more open system, they hope, 'would expose just what the government is up to'. They quote Peter Jay's statement that 'the conduct of public policy and the quality of politics improves or deteriorates in direct relation to the quality of public debate about it'; and go on to claim that if problems and policies were subjected to critical review from outside the government apparatus these same problems and policies would be identified and decided with a greater degree of attention to detail. To exemplify this point, they comment: 'Could the planners within the Department of Transport have gone on basing their motorway policies on inaccurate statistics for so long if the anti-motorway lobby had had the right of access to them? We think not.'[2]

Another aim in putting this book together was to draw attention to various key issues in the debate over official information, government secrecy and the role of the media. For it is not only the British political and bureaucratic élites who operate in a culture of secrecy; the mass media, too, are locked into this framework. They are part of our political system. In theory, the mass media should act as a free, two-way channel of communication between government and people. And the media do play a crucial role in the democratic process. Yet they are increasingly constrained – and intimidated – by legal and quasi-legal rules and conventions. Frequently, they seem content to accept official information at face value. It is easier, of course, to reproduce attitudes and assumptions which reinforce the status quo.

The book is divided into four parts. In Part One, Legislation, we look at the legal and quasi-legal framework of information control. This sets the parameters within which government releases information, and within which the media may report it. Unlike, for instance, the American Constitution, these are not a set of positive principles, but a series of negative constraints whose wide range and far-reaching scope may well be found surprising.

In Part Two, Interpretations, we illustrate the ways in which politicians and civil servants, journalists and academics, have interpreted their roles in this process of information management. Here, we are looking at informal behaviour: the reality, and not the myth. It becomes increasingly evident that senior members of the executive can, and frequently do, manipulate the system to their own advantage and for their own convenience.

With Part Three, Confrontations, the title is, perhaps, self-explanatory. Here, we have selected four case studies where a conflict has occurred between government ideology and what we will call, for the sake of convenience, 'the public interest'. In the discussion of nuclear power, and of the Concorde project, it is argued that traditional values of secrecy combined with closed systems of policy-making led, in each case, to policy failure. Reporting the crisis in Northern Ireland has placed a great strain on the media organizations. The pressure for an official consensus challenges the assumptions upon which broadcasting law and practice is based. The Crossman *Diaries* were written as a deliberate challenge to Britain's oligarchic political power. And while their publication was finally permitted, for the first time the Attorney-General was able to establish the principle of Cabinet secrecy on a legal footing. From now on, this sanction can be invoked to prevent or to penalize any future Cabinet leaks.

In Parts Two and Three, we concentrate on the last twenty years of British government, making comparisons with the American system where they seem relevant. With Part Four, we reach the present. Hugo Young, Political Editor of the *Sunday Times*, provides us with a lucid and entertaining account of Margaret Thatcher's government, its professed ideology and its day-to-day practices of information management. Official information, in this Prime Minister's view, is better seen as the property of the government than as ammunition for its critics.

REFERENCES

1. Peter Townsend, writing in *The Guardian*, 15 July 1981.
2. Joan K. Stringer and J. J. Richardson, 'Managing the political agenda: problem definition and policy making in Britain', *Parliamentary Affairs*, Vol. 33, No. 1, Winter 1980.

PART ONE

Legislation

This part is concerned with the legal and quasi-legal rules which both constrain the release of information by government and restrict the right of access to that information by the public. We do not claim to provide a comprehensive guide to all the legislation which affects the media. That would need several volumes. Instead, we have concentrated on the issues we believe to be important: the issues that illustrate the controversial nature of the legislation in this area. This part is subdivided into five sections: Official Secrets; Public Records (an area frequently overlooked in the discussion of official information); Law and the Press; Broadcasting and the State; and The D Notice System.

CHAPTER ONE

Official Secrets

Introduction

The Official Secrets Act

In a letter to *The Times* in 1920, a former Conservative Attorney-General (Sir Lionel Heald) commented that Section 2 of the [Official Secrets] Act is so restrictive that it 'makes it a crime without any possibility of defence to report the number of cups of tea consumed per week in a government department or the details of a new carpet in a minister's room'.[1]

British government is obsessed with secrecy. As Colin Seymour-Ure has pointed out, 'the right to know' is not a value deeply entrenched in British political culture.[2] This culture of secrecy is fostered by the absence of a written constitution. And it is further sustained by the operation of constitutional conventions, in addition to the legal constraints.

So before turning to the legal framework of information control, the subject of this first part, we will look briefly at two of these constitutional conventions. Perhaps the most important of them is the principle of collective Cabinet responsibility. Each individual minister is required to accept the decisions of the Cabinet, and to endorse the policies which underlie them. The Cabinet should, in other words, present a united front of public agreement. In recent years, this rule has been extended to junior ministers outside the Cabinet, who have no opportunity to participate in policy-making. Since the establishment of the Cabinet committee system (see pp. 126–33), it can also mean that ministers within the Cabinet are expected to endorse policy decisions of which they are ignorant. (See, for example, Lord Shinwell's claim that he did not know about the Attlee government's decision to make the atom bomb,[3] and, more recently, Hugo Young's account of the Thatcher Cabinet's decision to order the Trident missile system.[4]) It must be noted that the Labour government's EEC referendum – which acknowledged the fact that Cabinet members disagreed – marked a notable (and pragmatic) departure from this principle.

Another important convention in British political culture is the somewhat mystical doctrine of ministerial responsibility. Theoretically, every minister is answerable for the actions of his or her ministry, whether or not they are performed with his or her knowledge or consent. The corollary of this is obvious: it is that civil servants remain anonymous and unaccountable, whatever advice they may give or whatever blunders they may commit. So this convention, originally intended to ensure that ministers were accountable to Parliament, now serves to defend an increasingly centralized and secretive executive.

After looking at Parts Two and Three of this book, the reader might well come to the conclusion that these two principles are no more than myths. Certainly, they are convenient to both ministers and civil servants. They are useful within the two major political parties. And both conventions have been advanced as arguments against more open government (see Lord Trend's evidence to the Franks Committee, p. 139). They are important elements in the machinery of information management.

Our legal constraints are rooted in our political culture. In Britain, governments are given immense power by the threat of the Official Secrets Act, 'one of the bluntest of administrative instruments'.[5] The first Act, passed in 1889, concerned itself with spying and breaches of official trust. It was replaced in 1911 by an Act which had extended powers to include 'official' information which was not connected with national security. Section 1 of the 1911 Act concerned spying, and the communication of information to an enemy. This, on the whole, has not been controversial, apart from the notable case in 1962 (Chandler *v.* DPP) when it was used to prosecute and imprison six members of the Committee of 100, who had attempted to enter an airfield in a protest against nuclear weapons. It is Section 2 of the Act that has been a constant cause of controversy and debate. This Section makes it a criminal offence for any crown servant (from senior civil servants to private soldiers to temporary gardeners) to disclose *any information whatsoever* (regardless of its nature or importance) acquired in the nature of his or her work *to any 'unauthorized' person*. It is equally a crime to receive such information, knowing it to be unauthorized.

As Ronald Wraith points out, Section 2 provokes criticism because it is indiscriminate, though prosecutions under the Act have been relatively few (they need the consent of the Attorney-General). 'Authorization' is not a simple concept; and the Act does not define it.[6] Wraith argues that the indiscriminate nature of Section 2 makes it an objectionable measure. Does the fact that every crown servant must sign this Act subconsciously engender an attitude of mind whereby the citizen asking for information is expected to prove that he ought to have it, rather than the civil servant having to prove that he ought not to have it – 'perhaps the essential difference between "closed" and "open" systems of government'?

In the first extract, David Leigh, an investigative journalist currently working for *The Observer,* argues that the Official Secrets Act works primarily through its power to 'frighten' official sources of information. Intimidation in advance, he claims, has proved to be a far more effective technique of censorship than revenge after the event.

The Franks Report

In their 1970 election manifesto the Conservatives promised to eliminate unnecessary secrecy in government and to review the working of the Official Secrets Acts. The Franks Committee was set up specifically to inquire into Section 2 of the 1911 Act. Its Report was published in 1972.[7]

The Committee found Section 2 'a mess', and a 'catch-all' provision. They recommended that it should be repealed, and replaced by a more narrowly defined Official Information Act. This Act would only be applicable to certain specified categories of information: defence and internal security; foreign relations (a particularly vague category); the armed forces and weapons; intelligence services; treaties; matters connected with currency and national reserves; matters connected with law and order; Cabinet papers. But as one commentator, the barrister Michael Beloff points out, the balance was still tilted towards restriction.[8] The onus of proof (the 'why not?' approach, rather than the 'why?') would not be shifted. And the proposed Act, as Gavin Drewry argues in his analysis of the Report, 'does not get to grips with the basic social and psychological blocks to the diffusion of information'.[9] The quality of government, he believes, ultimately depends upon a free flow of information between governors and governed. But, Drewry concludes, the Franks Committee, in common with so many official inquiries, was not programmed to get to the heart of the problem.

In the extracts included in this volume from the evidence given to the Franks Committee, three distinguished witnesses provide us with an idiosyncratic selection of arguments in favour of retaining Section 2. First, Sir William Armstrong (the late Lord Armstrong), the then Head of the Home Civil Service, argues that the control of information is necessary in order that the government may have a positive policy of providing any information at all: 'for if an orchestra has no score you cannot get a melodic line through.' Next, Sir Martin Furnival-Jones, then Head of MI5 (billed anonymously in the Report as the 'Director General of the Security Services'), claims that civil servants positively enjoy the implicit threat posed by the Official Secrets Acts. They are proud, Sir Martin declares, to have been picked out as people who are doing work so dangerous that it brings them within the scope of the criminal law if they talk about it. And while this applies mainly to the lower orders in the civil service hierarchy, Section 2, he claims, does have a powerful effect on their minds. Finally, James Callaghan MP, at that time the Labour Opposition's spokesman on Foreign and Commonwealth Affairs, blithely dismisses the need for any change: for a 'satisfactory, ingrained tradition', he says, already exists. People know what they may say and what they may not say; the press, ministers, civil servants, the Director of Public Prosecutions and the Attorney-General all 'understand the limits'. Even if Section 2 were to be replaced by an Act which was more narrow and specific, things would, Callaghan declares confidently, go on much as before.

Open government and official secrets: British attempts at reform
The Franks Committee reported in 1972, under Edward Heath's Conservative government. As we have already pointed out, Franks did not concern itself with the concept of freedom of information; its proposals were solely addressed to the issue of Section 2 and to the question of what should be a criminal offence. It was later, as a result of events in America (Watergate, and the 1974 amendments to the Freedom of Information Act) that the secrecy debate widened to include the more positive question of public access.

The 1974 Labour government returned to power on a manifesto which implied the possibility of legislation on the Swedish or American pattern: it declared an intention to 'put the burden on the public authorities to justify withholding information'. When James Callaghan succeeded Harold Wilson as Prime Minister in 1976, backbench pressure had led to the establishment of a Cabinet committee to discuss the matter of secrecy. (The membership and existence of this committee were, naturally, officially secret; see pp. 126–34.) In November 1976, Merlyn Rees, who had replaced Roy Jenkins as Home Secretary, published a temporizing document which again ignored the issue of public access.

In a further attempt to pre-empt the growing pressure, on 6 July 1977 Sir Douglas Allen (later Lord Croham), Head of the Home Civil Service, sent, at Callaghan's insistence, a letter to all permanent secretaries. The letter, expressly designed to head off more radical demands for a public *right* of access urged the departments to release more background documents on policy-making.[10] This 'Croham Directive' only became publicly known through a leak to *The Times*. That newspaper then carried out a substantial monitoring exercise. Its conclusion was that very little of importance had been released.

By this time a number of groups, both inside and outside Parliament, were actively lobbying for legislation in the field of freedom of information (FOI). MPs had formed an All Party Committee for

FOI; the Liberal Party produced its own proposals in 1978. The independent Outer Circle Policy Unit and JUSTICE, the British section of the International Commission of Jurists, both published proposals for reform. The Law Society and the National Consumers' Council published statements calling for public access legislation. Private Members' Bills were tabled by Tom Litterick in 1977, by Robin Cook in 1978, by Michael Meacher and by Clement Freud in 1979.

In July 1978 the Labour government produced its White Paper on the reform of the Official Secrets Act. It was published without the accompaniment of policy papers. Described as 'a hotch-potch of Franks' proposals', it caused an uproar in the Commons. The Labour Party's National Executive Committee had drafted its own FOI Bill in 1978. It was unanimously endorsed by Conference, but was rejected by Callaghan and senior Labour ministers. Between January and March 1979, Liberal MP Clement Freud's Official Information Bill (drafted by the Outer Circle Policy Unit) went through the Committee stages in Parliament. It received an unopposed second reading in the House of Commons before the defeat of the Labour government in the general election of May 1979.

Shortly after taking office, Mrs Thatcher rescinded the Croham Directive and confirmed, in a confidential letter to the departments (the Whitmore letter) that her government did not intend to introduce public access legislation.[11] In autumn 1979 the Home Office's Protection of Information Bill was presented to the Lords. Although it was put forward as a reform of the Official Secrets Act, it proposed a situation in which ministers were to be their own judge and jury concerning official information. Journalists could have been prosecuted retrospectively over material which had not been classified at the time when they obtained it. It was the revelation that Anthony Blunt had been the 'fourth man' in the Burgess-Maclean-Philby affair – a fact that could not have been exposed if the Bill were in force – that finally caused this Bill to be withdrawn.

In December 1980 a further Official Information Bill, drafted by the Outer Circle Policy Unit, was sponsored by the backbench Labour MP Frank Hooley. It was defeated on its second reading, on 6 February 1981, when debate was adjourned.

In the third extract in this section David Leigh shows how some of the press have reacted to these ten years of 'Whitehall foot-dragging' and describes some recent cases of 'journalistic machismo' involving well-known unofficial leaks.

Why has none of the attempts at reform of the Acts succeeded? We include an article by James Cornford, formerly Director of the Outer Circle Policy Unit, who proposes one possible explanation.

The control and manipulation of information, he argues, is the key to the way in which Britain is governed. The political advantages of what Cornford refers to as 'private government' will always outweigh the claims of participation. Legislation, claims Cornford, is therefore essential. It is all too easy for governments to mistake their own convenience for vital national interest.

The US legislation and Canada's Access to Information and Privacy Act

The US Freedom of Information Act (FOIA) was initially enacted in 1966, and became operational in 1967. It was amended in 1974 (in the aftermath of Watergate) and was subjected to minor change in 1976. The FOIA incorporates nine exemptions to the general principle of public access. These are, very briefly: records on national defence and foreign policy; internal personnel rules and practice; information specifically exempted from disclosure by other statutes; trade secrets and confidential financial information; inter-agency or intra-agency memoranda; cases of invasion of privacy; investigatory records compiled for law enforcement; reports compiled in the course of supervising financial institutions; geological and geophysical information.

On 25 August 1980 the US Attorney-General gave a progress report on the impact of the FOIA in a speech to the Annual Meeting of the Canadian Bar Association in Montreal. While conceding that the implementation of the Act had caused both procedural and financial problems, he declared that freedom of access by members of the public 'to most public records' was a cardinal principle of democracy. He went on:

> The Act has, I believe, worked somewhat of a revolution. It has made our federal government far more open, and it has exposed government wrongdoing. The consequence has been that many of these wrongs have been righted. The Act tends to make our citizens better informed, and provides them with the data needed for intelligent debate. In addition to these benefits, the Act undoubtedly has served to deter wrongful conduct by government officials because of fear of disclosure as a result of the commands of the Act.[12]

Since these brave words, however, observers of US affairs have detected a perceptible hardening of attitudes towards the FOIA. Professor Aryen Neier, former Director of the American Civil Liberties Union, has described the new mood prevailing in the United States following the seizure of the hostages in Iran and the Soviet invasion of Afghanistan.[13] The FBI, whose role in carrying out political surveillance was largely discredited after Watergate, had been concentrating its energies on fighting organized crime and political corruption. Now, claims Neier, it has been put under considerable pressure from Congress to step up political surveillance once again. And the greatest immediate danger, he concludes, is a powerful move to modify the FOIA: he is doubtful whether the Act will survive intact for another year.

Neier's pessimistic view of the current situation is shared by (among others) Harold C. Relyea, of the Congressional Research Service, the Library of Congress, Washington.[14] Relyea argues that the climate of opinion surrounding the new Reagan administration has put the FOIA in peril. Both the President and the Republican majority in the Senate are committed to strengthening law enforcement, and to giving more power to the intelligence agencies. Recently, an influential Republican National Committee intelligence sub-committee singled out both the FOIA and the Privacy Act for modification. The scope of these Acts, Relyea believes, will be narrowed through 'backdoor' amendments which will, among other proposed changes, exempt intelligence files and FBI records from disclosure.

In 1980, Canada's Liberal government introduced a Bill (Bill C-43) to enact both an Access to Information and a Privacy Act. This Bill has received its second reading, and has now neared completion of a clause-by-clause study in committee. It is expected that the Bill will proceed to a third reading, and be passed through both Houses of Parliament and proclaimed by the autumn of 1981. Canada's constitution, it should be pointed out, is similar to that of the United Kingdom.

In the last extract in this section, Stuart Dresner, in a Report prepared for the Outer Circle Policy Unit, outlines the scope of the US FOIA; the Privacy Act; and the Government in the Sunshine Act. The Report as a whole argues that the benefits of open government are overwhelming, and that criticisms alleging that it is time-consuming and expensive have been greatly exaggerated, both in Britain and in America.

REFERENCES

1. Robin Callender Smith, *Press law* (Sweet & Maxwell, 1978), p. 146.
2. Colin Seymour-Ure, 'Great Britain', in Itzhak Galnoor (ed.), *Government secrecy in democracies* (New York, Harper & Row, 1977), p. 157.
3. Emanuel Shinwell, *I've lived through it all* (Gollancz, 1973), pp. 198–199.
4. Hugo Young, 'The death of Cabinet government', *Sunday Times,* 24 May 1981.
5. Anthony Smith (ed.), *The British press since the war* (David & Charles, 1974), p. 162.

6. Ronald Wraith, *Open government: the British interpretation* (Royal Institute of Public Administration, 1977), pp. 15, 17.
7. *Report and evidence of the departmental committee on Section 2 of the Official Secrets Act* (The Franks Report) (Cmnd 5104, HMSO, 1972).
8. Michael Beloff, 'Secrets: what now?' *New Society,* 29 July 1976.
9. Gavin Drewry, 'The Official Secrets Acts', *Political Quarterly,* Vol. 44, 1973, p. 92.
10. Christopher Price, 'Merlyn's final act', *New Statesman,* 30 March 1979.
11. Trevor Barnes, *Open up! Britain and freedom of information in the 1980s,* Fabian Tract 467 (London, Fabian Society, 1980), p. 4.
12. Tom Riley, *A review of freedom of information round the world,* International Freedom of Information Commission (London, 1980).
13. Aryen Neier, 'Political surveillance in the USA', *Index,* Vol. 10, No. 2, April 1981.
14. Harold C. Relyea, 'The FOI Act and the news media', *Transnational Data Report,* Vol. 4, No. 4, International Freedom of Information Newsletter, 1981.

The Official Secrets Act*

DAVID LEIGH

Beneath its dishonest flatulence, Section 2 has a fine simplicity. Everything except official statements, it says, is secret, and if the Attorney-General feels like it he can prosecute any of those who speak about the way the government is run. Civil servants do not know what is really secret and what is not, except by asking formal permission in writing. Therefore, apart from very senior officials, no civil servant dares to speak to a journalist who rings him up, without such permission. Hired public relations officials flourish, sent to these exposed positions like ambassadors.

Newspapers do worry about the Official Secrets Act, although 'receipt' is tricky to prove and the legislation has been heavily discredited by ludicrous occasional prosecutions, political abuse and promises of reform offered but never fulfilled between 1970 and 1980. Inside a newspaper or broadcasting company, the anxious huddles with the office lawyer often involve a kind of political guesswork: 'What we are about to print is technically illegal, but is an Attorney-General likely to act?'

Direct threats to newspapers are rare, although book publishers, with large amounts of capital tied up in a single project, are more vulnerable to hints. The Act works primarily by frightening official sources of information and inducing a 'clearance mentality' in them; it is best to say nothing dangerous unless it is cleared with one's superiors. Within newspapers and broadcasting companies, I have never in my own recent experience seen an article directly vetoed for fear of the Official Secrets Acts. What does happen is that sources of information are heavily disguised, one tries to avoid quoting directly from official documents and sources, and a generally muffled air surrounds the provenance of a piece. I once had publicly to apologize for printing an item of information I knew to be true (details would run into the law of libel) because the government official who had given it to me would have faced prosecution if he was called on to testify. But this is just as much the fault of civil service disciplinary codes as of the Official Secrets Acts: the man concerned not only feared prosecution; he feared the sack.

The retired defence journalist Chapman Pincher gives in his memoirs two direct post-war examples of the use of the Act to

---

*From David Leigh, *The frontiers of secrecy* (Junction Books, 1980) pp. 52–4.

intimidate in advance. In 1950, he says, the permanent secretary at the Ministry of Supply, Sir Archibald Rowlandson, rang the *Daily Express* and asserted it would be prosecuted under the Acts if it printed Pincher's discovery that embarrassing and expensive repairs were needed to a nuclear reactor being built at Windscale to make bombs. Poor workmanship was to blame. A year later Rowlandson admitted to the *Express* that his successful threat had been mere bluff. In the same decade, Duncan Sandys, Conservative Aviation Minister, used the Acts to stop the *Daily Sketch* printing pictures of the 'flying bedstead', an ungainly prototype of the jump jet. He wanted to announce the development personally two weeks later at the Farnborough Air Show.[1]

In 1967, Sir Anthony Nutting, former Minister of State at the Foreign Office, wrote a book about Suez after keeping secret for ten years the reasons why he had resigned from the Conservative government. He said secrecy 'allowed a government to deceive Parliament and people and, sheltering behind that deception, to lead the nation into war'. The Cabinet Secretary, Sir Burke Trend, was displeased: 'He told me in effect that the book could not be published. Sir Burke went through the book with me page by page objecting to almost all. . . . He referred to the oath taken by a Privy Councillor and also to the provisions of the Official Secrets Acts as being the bases of his objection to publication.' Sir Burke also sent a letter to *The Times*, which planned to serialize extracts, telling the editor, William Rees-Mogg: 'Objection was taken to these memoirs on the grounds that they infringed official secrecy.'[2] Neither Nutting nor Rees-Mogg was frightened off by these threats.

But unpublicized bullying beforehand is always a much more efficient censorship tactic than efforts at revenge after the event. Those inevitably have to be conducted more or less in the open, in a courtroom, and be unsympathetically reported by the professional colleagues of the people in the dock. Before the last war, such figures as Compton Mackenzie and the son of the Labour minister George Lansbury, fell foul of the Act for describing long gone intelligence activities and Cabinet meetings. In the post-war period there was the occasional minor prosecution or threat of prosecution against young left-wingers for printing military material. (In 1958 there was a case suppressing an article on radio eavesdropping.) But most actual prosecutions were properly aimed at leaks to foreign intelligence agencies, or dishonest dealings by policemen, prison warders and postmen. Between 1946 and 1971, there were twenty 'Section 1' cases, almost all about Russian intelligence-gathering. There were twenty-two 'Section 2' cases under the blanket clauses making all government information a theoretical secret – only three were aimed at publications.[3]

In 1970, however, the Labour government lost its head and let Sir Norman Skelhorn, the DPP, prosecute the *Sunday Telegraph* and a young man called Jonathan Aitken (later to become a Conservative MP) for printing an official report on the civil war in Nigeria which annoyed the Nigerian government. Government troops were winning at the time, and had the backing of the British, despite an emotional campaign on behalf of the breakaway insurgents in Biafra, which Aitken supported. It became a *cause célèbre* – there had been growing public unhappiness about the Official Secrets Acts and other instruments of press censorship since the Vassall Tribunal of 1963, which jailed two journalists for refusing to name their sources in an uproar about Whitehall's competence at winkling out blackmail-prone homosexuals.

Technically the case turned on the culpability, under the law as drafted, of members of a 'chain' passing the key document from hand to hand. Written by the Defence Adviser posted to the British High Commission in Lagos, the report went through several hands. Only two links in the 'chain' were put in the dock along with the newspaper and its editor, the others acting as witnesses. All the defendants were acquitted and the judge, Mr Justice Caulfield, remarked caustically that Section 2 was a legal mess which should be 'pensioned off'. This affair was nectar to secrecy's opponents; Aitken wrote a sarcastic book about the Official Secrets Acts[4] and the Franks Committee, set up to study them as part of a secretive Whitehall's slow retreat under fire during the 1960s, began to work in an atmosphere of controversial excitement.

REFERENCES

1. Chapman Pincher, *Inside story: a documentary of the pursuit of power* (Sidgwick & Jackson, 1978).
2. Attorney-General *v*. Times Newspapers, 22 July 1975.
3. *Report and evidence of the departmental committee on Section 2 of the Official Secrets Act 1911* (The Franks Report) (Cmnd 5104, HMSO, 1972).
4. Jonathan Aitken, *Officially secret* (Weidenfeld & Nicolson, 1971).

Some evidence to the Franks Committee*

1 *Question* I suppose very generally most people in this country understand a threat to the safety of the nation in terms of old-style espionage quite directly, and this is not a controversial problem as such, whether or not in a particular case it is. These ultimate issues of international finance are in a sense more controversial, people have been arguing when a crisis is approaching about alternative solutions, etc. etc., and therefore the interest of quite a large number of people in the country and the press will be very lively about that in a way that I think it is not lively about particular elements of espionage. Do you regard that by itself as affording a special difficulty to including it in matters that go to the safety and security of the nation or not?

Sir William Armstrong I think it does increase the practical difficulty of it, yes. The espionage defence is well known and well understood, but in these other matters the appropriate action to be taken by the government is a matter of controversy, the degree of crisis can also be a matter of controversy and, put it this way, there can be large bodies of people who genuinely believe that more and greater information about the degree of the crisis and the likely measures of the government would be in the interests of the state, and that they fear the government may take wrong action, or foolish action, and so I think it would be very difficult to get a consensus of opinion about this, and that does add to the practical difficulty of it.

Question Is there not another practical difficulty? Lord Franks mentioned the period leading up to the last devaluation, but when one gets one of these large international financial exercises going on a great deal is being said, and this certainly happened in that period, I think in the middle of that particular week. It is not always accurate information, but so far as newspapers are concerned it is flowing into their offices.

Sir William Armstrong Yes. I can only tell you how that appeared to us. It certainly had appeared to us that other governments and other financial authorities were actively putting out opinions of their own

*From *Report and evidence of the departmental committee on Section 2 of the Official Secrets Act 1911* (The Franks Report) (Cmnd 5104, HMSO, 1972) Vol. 3, pp. 118–19, 261; Vol. 4, p. 190.

and views of their own, and this led us to want to counteract that, to do the same sort of thing. Now in order to do that, in order to have a positive policy of providing information, you have to have control. If the thing is uncontrolled you cannot create a policy, if an orchestra has no score you cannot get a melodic line through. So that led us to wish to control what was being said in order that we should in fact be able to say what we wanted to be said.

Question When you say 'control', what exactly do you mean by that?

Sir William Armstrong We were working of course in the existing situation and with the existing apparatus. There were things we very much did not want known, and there were other things we were anxious should be known, and we operated in this way. The conclusion I am drawing from that is that if we had no control, if the thing were freely open, we would not have been able to have such a policy because we would have been at the mercy of the free flow of information, good bad or indifferent, inaccurate or accurate, embarrassing or unembarrassing.

Question I would like to put one or two very brief questions on the position of the recipients of information who are also covered by this Act, because really it follows on from what you have just been saying. You were talking about your relations with economic journalists, and, to put it mildly, this was not the only relationship of its kind in Whitehall. Now, as I understood you, you were saying that you were not in any way deterred by the Official Secrets Act. You were, however, deterred by the effect on your career if you made a serious blunder. Would you accept that in a sense the same position could affect the recipients? In other words, if you said to one of those journalists, 'This is the position, but you really must not say it,' he will know perfectly well if he did none the less print it not only would you not speak to him again but the news people would freeze him out of the Treasury and it would be difficult for him to do his job. There was the Anthony Howard case where it was quite impossible for him to do the job which his newspaper wanted him to do and he had to change his job. Therefore it is reasonable to say that at the highest policy level the Official Secrets Act is no more applicable to recipients of information – and let us leave aside whether it should be or not – but it is no more applicable in practice than to the civil servants?

Sir William Armstrong I would find it difficult I think to go quite as far as that. Naturally I was aware that there was some kind of constraint on the journalists' writing, as you say, but it is obviously in the nature of journalism that information obtained should be published, and there is always a question of degree. If he goes too far he is going to be frozen out, but he is continually probing to find out how far he can go. I took the view that the object of a journalist was to publish, and therefore it was almost wrong of me to burden him with information that I did not want him to publish, and I really tried to avoid that. It is an accepted convention that information may be published without attributing it to individuals, and frequently the kind of thing I was doing was putting a construction on known public information and saying, 'This is the construction I put on it. That may be of interest to you that I put that on it. I wish you to consider whether you put that construction on it, and what I am asking you not to do is to say that William Armstrong puts that construction on it, to print that. If you think this a wrong construction you can say the government must be looking at events this way, but because of this reason they are quite wrong. On the other hand if you agree with it then you use it as your own [but unattributably] . . .,' and that kind of thing. I never found any difficulty at all; I found they understood.

There is another area I think that journalists call operational information, and if they are told that a press conference is going to take place in twenty-four hours' time you can draw interesting inferences from that, but it is accepted that you do not, and sometimes they are under very great pressure to do so.

Question If none the less the journalist broke the confidence and did draw the inference and published a report twenty-four hours earlier, you would never take him to court on the evidence.

Sir William Armstrong No, I agree with you; you would take other sanctions.

2   *Question* What you have already said, as I understand it, is that, not talking about the senior civil servants or Ministers, but talking about the great body of the service, people who may not have been there very long, people who have not such a clear notion of what their responsibilities are and what their responsibilities to Ministers are, something would be removed from their state of mind and the total circumstances in which they work if Section 2 in its present form were withdrawn, which would really make a difference. May I invite you [to comment on this]?

Sir Martin Furnival-Jones Of course, you have set me a very difficult problem, because one is dealing with a situation which does not exist. The number of prosecutions under Section 2 is minimal, and the number of prosecutions of ordinary civil servants is smaller still; there are hardly any. I doubt whether civil servants are frightened of prosecution, but I believe – this is a peculiar state of mind – and some have told me that it is so, that they find a kind of pride in being subjected to the criminal law in this way. I do not know whether you can understand this. I think I do understand it. You may think this is very naive, you may think this is a very illogical emotional reaction, but the fact that they, along with, of course, other classes of people, are picked out as being people who are doing work so dangerous, if you like, that it brings them within the scope of the criminal law if they talk about it, has a very powerful effect on their minds. I cannot prove this to you, possibly. All I can say is that some civil servants have put it to me, not precisely in those words, but this is what they meant. It is not that they are deterred by the fear of prosecution, but in a sense it is a spur to their intent. I do not say that this applies to very large numbers of the administrative grade; I do not think it does apply to the administrative grade, this applies lower down. When you get outside the civil service – perhaps this partly illustrates what I am saying – you get different considerations, for example the employee in industry has no tradition of this kind, but there is equally no doubt that, for I think quite different reasons, Section 2 is effective: you know, there comes a day, in some factory or other, where the Official Secrets Act posters go up, and there is education of staff, lectures, and all this has an effect on the mind for the first time. Now this is quite a different situation, quite a different one I think from the civil servant who grows up with this almost from the moment of entry to the civil service. I cannot prove it, it is an assertion; it is certainly one I believe.

3   *Rt Hon. James Callaghan, MP* [There is] something which we have in this country, and of which I feel very proud, and that is the great sense of responsibility among all the people concerned. I would say a lot of other people do not have it, but I think we have got it very much here. I think our sense of civic responsibility is something which, if we were to destroy, would make us a much worse country than we are. The press understand the limits, I think ministers broadly understand the limits, the civil service understands the limits, the Director of Public Prosecutions and the Attorney-General, and they all work together I think to produce a situation in which most of the information is available. Now I fully agree with the critics – and I think this is the press – who say there is an unnecessary air of secrecy about government departments, and I think there is a lot in that, but of course it is inevitable, is it not, when you consider that at any one time only half the country is in favour of the government, and the other half want to get rid of them

tomorrow. So a government is not like an ordinary institution, it is not like a cricket club where on the whole all the members belonging to the club want it to go on, provided it wins games, and are not so concerned, whereas frankly half the people in this country are concerned to find things that will redound to the discredit of the government, every day. It is inevitable in this case that a government is going to have some defensive reaction and say, 'We are not going to tell you anything more than we can about what is going to discredit us,' and I think this battle will go on, but frankly I do not think altering Section 2 is going to alter it very much. It will depend to a much greater extent upon the atmosphere and attitude of the minister, of his advisers, of the press generally, and of the general atmosphere of public opinion. I sometimes think we almost make it impossible for a government to govern here. . . .

Question If it were thought desirable to categorize, as the Chairman suggested, and under the category of safety and stability of the state one included things like defence, foreign affairs, and particularly some Treasury element, from your experience in the Treasury do you think it would help if there were a further element of categorization by saying it should be those matters which are covered by top secret or secret classifications?

James Callaghan I do not think it would make any difference, frankly. I think the practice would go on unchanged. My own feeling is that, however you categorize this, even if you can make a separate definition of safety and stability and categorize these matters, I do not think the effect would be any different from the existing Section 2, not even in atmosphere. I would be inclined to say things would go on much as before. I think you are confronted by a satisfactory engrained tradition and approach to the job, as to what you may say and what you may not say and in what circumstances, and I think that is the most important consideration.

The last ten years*

DAVID LEIGH

The last decade has left journalists relatively carefree about prosecution under the Acts. Franks discredited them, and proposed they should be confined to properly classified areas of security and privacy, but after ten years of Whitehall foot-dragging and unacceptable proposals, nothing has yet been done.

The only attempt to mount another trial of journalists came at the end of the decade in the ABC affair, and that too was a legal and political fiasco. By the spring of 1980 journalists and newspapers were acting as though the Acts were a total dead letter. Duncan Campbell, one of the ABC defendants, printed, for example, a long, accurate account of the government's secret and extensive telephone-tapping system in the *New Statesman* magazine, based on leaks by a GPO engineer.[1] He was clearly in breach of the 'receipt' clauses of the Acts and did not try to disguise this. The Conservative government made no move to prosecute, although the D Notice Committee sent a plaintive 'private and confidential' letter, asking him to stop.

Unfortunately, contemporary displays of journalistic machismo have a flimsy basis. A journalist is only as good as his unofficial sources, and these sources still have much to be scared about. Whenever sensitive information reaches newspapers, the government aims as a rule for the vulnerable source, not the self-righteous and vociferous journalist. It sets up what Mrs Thatcher insouciantly termed in 1980 'the customary leak inquiry'.

The *Railway Gazette* affair of 1972 is a case in point. The magazine was shown a railway policy review document classified 'Confidential', from the Department of the Environment, which had found its way to one of the best campaigning newspapers in Britain, the *Sunday Times*. The *Sunday Times* published a story[2] pointing out, to some public debate, that civil servants were urging the Transport Minister to close down 4600 miles of the 11,600 mile rail network. Scotland Yard were summoned by the Department under a Conservative government. The *Railway Gazette* was raided and its editor complained that staff telephones were being tapped and one young employee threatened with embarrassing personal

*From David Leigh, *The frontiers of secrecy* (Junction Books, 1980) pp. 54–70.

disclosures unless he named sources. Under the Franks Report proposals, published only the previous month, no one would have been committing any illegality by viewing departmental documents about railways.

Harold Evans, the editor of the *Sunday Times,* was interrogated and cautioned under the Official Secrets Act. The offices of the *Railway Gazette* were searched, under, it was claimed, the provisions of the Theft Act. The document might, it was explained, have been stolen. No prosecutions ensued. They had never been likely.

Nor were prosecutions the real point of the 1976 Frank Field affair, in which all the Labour government's young political advisers were solemnly finger-printed in an effort to discover who had leaked a set of Cabinet minutes to the magazine *New Society.*[3] The minutes detailed the Labour Cabinet's rather shabby efforts to postpone the costly introduction of child-benefit payments and palm off the blame on to trade-union leaders (typically, by unattributable 'lobby' briefings of journalists). A Whitehall source passed the minutes, which had been quite widely circulated, to Frank Field in a London restaurant. Field was then heading a welfare lobby, the Child Poverty Action Group. His informant told Field to print them in *New Society*, which was done anonymously after Field burnt his documents. Field's authorship rapidly became known. No proceedings were taken against either him or the magazine, although all Cabinet documents had been recommended by Franks for continued protection by the criminal law. The indignant Whitehall source was never traced by police. Field subsequently became not only an ardent campaigner against official secrecy, but also a Labour MP. Some time afterwards, the government dropped the Franks scheme to make all Cabinet document disclosures a criminal offence, marking a small political retreat. Field asserted proudly: 'It was only the leak which persuaded the government, shamefacedly, to introduce the child benefits scheme.'[4]

In the same spring, Sir Phillip Allen, retired permanent secretary at the Home Office, was called in to conduct a 'customary leak inquiry' into the disclosure that some names on the resignation honours list of Sir Harold Wilson had been queried. The leaks named as honours candidates, accurately enough, a right-wing financier, James Goldsmith, and a businessman friend of the Prime Minister's who later left Britain after a customs investigation – Sir Joseph Kagan. These leaks caused some pain to Sir Harold and even more distress to naïve Labour supporters up and down the country. Mr Callaghan set the mark on his prime ministerial style by ordering this inquiry. Sir Phillip interrogated more than fifteen witnesses, but no prosecutions followed.[5]

In 1976 I had my first personal experience of the direction these leak investigations take. One of the things the Official Secrets Acts are supposed, properly, to protect, is the confidentiality of police records about individuals. In fact, this being an issue of privacy and not of bureaucratic convenience, secrecy is not scrupulously observed. Police used to assert in public that there was little danger of details of criminal records falling into unauthorized hands because they were never handed out by telephone, but only transmitted to police stations.

A young man from Swindon, who in the interests of his welfare I had better call George, gave me a personal demonstration that this piece of public relations was simply untrue. He had various petty convictions himself and, claiming to be motivated by outrage at the way his background always leaked and prevented him gaining honest employment, he found out how Criminal Record Office records were released. Simply by getting hold of the ex-directory phone numbers of central and regional CROs (which he did originally by accident), he rang up, announced he was a PC from various police stations, and obtained CRO details for any sample name one gave him.

The Times, for whom I was working at the time, printed this disclosure of police malpractice. Scotland Yard with gratifying speed appointed a chief superintendent to investigate. But he did not investigate the police abuses; he started investigating me and my source. Policemen arrived in the *Times* office armed with a long questionnaire aimed at discovering the source. Belonging as I did to the staff of a relatively powerful establishment newspaper, I merely sat comfortably through the interview, flanked by a Times Newspapers Ltd solicitor, not answering dangerous questions, and declining on the lawyer's instructions to make a statement. [. . .]

In Sweden it is considered unconstitutional under the Freedom of the Press statutes to try to trace the source of leaks to the press about government. This is a genuine restriction: in Stockholm visiting journalists will be proudly told that a finance minister who sought to trace a recent budget leak was prevented from doing so. The 'customary leak inquiry' is merely part of the authoritarian British governmental tradition, not an integral feature of democratic systems.

REFERENCES

1. Duncan Campbell, writing in the *New Statesman*, 1 February 1979.
2. *Sunday Times*, 8 October 1972.
3. *New Society*, 17 June 1976.
4. Shelter Housing Conference, London, 28 July 1978.
5. *Sunday Telegraph*, 23 May 1976.

The right to know secrets*

JAMES CORNFORD

Twenty years ago, the American sociologist, Edward Shils, wrote a book called *The Torment of Secrecy*. In it, he compared reactions in the United States and Britain to the cold war and to threats of internal subversion. In the United States, he found relatively open government; but, combined with it, popular suspicions about guilty secrets in high places – suspicions which Senator Joe McCarthy exploited so skilfully. In Britain, by contrast, he found a system of closed government; but, paradoxically, little apparent public concern about what was going on behind closed doors.

Shils applauded both the confidence of the rulers and the tolerance of the ruled which allowed Britain to be governed in this traditional aristocratic manner. For the important thing which Shils observed about British government was not that it was closed, but that it was private: public men, whether politicians or civil servants or leaders of the great interest groups, treated government as a private affair. And so it has continued. They may call themselves Tory or Labour or Liberal, or by no party label, but, as far as the practice of government is concerned, they are all Whigs: liberal-minded and public spirited, but also skilful defenders of their privileges.

The political world is open to those with the determination and ability to climb the long ladder of promotion in party or civil service. It is equally open to the journalist, the lobbyist, the political academic, as long as he understands the rules. The rules enjoin privacy: you may know what is going on if you are trusted – which means, if you will use your knowledge in ways which are acceptable to those in a position to tell. The control and manipulation of information is, in fact, the key to the manner in which Britain is governed; and this explains why the government's recent White Paper on the reform of Section 2 of the Official Secrets Act 1911 has caused a political row out of all proportion to its apparent purpose.

On the face of it, the White Paper is important, but not controversial. It follows closely the recommendations of a much respected report by the Franks Committee, and its aim is to clean up, to make more precise and certain, the law in relation to Whitehall leaks; or, in official language, unauthorized disclosures of official informa-

*From *The Listener*, Vol. 100, No. 2575, 31 August 1978.

Manipulated by media?

tion. The storm has arisen for two reasons: first of all, because Section 2 is a symbol of all that the critics most dislike about private government; and secondly, because expectations had been raised that the government was at least considering the much more difficult question of legislation on what is sometimes called freedom of information, but what is more precisely described as a public right of access to information held by government departments.

I think it would be fair to say that Section 2 is not important to ministers and senior civil servants. They are held to be authorized to publish or release information as they think fit, and the constraints on them are political rather than legal: their relations with colleagues, their chances of promotion, and so forth. Where Section 2 is important is in relation to the civil service as a whole and in relation to outsiders, among whom I include Members of Parliament. Section 2 reinforces civil service discipline and helps to maintain the convention that no one outside the executive branch of government has a *right* to know anything. It reinforces the assumption at lower levels of government that the correct and safe thing to do is to refuse information. And it may be an effective deterrent against both internal and external critics of government.

The notion that information held by government is the private property of government is, of course, immensely convenient to ministers and civil servants alike. It gives ministers a great superiority in dealing with Parliament and useful opportunities for manipulating the media. It gives the civil service a large degree of immunity from parliamentary or public scrutiny. And it enables the constitutional convention of ministerial responsibility to be preserved, despite the enormous changes in the scope of government that have taken place in this century.

Even in the nineteenth century, when government departments were small and their responsibilities restricted, there were civil servants like Edwin Chadwick who wielded great influence on policy. Nowadays, the responsibilities of government have multiplied, and a handful of ministers preside over enormous departments which they can supervise and direct only in the most general sense. Apart from their contribution to policy-making through consultation, research and advice, it simply is necessary for civil servants to make many important decisions. These may not be policy decisions in a formal sense, but they are in fact, because it is through these decisions that policy becomes a reality.

Ultimately, of course, there is accountability, through ministers, to Parliament; but it is an accountability of last resort. The high standards of integrity in the civil service reflect far more credit on the self-discipline and traditions of the service itself than on the system of accountability; and it is public confidence in these standards that has permitted the constitutional fiction to survive. But there has been a growing feeling that integrity is not enough. That, if we are to understand and accept the government decisions we have to live with, we shall need to know a great deal more about how they are made.

This decline in readiness to acquiesce in private government I attribute to a number of things, the most important of which is simply the poor record of British governments. An unfriendly critic might even say that the last twenty years had been a chronicle of slowly accumulating disasters, punctuated by expensive follies and the occasional scandal. It is no longer convincing to say of our system of government, 'Well, at least it works.' There is a sense of failure about.

This sense of failure is reflected in Parliament, where the comfortable doctrines of two-party government have been upset. Minority government has involved more advance discussion of legislative proposals and greater possibilities of upsetting government policies in Parliament. While party loyalty is still far and away the strongest feature of the House of Commons, there is a new atmosphere of wheeling and dealing for majorities, of cross-party alliances, guerrilla opposition and ambush in committee.

This relaxation of party lines has allowed the issue of Parliament *v.* executive to emerge more strongly; and this may result in some positive outcome to the long-mounting frustration of many members, with their powerful but unusable deterrents and their inadequate means for scrutinizing administration or contributing towards the formation of policy. The proposals of the Select Committee on Procedure for a new committee system are a positive step in this direction.

There is also much evidence of discontent among a better-educated and more assertive public. This is particularly evident in local government, where a similar attitude to information prevails, without benefit of an Official Secrets Act. But this discontent is also directed at central government, and not just at the administration of taxation or welfare, where it touches individuals, but against the way in which decisions – whether they affect, say, one area in the Cotswolds or the whole of the country – are taken without adequate knowledge of what possibilities the government is considering or full discussion of the alternatives.

More and more people, whether they are interested in the administration of welfare, or transport policy, or the protection of consumers, are coming to feel that what they need is a right of access to official information – to the supplementary benefits 'A' codes, to the traffic forecasts of the Ministry of Transport, to information on chemical additives in processed foods, and so forth. Looking abroad, they see that such rights of access can and do exist.

This is what was promised in the Labour Party manifesto of October 1974, which undertook 'to replace the Official Secrets Act by a measure to put the burden on public authorities to justify withholding information'. The White Paper, on the other hand, approaches the possibility very gingerly indeed: the government, it tells us, has an open mind. But, in so far as it has registered anything, it is objections. No serious work has been done inside Whitehall on what a British Freedom of Information Act should look like.

The difficulties of switching from the present system to one in which there is a public right to information are real. There would be less impatience with the government's doubts if the difficulties had been thoroughly investigated and not accompanied with a lot of eyewash about Parliament's vigilant scrutiny of the executive. It is doubly insulting to be told that a cardinal weakness in our present system is the virtue which makes change unnecessary.

But the difficulties do deserve attention. First, there is the constitutional problem. The countries in which a public right to information is established, notably Sweden and the United States, have different constitutional arrangements from our own. In Sweden, where access to information has been an accepted part of the government for more than 150 years, there is a separation between ministries and departments; the minister has no responsibility, either legally or politically, for the way in which the administration carries out his policies, or for their day-to-day work.

Here in Britain, the minister is formally accountable to Parliament for the slightest thing done by his department, a fiction with real political consequences, since civil servants must live in fear of embarrassing ministers, and ministers must defend actions of which they neither knew nor approved, and which may, indeed, have been taken when they were not even in charge of the department. Freedom of information would certainly threaten this fiction. That is no reason for denying information, but an added reason for finding more sensible ways of controlling administration.

Apart from the constitutional problems, there are also real administrative difficulties. In Sweden, the recording and filing of documents in such a way as to make public access easy has long been established. The problems of starting such a system from scratch, or, rather, from a complex administrative system which has grown up on different assumptions, are illustrated by experience in the United States, whose freedom of information law is now some twelve years old.

There *have* been large administrative costs in deciding which documents should be available, and a rising tide of litigation and counter-litigation. Litigation is less of a problem in the United States than it would be here, because the political role of the courts is a recognized and accepted part of the American constitution. But what these things tell us is, first, that we must devise arrangements which fit in with our own constitutional traditions, even while modifying them. We cannot borrow wholesale, but we can follow the example of the Danes, the Canadians and the Australians and adapt the principle to our existing practices.

Secondly, we must face the fact that creating a public right of access is not going to be cheap. Administrative practices and methods of record-keeping will have to be adapted. The time of experienced officials will be taken up, especially in the initial stages. Facilities for discovering, consulting and copying documents will have to be provided. And whatever means is adopted for resolving disputes between departments and the public will also cost money. How great these costs will be will depend on the exact form of the scheme and how much people use it, and on the spirit in which it is administered. But there is no point in pretending it will be a cheap or anything but a damnable nuisance to civil servants, at least in the short run.

These, however, are not the crucial objections. The crux is that any right to information is a breach of private government; it is the thin end of the wedge, the first domino, the first step on to the slippery slope which leads down to the transatlantic follies of government in the sunshine. That is why ministers and senior civil servants who acknowledge that more information should be available would still prefer information to be available at the discretion of government: more white papers, more green papers, more background papers, more statistics, more consultation – in fact, a general loosening of the reins which could be backed up by a code of good administrative practice voluntarily adopted by government and policed by the ombudsman.

Now, there is a decent, practical, gentlemanly offer which no right-minded person would refuse. But there are objections. First, voluntary disclosure does not deal with the problems of the individual citizen. And much of the steam behind the campaign for freedom of information has been generated by concern about what information is kept on individuals by government, and what use is made of it. Nobody with that interest at heart is going to be satisfied with voluntary, discretionary disclosure.

Secondly, there is an assumption in this official approach that information will be specially prepared for publication. But no sophisticated critic of government policy wants a special public brief; he wants to see the actual advice given to ministers and the evidence and assumptions on which it is based. Facts, let alone opinions, are slippery things, and the definition, selection and presentation of facts can determine a decision before judgement is exercised. It is the facts that critics often want to question.

But thirdly, and most important, comes an unkind thought: 'I fear the Greeks even bearing gifts.' A year ago, Sir Douglas Allen, then Head of the Home Civil Service, wrote to his senior colleagues about the disclosure of official information. Sir Douglas – or Lord Croham, as he has since become – urged his colleagues to be more liberal in granting access to information; in particular, to publish more background material relating to policy studies and reports. But, of course, the decision about what to publish still lies with the minister, and, sad to relate, assiduous inquiries have revealed very little new material being made available. In some cases, there have even been denials that any background papers exist at all.

It is a reasonable suspicion that, when publication is left to the discretion of ministers, they will publish only what suits them. It is at least as reasonable as the view that any public right of access will lead to the absurdities of government in a goldfish bowl. The people who have been campaigning for freedom of information know perfectly well that political decisions will still be made in private; if one meeting is made open, another private one will be arranged beforehand, and so on. They also know that not all government information could, or should, be made public. They accept that there is, in the words of the White Paper, 'an inescapable tension between the need to keep some information secret and the requirements of openness if people are to participate in government as they should'.

But, in Britain, the balance is hopelessly out of true. Things are concealed whose revelation could not conceivably threaten the vital interests of the nation. And the balance will remain that way as long as governments are free to decide what to release and when. The temporary political advantages of private government will always outweigh the claims of participation. Governments will too obviously mistake their own convenience for vital national interest. This is why it is essential to have some public *right* of access.

It is important to stress two things about demands for a public right of access. The first is that what reformers are working for does take account of the need for secrecy in relation to defence and foreign relations, to the need to protect the privacy of individuals and the process of law enforcement, and for confidentiality in the process of decision-making. What is needed as a right, rather than a tentative, incomplete and reversible policy, is the publication of administrative rules and regulations, access to government reports and inquiries, and the opportunity to examine the factual material on which government decisions on current domestic issues are based; as well as the opportunity to check, as individuals, on what information government holds about us and what use is made of it.

The second point is that a right to information is not simply a means to check abuses of power or injustices against individuals: it is intended to improve the quality of government in the general interest.

In judging the quality of government, I would ask three questions: Are decisions taken properly? Are they taken with good reason? Do the people affected accept that they have been taken properly and with good reason? In this last respect, particularly, greater openness of government is essential, and it will only be achieved by creating a public right of access. It is simply no good civil servants comforting themselves that they have behaved properly if the people they are dealing with neither know nor understand the rules being applied. Nor is it any good going through the process of consultation if it only involves the respectable vested interests, who can be relied on to play the game of private government. Greater openness is necessary to convince the public both that they are getting fair treatment and that the whole range of views and opinions has been considered.

Finally, it is important for the quality of decisions that the internal debate in Whitehall should be opened up. Whitehall has no monopoly of wisdom, and, in some areas, there is evidence of ignorance and insularity. Government proposals need to be submitted to the test of expert opinion in public debate, especially in those spheres of technical and scientific policy which involve irreversible decisions with momentous long-term consequences.

It is for this reason that I do not think that changing the rules and abandoning the assumptions of private government is a matter for leisurely debate. A Concorde or two may not matter much, nor a Gothic tax system, but spectacular mistakes about nuclear energy, for instance, had better be made with full public awareness of the reasons, and the widest and most open debate. If that is not granted, opposition will be forced into irrational channels, and existing forms of protest, such as the disruption of planning inquiries, will acquire an aura of antique gentility.

The Freedom
of Information Acts*

STUART DRESNER

Scope of the Freedom of Information Act
The Freedom of Information Act (FOIA) applies to all agencies of
the executive branch of the federal government including 'any
executive department, military department, government corporation, government controlled corporation, or other establishment in
the executive branch of the government (including the executive
office of the President) or any independent regulatory agency'.[1] The
FOIA, therefore, covers agencies in the executive office of the
President holding sensitive information, such as the Central Intelligence Agency; executive departments headed by a cabinet member, such as the Treasury Department; independent agencies, such
as the Consumer Product Safety Commission; and a government
controlled corporation, such as Amtrak, the railway corporation.
The FOIA does not apply to the legislative or judicial branches of
the federal government nor to any part of state or local government.
Nor does it apply to 'the President's immediate personal staff or
units in the executive office whose sole function is to advise and
assist the President'.[2] Thus when the *New York Times* asked for a
copy of notes taken by General Snowcroft, the then Assistant to the
President for National Security Affairs, on a report by former
President Nixon on his talks with Chinese leaders, the request was
denied on the above 'personal staff' grounds.[3]

The FOIA is available for use by 'any person'[4] and this literally
means residents of the USA, residents of all foreign countries, all
private and commercial corporate bodies and any other group
anywhere. Therefore, a person who seeks information does not
have to establish any right to seek access, because it is automatically
given by the law, and neither does he have to give any reason why he
wants the information, unless there is a question of 'clearly unwar-
ranted invasion of personal privacy'.[5] However, there are two
possible advantages to a requester in giving reasons for the application for information. Firstly, the agency official has the discretion to

*From Stuart Dresner, *Open government: lessons from America* (Outer Circle
Policy Unit, 1980) pp. 9–10, 25–26, 31–32.

release material which may be technically exempt from disclosure; secondly, he may be more sympathetic to a request to waive fees, as he also has discretion in this respect if 'furnishing the information can be considered as primarily benefiting the general public'.[6]

Access to government information means, in practice, inspection and copying. Many government departments have established public records offices where the public may inspect records at their leisure and make copies. Information covered by the exemptions is not available to the public in these offices. The FOIA provides for the copying of information for those unwilling or unable to visit a public records office. The principle of the FOIA is access and so if any person wants to inspect, say, a considerable bulk of information, but is likely to want to copy only portions of it, officials can work out a means of access, such as making the information available for the requester's inspection at the federal office nearest to the requester's home.

Finally, making the information available is not a boundless commitment. There is no provision in the FOIA for disputing the accuracy of the information nor for seeking its amendment. Nor is there any provision to require an agency either to obtain information which it does not already possess or to analyse the information in any form the requester might choose [. . .]

Scope of the Privacy Act

The Privacy Act covers the same federal executive branch agencies as the Freedom of Information Act and, similarly, does not apply to the legislative and judicial branches of the federal government nor to state or local government agencies. Information 'maintained by the state department, the Central Intelligence Agency and other agencies for the purpose of dealing with non-resident aliens and people in other countries'[7] is not covered and certain categories of files held by criminal law enforcement agencies, such as the Federal Bureau of Investigation, are permitted to be exempt from the disclosure requirement.[8] There are also certain other permissive exemptions from parts of the PA, covering, for example, national security, statistical records and civil service examination material. An important category of organizations covered by the PA are private companies which have a contract with a federal agency to maintain or process 'a system of records to accomplish an agency function',[9] such as processing to insurance claims, on the agency's behalf.

Only individuals may use and are protected by the PA and as this term is defined as 'a citizen of the United States or an alien lawfully admitted for permanent residence',[10] it excludes foreigners, businesses and groups of any type [. . .]

Scope of the Government in the Sunshine Act

The SA applies to all agencies of the executive branch of the federal government headed by at least two members, of which a majority are 'appointed . . . by the President with the advice and consent of the Senate . . .'. Also covered are their subcommittees 'authorized to act on behalf of the agency'[11] and advisory committees[12] (consisting, typically, of consumer, industry, trade union and any other recognized interested group) to every agency. The SA applies to the heads of some fifty agencies, such as the Federal Trade Commission and Nuclear Regulatory Commission, whereas agencies headed by an individual, such as the Commerce Department and the Environmental Protection Agency, are not covered. The SA also applies to a committee governing an agency whose day-to-day management may be under the authority of an individual, such as the Postal Service and Amtrak, the railway corporation.[13]

The SA deals with the question of who may attend meetings by simply stating that they should be 'open to public observation'.[14] This phrase 'is intended to guarantee that ample space, sufficient viability, and adequate acoustics will be provided'.[15] From the purely practical point of view, this is not the problem that it might seem. Experience of them under both the Federal Advisory Committee Act in various agencies and the voluntary open meetings policy of the Consumer Product Safety Commission suggests that they do not become over-crowded.[16]

REFERENCES

1. From Freedom of Information Act (e).
2. Joint explanatory statement of the Congressional Committee of Conference in 'Freedom of Information Act and Amendments of 1974' (PL 93–502) in *Legislative history, texts and other documents*, p. 232.
3. Letter from Phillip Buchen, Counsel to the President, to the *New York Times,* quoted in interview with Mr Alex Greenfeld, a *New York Times* attorney.
4. From Freedom of Information Act (a) (3).
5. From Freedom of Information Act (b) (6).
6. From Freedom of Information Act (a) (4) (a).
7. Senate Report 93-1183 p. 79 in Office of Management and Budget's 'Privacy Act implementation – guidelines and responsibilities' in *Federal register*, 9 July 1975, Vol. 40, No. 132, Part III, p. 28951.
8. From Privacy Act (j) (2).
9. From Privacy Act (m).
10. From Privacy Act (a) (2).
11. From Government in the Sunshine Act (a) (1).
12. From Government in the Sunshine Act Sec. 5 (c).
13. Sunshine Act Conference Report Senate, No. 94-1178, p. 10.
14. From Government in the Sunshine Act (b).
15. Sunshine Act Conference Report Senate, No. 94-1178, p. 11.
16. Interviews with Clarence Ditlow, Director of the Center for Auto Safety, Vincent de Luise and others.

CHAPTER TWO

Public records

Introduction

Without good records, current administration is seriously impeded, and posterity can have only an inadequate picture of the activities of government and of the most important social developments of our time.[1]

Control over the selection and release of government records is a powerful propaganda weapon in the armoury of the state. If documents are lost, hidden or destroyed, scholars and researchers cannot gain access to them. And when information is not available, or is deliberately withheld, informed public debate cannot take place. In Britain, which government records are preserved and which are destroyed? Who can have access to official records, and when and why is access granted?

The most recent report on the administration of public records in Britain claims that many valuable records are being indiscriminately destroyed by government departments.[2] Important documents were not available when administrators or researchers had needed them. But, declared the report, it was difficult to know whether papers had been destroyed through bad judgement or whether they had been mislaid; whether they had been misfiled or had been kept in private caches; or whether they had been deliberately destroyed outside the reviewing system.

The present reviewing system was initiated by the Grigg Committee in 1952.[3] Grigg recommended a two-tier review system for all government departments. All files were to be given a First Review by a departmental officer, five years after they had ceased to be in active use. Files which survived this First Review would be subjected to a Second Review after twenty-five years, this time by a Departmental Records Officer in conjunction with a senior official from the Public Record Office (PRO). It was only at this second stage that historical considerations would be taken into account. In practice, commented the Wilson Committee, the criterion for the efficiency of the First Review had proved to be maximum destruction. And this approach, unfortunately, appeared to pervade the whole records system. One directive from the PRO in 1962, addressed to all government departments, stated that the records produced each year amounted to a hundred miles of shelving; out of this, the PRO would expect to receive about one mile. The problem was, the guide went on, one of how to reduce the hundred miles to one mile worth keeping. Some departments had taken this literally, and had destroyed 99 per cent of their records. Others had been more circumspect. The Foreign Office – 95 per cent of whose material, according to Leigh,[4] has a security classification – kept an average of 60 per cent of material. The Ministry of Defence, predictably, was commended by the Committee as being the only department which had established an advisory panel of academic experts. This panel, in conjunction with a senior civil servant and a senior officer from the PRO, advised records staff on the problems of selection. But in general the work of reviewing files was being carried out by poorly-trained staff, without senior advice or support. The way in which the Grigg recommendations had been either ignored or frustrated was, the Wilson Report concluded, 'a sobering commentary on the ability of government to implement administrative reforms which it accepted wholeheartedly and embodied in legislation'.

Access to government information is also circumscribed by law. The 1958 Public Records Act stated that official records in general should be opened to the public fifty years after their creation. In practice, this means that government papers should be placed in the PRO, and made available to the public on request. An advisory Council on Public Records was set up, in conjunction with the Act; its members included lawyers, senior civil servants, MPs and historians. This Council, however, did not have the power to advise on the selection of material. It still suffers from this fundamental limitation. It can only concern itself with documents which government departments choose to release. Therefore its members have no means of knowing which records have been withheld, and why. Security records, for example, usually stay in the department where they originated, and do not get transferred to the PRO at all. A specially constituted Cabinet Office Committee scrutinizes policy regarding material which is looked upon as sensitive to national security.

In 1967, following pressure from the Advisory Council and from an outside group of academic historians, the period of closure was reduced to thirty years. This brought Britain into line with practice in the United States. But certain categories of documents continue to be withheld *en bloc*. Leigh[5] cites the example of the papers concerning the abdication of Edward VIII; we know from Moorhouse's account that the files on the Suez affair will not be opened for a hundred years.[6] In 1970, the following categories were recommended for extended closure:[7]

1   'Exceptionally sensitive papers, the disclosure of which must be contrary to the public interest, whether on security or other grounds.'

(This category is so broad that it leaves virtually unlimited scope for interpretation. And who defines 'the public interest'?)

2   'Documents containing information supplied in confidence, the disclosure of which would or might constitute a breach of good faith.'

3   'Documents containing information about individuals the disclosure of which would cause distress or embarrassment to living persons or to their immediate descendents.'

(Could this category, we might ask, cover embarrassing errors in judgement made by civil servants?) A later guide for Departmental Record Officers (published in 1971) introduces a still more all-embracing description for documents to be put into the 'closed' category: papers of 'political or commercial sensitivity'.

Former ministers are allowed access to cabinet documents (whether thirty years old or not) which they saw when in office. This rule has now been extended to include certain officials, including special advisers. A few researchers, official historians in particular, may be granted what is called 'privileged access' to selected government records. Procedures vary, but applicants will probably have to sign the Official Secrets Act plus an undertaking to submit drafts of their work for official approval. Journalists are never granted this type of access.

The Wilson Committee recommended that a series of advisory panels should be set up, along the lines established by the Ministry of Defence. These panels would advise on the selection of material, and also on access to 'sensitive' records. The Public Record Office is nominally under the command of the Lord Chancellor and his department. His response to the Committee's findings has, so far, not been encouraging.

In 1978, two historians, Chris Cook and John Stevenson, wrote an article in *The Guardian* complaining about the difficulties they had encountered working in the PRO. Their researches concerned the hunger marches of the 1930s. After a request from Scotland Yard, the Lord Chancellor gave instructions for forty-eight files to be removed from public access, files which had already been available for eleven years. This incident, described below in the original article, gave rise to considerable debate about the administration of public records. According to the Wilson Report, all but one of the files in question have now been returned to the PRO.

REFERENCES

1. *Modern public records: selection and access. Report of a committee appointed by the Lord Chancellor* (The Wilson Report) (Cmnd 8204, HMSO, March 1981), p. 157, para. 554.
2. The Wilson Report (1981); see Reference 1.
3. *Report of the committee on departmental records* (The Grigg Report) (Cmnd 9163, HMSO, July 1954).
4. David Leigh, *The frontiers of secrecy* (Junction Books, 1980), p. 41.
5. David Leigh (1980), p. 43; see Reference 4.
6. Geoffrey Moorhouse, *The diplomats: the Foreign Office today* (Jonathan Cape, 1977), p. 173.
7. The Wilson Report (1981); see Reference 1.

Historical hide and seek*

CHRIS COOK AND JOHN STEVENSON

The exclusive revelation in yesterday's *Guardian* of the recent removal from the Public Record Office of forty-eight Metropolitan police (MEPOL) files concerning the hunger marches of the thirties (files already extensively used, researched, and quoted from by a succession of contemporary historians) has led to a storm of indignation. Scotland Yard, which persuaded the Lord Chancellor, the man responsible for public records, to withdraw this material has denied historians (except those willing to wait thirty-two years) access to important documents on a significant and controversial period of recent British history.

The action has caused serious embarrassment to the PRO which happily let scholars (including the authors of this article) consult and even photocopy the material for over a decade. These files revealed the bizarre nature of police intelligence and activities at the time. They were evidence that the police not only maintained surveillance over 'extremist' organizations in the thirties (most particularly those of the left) but also kept constant watch on the national unemployed workers' movement (NUWM), the organization formed in 1921 with a militant left-wing stance to campaign for increased benefits and other action for the country's almost three million unemployed.

It was clear from the missing police files that police informers operated in the highest councils of the NUWM, feeding their masters a constant and at times lurid account of proposed NUWM activities. The material made extraordinary reading. For instance, Scotland Yard was informed during the preparations being made for the 1932 national hunger march that NUWM supporters would indulge in widespread disorder. The police duly prepared themselves to meet what was treated as a full scale challenge to the authorities. Eighteen contingents of NUWM hunger marchers were making their way to London to gather in a mass demonstration in Hyde Park followed by the presentation of a million-signature petition against the Means Test. The files revealed that the authorities kept a close watch upon the contingents marching on the capital. Amongst the information sought by Scotland Yard was advance notice of prominent militants amongst the marchers.

*From *The Guardian*, 25 August 1978.

This was supplied by provincial constabularies such as those at Glamorgan and Norwich and it is this information which has perhaps been regarded as most damaging. The profiles of known 'agitators' contain not only physical descriptions of the persons concerned, but also a précis of their previous criminal record and political activities.

As well as a report on Will Paynter, later general secretary of the NUM, describing him as 'a very dangerous agitator' the now closed file for 1932 also contains such entries as

GP . . . age forty-five, a man of most extreme and antagonistic views . . . always foremost in getting something for nothing. Always prominent in marshalling processions and is an avowed revolutionary. He is a dangerous man and should be well noted. Previously convicted of riot.

EB . . . aged thirty-four years . . . he is a man of the lowest possible type. And since his advent to this locality he has allied himself to the Communist Party. He is in all demonstrations on look out for trouble and will join in any bother at the slightest chance. A convicted thief and disturber of the peace.

Not only do these files reveal a contemptuous attitude towards the political militants of the day but they show a degree of alarmism which undoubtedly influenced government attitudes towards the hunger marchers.

Marchers in 1932 were reported to be preparing to attack Parliament and the police with vitriol, staves studded with nails, and even with firearms.

In fact, the NUWM was pedantically constitutional in its action, often being criticized by Moscow for its 'trade union legalism' and its concentration on day-to-day case work on behalf of the unemployed.

The record of police involvement with the NUWM, and later in the thirties with anti-fascist demonstrators, often revealed that the police were taking a tough line against any group they saw as posing a potentially subversive threat. The protests of such groups as the newly formed National Council for Civil Liberties were dismissed as being the special pleading of a front organization, one of the files recording that 'although it has a long nominal roll of distinguished persons as vice-presidents and no doubt attracts a considerable body of support for the ideals for which it professes to stand, its *modus operandi* is to vilify the police on all possible occasions'.

As well as suppressing revealing insights into the attitudes of the authorities towards demonstrations and protest movements in the thirties, the blanket censorship of these files has also deprived historians of information on one of the most emotive and famous episodes of the whole inter-war period. The files on 1936 containing the police account of the Jarrow march are now lost to historians till 2010, although these accounts contained little that was obviously damaging or sensational, apart from illustrating a patronising attitude to the Jarrow crusade.

The MEPOL affair presents a new dimension on the 'open government' debate. For many years historians have questioned the criteria on which the Public Record Office selects and preserves historical documents. Doubts have been cast on the historical skills of career civil servants to know what the requirements of future historians will be – not least in scientific and technological records. The MEPOL affair must greatly intensify these doubts.

It is difficult to understand the logic which makes material available to both scholars and the public for eleven years and then withdraws it on the instructions of the Lord Chancellor. Historians will clearly want to know on whose advice (if indeed advice was taken) the Lord Chancellor took the decision to agree to the request from Scotland Yard. Equally historians will now be asking what logic allows the MEPOL files to be closed until 2010, while the files on the Left Book Club are closed for no less than one hundred years (yes, the police kept surveillance on this organization and no doubt on such 'dangerous' figures as Michael Foot!).

The affair also raises once again the question of the preservation of the archives of the Special Branch, archives which do not appear to feature in any existing catalogue of the holdings of the PRO. If indeed the archives of the Special Branch are public records, historians will want to know if these archives are held by the PRO. And if not, who holds them? What arrangements exist for their transfer to the PRO? For historians the MEPOL affair represents a serious setback. Having fought for greater availability of documents, they now find the tide has turned against them. This is the issue and the occasion for historians to take a stand.

CHAPTER THREE

Law and the press

Introduction

Prior restraint

The government was fundamentally aristocratic; the press was a vulgar and commercial activity conducted by opportunist tradesmen. It was not seen, despite some self-consciously campaigning attitudes over the years by *The Times*, as inherently valuable. Indeed most of the British press has been seen by the authorities for most of the time as inherently seditious. This is reflected in the extensive legislation about it.[1]

The primary role of the press should be to expose, discuss and criticize the institutional structure of established authority and of political power. Yet traditional attitudes towards the press have resulted in a set of legal constraints on its freedom to pursue this role. The law stresses its negative qualities. The press is seen to be irresponsible; and therefore it is inconceivable that its inquiries could possibly assist the course of justice. Hence the laws of libel and contempt. Despite the 'responsibility', indeed, the conservativism of the quality press in Britain, and despite the importance of a free press in an increasingly bureaucratized and centralized state, recent years have seen, if anything, a hardening of attitudes.

The fear of uttering libel, writes Anthony Smith, is deeply ingrained on the professional subconscious of the British journalist; as a consequence, there are many subjects that are difficult to tackle. But despite press campaigns and the recommendations of the Faulks Committee[3] the press has gained no further protection from the libel laws. In fact the reverse is the case; Sir James Goldsmith's success in 1976 in getting *Private Eye* prosecuted, as Harry Street points out, marked a new threat to press freedom.[4]

The principle of free speech – the right to investigate and publish freely – is hampered to an even greater extent by the law of contempt. The reporting of any issue of public concern that *could* become the subject of legal proceedings is inhibited. So attempts by editors, academics or 'investigative journalists' (a term of abuse in the Contempt Bill debates) to preempt, criticize or even research the workings of the legal process, Geoffrey Robertson argues, are deemed to merit prison sentences.[5]

So do the legal constraints on the press increasingly stand in the way of informed public debate, as Harold Evans, once editor of *The*

Times has claimed?[6] A Royal Commission on the Press was set up in 1974 to consider this very issue (though it may have owed its existence more to a belief that Labour politicians and policies received unfair treatment in the press). The Commission acknowledged that the press's role in disseminating information is crucial in the democratic process. It argued that the press needs that degree of freedom from restraint which is essential for it 'to advance the public interest by publishing facts and opinions without which a democratic electorate cannot make responsible judgements'.[7]

But how is the 'public interest' to be defined, and what constitutes a 'responsible' judgement? Comment on the Report was critical. 'Press freedom will not be secured by broad and bland safeguards calculated to preserve within the newspaper industry a structure of relationships unconducive to freedom in the sense of diversity and independence of newspapers.'[8] And the editor of *The Observer* described it as conservative, derivative and banal – like the press itself.[9] Criticism was also directed at its failure to advocate the external reforms necessary for a better quality of journalism. Its refusal to go beyond the modest proposals of three other official inquiries into press law (Franks on Official Secrets, 1972;[10] Faulks on Defamation, 1975;[11] and Phillimore on Contempt, 1974)[12] was, Geoffrey Robertson claims, a serious abdication of responsibility.[13] In his view, all these Reports reflect an attachment to secrecy and to a view embodied in traditional legal philosophy that the Fourth Estate cannot be trusted.

In the first extract in this section, Geoffrey Robertson, a barrister specializing in media law, writes of the inhibiting effect of the injunction and contempt law on investigative journalism. He shows how the resulting prior restraint provokes bad press practice.

Postscript on prior restraint
In March 1979 the US government moved to stop publication in *The Progressive* of an H-Bomb design outline by a freelance journalist who had used unclassified sources. This is the first case in US history to extend prior restraint.[14]

Contempt of court
I probably spend more time worrying about the possibility of contempt of court than I do about all other legal restrictions put together. This is because the law of contempt is vague in detail, the penalties harsh, and usually though not invariably inflicted on the editor.[15]

The law of contempt, which was established in the seventeenth century to protect an individual's right to a fair trial and which gave

judges summary powers to indict anyone thought to be hindering
this process, has in principle remained unchanged to this day. The
law of contempt is of great concern to the press. It is effective in
inhibiting investigative journalism because violation of the law may
be a criminal offence resulting in imprisonment as well as fines. The
law does, however, recognize both civil and criminal contempt. The
former occurs when a court order is disobeyed – for example, an
injunction not to publish a particular article. Criminal contempt
falls into three categories:

i   publishing matter which may prejudice a pending trial;
ii scandalizing the court; or
iii interfering with judicial proceedings or refusing to reveal
     sources of information to the courts.

The law, which even its critics recognize as 'a potentially valuable
piece of our judicial system which needs to be respected and
upheld'[16] ideally should '. . . strike a balance between allowing
individuals a fair trial and permitting the press to reveal situations
that might otherwise rest without correction'.[17] So why has it been
the subject of so much criticism and why is it deemed to pose such a
threat to press freedom?

According to the *Guardian* editorial quoted above, the law has
been both abused and defied. It provides a legal shield for litigants
who were not otherwise entitled to it.[18] And, as David Leigh
describes in the second article in this section, the most spectacular
abuse of the law was the *Sunday Times* thalidomide case. Calls for
reform therefore stem from the concern that contempt law tends to
protect the judicial machine rather than those who use it. Further-
more, the operation of the law is seen to be totally inconsistent:
for example, it is now standard practice for the media, at the request
of the security forces in Northern Ireland, to publish details of
wanted or suspected terrorists.

The Phillimore Committee, set up by the Conservative government to inquire into the law of contempt, reported in 1974. It
proposed a number of reforms, notably to shorten the period of
time that the law could be applied. Harold Evans, who, as editor of
the *Sunday Times*, had alerted the British public to the fact that laws
of contempt made a Watergate type of exposure impossible in
Britain, was hopeful about the response to Phillimore.[19] By 1979 his
optimism had faded. '. . . Not a single clause of this legal reform,'
he declared, '. . . has passed into legislation. On the contrary:
judges taking a narrow view have made matters worse and worse in
case law.'[20]

Parliamentary privilege and the media

The reluctance of successive governments to reform the law of contempt is less surprising when looked at in the context of the persistence of other similar conventions within the political system.

Both Houses of Parliament possess the power – a power which dates back to the medieval concept of Parliament as a High Court – to judge and punish individuals who are considered to have committed an act which 'obstructs or impedes' either House, its members or officers, in the performance of their respective functions. While this right to punish for contempt applies to persons within the precincts of Parliament itself, it may also be used to proceed against journalists who have allegedly offended against Parliamentary privilege by bringing the House into disrepute. In such cases, the Committee of Privilege, an all-party Committee chaired by the Leader of the House of Commons, meets in private and acts as both judge and jury. An individual summoned to appear before this Committee is not allowed legal representation, and cannot cross-examine his accusers. Bradshaw and Pring[21] cite the case of the editor of a Sunday newspaper who was summoned to the Bar of the House and formally reprimanded by the Speaker for alleging that MPs were giving themselves special treatment at a time of petrol rationing. Callender Smith describes how, in 1975, the Committee recommended a six-month ban on the editor of *The Economist* and one of his staff for leaking Select Committee conclusions.[22]

The Contempt of Court Bill 1981

Too many clauses of the Contempt Bill . . . treat 'the public interest' as synonymous with 'the interests of those involved in the legal process', imposing secrecy and censorship without regard for the countervailing benefits of a free flow of information.[23]

Towards the end of 1980 the Thatcher government finally published the Contempt Bill to pull together the frayed ends of the contempt law and, nominally, to meet the Phillimore Report's recommendations. But, as David Leigh points out in the second article in this section, where he sets out the political background to the Bill, the government has almost totally failed to do this. And he is not alone in his view that the Bill is a sorry outcome of ten years of deliberations. A blistering editorial in *The Guardian*[24] and a highly critical analysis by Geoffrey Robertson in *The Listener* set out the defects of the Bill.[25] They both refute Lord Hailsham's claim that it is intended as a liberalizing Bill. On the contrary, they argue, it vastly extends the power of the courts to suppress the freedom of speech. Contempt will apply from the point of arrest in criminal cases, though Phillimore wanted the starting point at the time of charge. The Bill fails to address itself to prejudicial reporting – a deficiency well illustrated in the Peter Sutcliffe case – and police disregard for current contempt laws is not resolved. One of the main aims of the Bill was to bring British law into line with the European Court of Human Rights which upheld the *Sunday Times* in the thalidomide case. But even in this, *The Guardian* claims that the Bill misrepresents the Court's ruling.

The contempt of Court Bill became law 27 July 1981.

Law and the press: present and future?

In an atmosphere where even the fairly modest reforms proposed by Committees such as Franks and Phillimore have been ignored or overruled it appears unlikely that more radical suggestions for freeing the press will see the light of day. Robertson argues, however, that there are four political principles which could be translated into British law which would free investigative journalism at the same time as restraining the worst excesses of sensationalism.[26] A law to curb the invasion of privacy would in itself make unnecessary the laws of libel and contempt. But in addition to this, Robertson demands a formal doctrine against prior restraint, because he argues the press can only serve the public interest if it is freed from the various forms of pre-censorship. To protect individuals whose reputations are damaged he advocates a press ombudsman rather than the delays, uncertainties and expense of libel proceedings. Finally, and perhaps most importantly, he argues for freedom of information legislation which would establish the principle in law of the public's right to know the basis on which government decisions are made.

The present laws of official secrets, contempt and defamation neither serve the public interest nor protect individual rights.

REFERENCES

1. David Leigh, *The frontiers of secrecy* (Junction Books, 1980), p. 37.
2. Anthony Smith, *The British press since the war* (David & Charles, 1974) pp. 213–4, for a comprehensive account of the legal position and the implications of the 1952 Defamation Act.
3. *Report of the committee on defamation* (The Faulks Report) (Cmnd 5909, HMSO, March 1975).
4. Harry Street, *Freedom, the individual and the law* (Penguin Books, 1979) pp. 164–5.
5. Geoffrey Robertson, 'The Contempt Bill', *The Listener,* Vol. 106, p. 34, 9 July 1981.
6. Harold Evans, *The half free press,* Granada Guildhall Lectures (Hart, Davis & MacGibbon, 1974).
7. *Final report of the Royal Commission on the Press* (Cmnd 6810, HMSO, 1977) paras 2 and 3.

8. D. A. Burnet and W. M. Rees, 'Press freedom and a journalists' closed shop', *Industrial Law Journal,* Vol. 7, No. 1, p. 54, 1978.
9. *The Observer,* 10 July 1977.
10. *Report and evidence of the departmental committee on Section 2 of the Official Secrets Act* 1911 (The Franks Report) (Cmnd 5104, HMSO, 1972).
11. The Faulks Report; see Reference 3.
12. *Report of the committee on contempt of court* (The Phillimore Report) (Cmnd 5794, HMSO 1975).
13. Geoffrey Robertson, 'Law for the press', in J. Curran (ed.), *The British press: a manifesto* (Macmillan, 1978).
14. An account of this can be found in A. Devolpi, G. E. Marsh, T. A. Postol and G. S. Stanford, *Born secret: the H-bomb, the Progressive case and national security* (New York, Pergamon, 1981).
15. Charles Wintour, *Pressures on the press* (Deutsch, 1972), p. 129.
16. See 'Sliding back on Phillimore' in *The Guardian,* 29 November 1980.
17. R. Callender Smith, *Press law* (Sweet & Maxwell, 1978) Ch. 5.
18. See Reference 16.
19. Harold Evans (1974); see Reference 6.
20. For Harold Evans' discussion of what he sees as recent curbs on free speech and free inquiry see Evans 'Ever-increasing shackles on the freedom of the press', *The Guardian* 17 February 1979.
21. K. Bradshaw and D. Pring, *Parliament and Congress* (Constable, 1973) p. 99.
22. R. Callender Smith (1978) pp. 261–2; see Reference 17.
23. Geoffrey Robertson (1981); see Reference 5.
24. *The Guardian,* 29 June 1981.
25. Geoffrey Robertson (1981); see Reference 5.
26. Geoffrey Robertson (1978); see Reference 13.

Prior restraint*

GEOFFREY ROBERTSON

Once the journalist has extracted information of public importance, and convinced the editor and the editor's lawyers that it deserves publication, he or she must still run the gamut of legal action by some aggrieved party which will prevent the story hitting the streets. At any hour of the day or night a High Court judge may issue an injunction against publication if it is suggested that a forthcoming article is based on confidential information, copyrighted documents, or else passes comment on pending litigation. This power to restrain publication is in effect a power to censor – upon hearing claims which may never subsequently be justified. It has been used in recent times to suppress material as diverse as the background to thalidomide manufacture, the financial manipulations of James Slater and the sex life of the Rolling Stones. Aggrieved parties have the right to sue for damages if published material injures them in an unconscionable way, so why should they have the right to persuade an idiosyncratic judge, late at night, to kill a major story for readers on the morrow? The law provokes bad press practice, because newspapers which decide to publish a contentious story hesitate to ask for comments prior to publication, for fear that any forewarning will prompt a restraining order. The *Sunday Times* endeavoured to be fair by sending Distillers the thalidomide article for comment prior to publication – a kindness reciprocated by an avalanche of writs. After that experience, the press is understandably chary of seeking advance comment to balance its big exposés. The *Daily Mail* failed to put its Leyland bribes allegations to Lord Ryder, doubtless fearing that he would rush to a secret court and suppress the whole story. Had advance comment been sought, the newspaper would have been alerted to the false aspect of its scoop in time to alter it. Legal remedies should never lead to a practice which is in the interests of neither newspapers nor their targets, by inhibiting balanced treatment of matters of public interest.

The US Supreme Court ruled prior restraint impermissible in its historic *Pentagon Papers* decision. The government got wind of the *New York Times* plan to publish a set of army research papers on the

*From 'Law for the press', in J. Curran (ed.), *The British press: a manifesto* (Macmillan, 1978) pp. 212–15.

history of American involvement in Vietnam. It sought to injunct the newspaper on the ground that the papers contained military and diplomatic secrets, disclosure of which would substantially damage the national interest. The Supreme Court refused to allow any restraint on publication, on the principle that

> the only effective restraint upon executive policy and power in the areas of national defence and international affairs may be in an enlightened citizenry – an informed and critical public opinion which alone can here protect the values of democratic govern-ment. For this reason, it is perhaps here that a press that is alert, aware and free most vitally serves the basic purpose of the first amendment. For without an informed and free press there cannot be an enlightened people. [. . .][1]

The other broad area of prior restraint concerns the doctrine of contempt of court. Injunctions will be granted against newspapers which desire to publish material tending to prejudge any question which is at issue in likely or current civil litigation, or in a dispute which is the subject of negotiation with a view to settlement. There is much to be said in favour of curbing press comment on issues involved in current criminal proceedings, where jurors might be swayed by what they read. But there can be no justification for prohibition of public debate on issues arising in civil cases, which are tried by judges alone – persons supposed to have sufficient fortitude to decide cases on the evidence heard in their court, not outside on Fleet Street. None the less, the *Sunday Times* was injuncted from telling the full thalidomide story on the pretext that writs for damages had been issued against Distillers over the previous de-cade, and some had not yet been settled. The House of Lords justified its ruling by the popular judicial assumption that British people overwhelmingly deplore 'trial by newspaper'. 'If we were to ask the ordinary man,' pontificated one Law Lord, 'or even the lawyer in his leisure moments why he has the feeling (i.e. that trial by media is a "horror" which is "wrong and should be prevented") I suspect that the first reply would be – well, look at what happens in other countries where that is permitted.'[2] Leaving aside what happens in some countries where it is *not* permitted, it is at least possible that the ordinary man has a good deal more respect for the press which uncovered Watergate than for the press which for two years ignored the Poulson bankruptcy. And it is distinctly probable that he is inured to 'trial by newspaper' because his Sunday reading is devoted to little else, although the victims of Rupert Murdoch's Kangaroo Courts do not normally have Distillers' pre-tax profits of £73 million. 'Lawyers in their leisure moments', of course, abhor trials by newspaper, because they sometimes cast aspersions on lawyers in their professional moments. The Law Lords were openly paternalistic: 'If people are led to think that it is easy to find the truth, disrespect for the processes of the law could follow and, if mass media are allowed to judge, unpopular people and unpopular causes will fare very badly.'[3] The corollary – that if the mass media are not allowed to judge, bad people may remain undeservedly popular – did not seem to trouble them. Nor did the naïvety of the view that truth will ultimately emerge, butterfly-like, from the cocoon of litigation. How much 'truth' has emerged from legal actions against Distillers?

REFERENCES

1. *New York Times v.* US, 403 US 713, at p. 729.
2. Attorney-General *v.* Times Newspapers Ltd (1974) AC 273, at p. 300 (per Lord Reid).
3. Attorney-General *v.* Times Newspapers Ltd; see Reference 2.

Ten years that brought the law into contempt*

DAVID LEIGH

Clouted by the European Court of Human Rights, nagged at over the years by the press and struck down by embarrassing court cases, the politicians and legal civil servants have finally produced a Bill to reform Britain's peculiar law of contempt of court: it has taken almost ten years.

And although it is supposed to be a contribution towards a little more free speech in Britain, the Contempt of Court Bill, introduced in the House of Lords yesterday [26 November 1980], is bound to face storms. It makes a string of new offences, as well as some relaxation.

It was June 1971 when the Heath government set up a committee under Lord Justice Phillimore to look into contempt, under which courts had been punishing newspapers in a haphazard fashion since 1720.

While Phillimore was still coming to its conclusion that the way the law worked was unfair and 'contains uncertainties which impede and restrict reasonable freedom of speech', the *Sunday Times* was hauled into the dock in the famous thalidomide affair.

Fighting up to the House of Lords, the *Sunday Times* was solemnly told by the judges (with the exception of Lord Denning's appeal court) that they had 'pre-judged' the Distillers Company, by trying to print an article showing that the company ought to offer large sums of money to children who had been horribly deformed by taking the drug sold by Distillers.

The House of Lords said in theory the children's parents were still trying to sue the company, although the case was dormant because it would have been a hard one to win. In a clash between the idea of 'prejudice' to some future trial conducted by a judge and the idea of free speech, the notion of prejudice must win, they said.

Phillimore said the House of Lords was wrong, when they reported in 1974. So, to the embarrassment of the Attorney-General, did the full Court of Human Rights at Strasbourg, after the *Sunday Times* had spent £40,000 in costs, only half of which it eventually recovered, against the government's reluctance to pay.

*From *The Guardian*, 27 November 1980.

Phillimore made some commonsense suggestions, which the Strasbourg decision turned into a semi-legal obligation. People ought to be allowed to try and influence litigants, provided they did not intimidate them, it said.

Phillimore said that newspapers and TV should be free to discuss issues, even though someone had issued a writ of some kind about them, until the point when the hearing was actually due to come on. Publications should only be counted as contempt if there was a risk of 'seriously prejudicing or impeding justice'. It also proposed other clear guidelines.

The five years of Labour government, from 1974 to 1979, saw a complete failure to do anything about these proposals. Nor did those five years see any moves on the other freedom of the press issues which had seen weighty studies and recommendations.

Labour did not enact Phillimore. Nor did they enact Franks, which urged reform of the Official Secrets Act: Faulks, which urged reform of libel law; Younger, which urged privacy reforms; or their own manifesto proposal for a freedom of information act.

Harold Wilson, then Prime Minister, made his own attitude clear in 1976, when he demanded some sort of voluntary embargo on gossip columnists and investigations then going on into the private life – as he called it – of Jeremy Thorpe, the leader of the Liberal Party.

In return, the press could have some of its shackles lifted, he said. Last year, he lamented 'from my own experience since leaving No. 10, I would suspect that certain organs of the press cherish the right to invade privacy more than they would welcome any easement of the law in relation to defamation and contempt'.

In 1978, the government's lawyers were sinking at Strasbourg, where one judge, Judge M. Zekia, declared free speech was impossible with British contempt laws 'which are not predictable or ascertainable – even by a qualified lawyer'.

But, instead of reform, Whitehall produced a 'discussion document', raising doubts about Phillimore. Allowing attempts to influence a litigant 'would tip the balance too far', they said. It is not in the new Bill.

Phillimore wanted comment allowed about crime and criminals until the moment of charge. 'The Phillimore recommendation goes too far,' the discussion document said. Instead, the Bill wants to invoke contempt from the moment a warrant is issued for someone's arrest, which newspapers fear will make a new handicap.

Finally, in 1978, the Jeremy Thorpe case (he has been acquitted of conspiracy to murder at the Old Bailey) caused a new flurry. The *New Statesman* published an interview with a juror, following the

1967 Criminal Law Revision Committee finding that to do so was legal.

The new Attorney-General, Sir Michael Havers, mounted a contempt prosecution against the journal. The Lord Chief Justice, Lord Widgery, threw the case out, and awarded costs against the government.

The Whitehall lawyers immediately set to work to rewrite a draft bill. They also wanted to tighten the law further because a radical journalist, Paul Foot, had named a witness in the Janie Jones blackmail case, for what he thought were good political reasons.

And so, finally, the Contempt of Court Bill emerged. In return for Phillimore's main proposals, Mrs Thatcher's Cabinet proposes curbs on the press which at present do not exist. Judges can explicitly ban the reporting of names; they can explicitly postpone the reporting of any evidence in open court; jurors are forbidden to talk to journalists about named cases, under all circumstances, and journalists are to be forbidden to print what they say.

It may be contempt if newspapers say anything about fugitives with warrants out, such as Lord Lucan. And it may be contempt if they say anything about convicted people who plan to appeal. It may be contempt to write about convicted people who have not yet been sentenced.

The new Bill offers some definite bans on free speech and some new areas of uncertainty. One thing it is unlikely to do is end the uneasy relationship in Britain between the courts and the media. But Mrs Thatcher's government is the first one to grasp the nettle of press freedom and the law for many years.

CHAPTER FOUR

Broadcasting and the state

Introduction

[The legislation on broadcasting] has become the most powerful vehicle for censorship in the history of communications.[1]

Independence and government control
> We have no reason to suppose that, in practice, divergent views of the lines of public interest have been held by the Corporation and by government departments, or that the Corporation has suffered under any sense of constraint or undue interference.[2]

Broadcasting media are subject to all the laws that constrain the press. But in addition to this they are regulated by a series of specific statutory obligations and a number of historically agreed conventions which affect the content and balance of programming. The right to broadcast which is given by government through Parliament is tied up with these obligations. The scarcity of broadcasting frequencies and the ultimate responsibility of government for the airwaves, is the conventional explanation for the origin of this reciprocal relationship.

The Annan Report[3] describes how the foundations of public service broadcasting in Britain were laid by the first two Committees of Inquiry into Broadcasting: Sykes[4] and Crawford.[5] Both inquiries recognized the potential power of the medium – 'We consider that the control of such a potential power over public opinion and the life of the nation ought to remain with the State,' concluded Sykes – but both committees rejected the idea that the service should be directly operated by the government. The new corporation, according to the then Postmaster General, must not be seen in the public mind as the creature of Parliament.[6] Thus the organization was anchored to Parliament not by an Act, but by Royal Charter, under the technical supervision of the Post Office.[7] But even before the corporation had officially come into being, the Postmaster General had already asserted his powers over the content of broadcasting. And while these powers have never been exercised 'publicly and officially', claims Burns, he goes on to argue that it has hardly been necessary to do so. The arrangement arrived at between the BBC and the government at the time of the 1926 General Strike (while the

Crawford Committee was still sitting) was to provide a model for their future relationship.

The Ullswater Committee set out the formal terms of the relationship between the BBC and the government in 1936: the BBC having independence in day-to-day management of business but the government retaining ultimate control. But since then the assumption of a shared view of the public interest has placed increasing strain on the relationship. Most historians of broadcasting agree that the BBC's handling of current political affairs in the context of its special relationship with and obligations to Parliament can confront it with almost unresolvable dilemmas.[8]

The problem of reconciling independence with government control is analysed in the most recent of the inquiries into British broadcasting.[9] The report recognizes that the offsetting of government control with the formal accountability of broadcasters to Parliament does not resolve the conflicting obligations of the broadcasting Authorities (the Independent Broadcasting Authority as well as the BBC). They have a public duty to protect the freedom of their staff to investigate and report. But this may not in all cases square with a parliamentary or government interpretation of the public interest – indeed, of the national interest. The ability of the Authorities totally to resist government pressure is doubtful, as Asa Briggs' case histories demonstrate. The form such pressure takes may be felt implicitly or explicitly. But for the outside commentator it is difficult to tell whether censorship is covert or overt. The decision of the Director General of the BBC, Sir Ian Trethowan, to edit the 'Panorama' programme on the British security services in January 1981 is a case in point.[10] Was it a result of direct government pressure, which Sir Ian denied, or of his own prediction of possible government response in light of his own responsibility to the Corporation not to jeopardize a future increase in the Licence Fee? (The rate is decided by government.)

The Independent Broadcasting Authority, first set up in 1955, shares the same dilemmas *vis à vis* government despite the commercial basis of the stations it runs.[11] The structure of British broadcasting encourages editorial intervention on the part of the governing bodies rather than a championing of freedoms. It is their responsibility to see that specific conventions and statutory obligations are adhered to. The BBC, for example, is required to broadcast an impartial day-by-day account of the proceedings in the House of Commons. Both the IBA and the BBC must broadcast ministerial statements if asked to do so. And by the mid 1960s a common set of rules had emerged with the aim of ensuring good taste and decency, political impartiality and that no programme likely to be 'an incitement to crime' be shown. These are set out for the IBA in the 1964 and 1973 Acts but in the case of the BBC they have always taken the form of a self imposed obligation.[12]

So in practice broadcasting stays above the law by dint of self-censorship and by careful and sometimes ridiculous adherence to the impartiality rule. This is, in effect, an important function of the editorial hierarchy. But the disadvantage of this procedure is that the mass public, for whom television is a chief source of information, are almost totally unaware of the editorial or censorship decisions that do take place.

In the first extract in this section, Anthony Smith, a historian of broadcasting, argues that the fundamental constraints on broadcasting derive from the institutional framework itself. He suggests that the only route back to a greater freedom would involve a devolution of power from the broadcasting authorities.

Broadcasting and the political parties

It was not until 1953 that the political parties in Britain accepted the BBC's offer of television time and facilities for party political and budget broadcasts. Prior to that the only use they had made of television was for ministerial broadcasts. The rules governing ministerial broadcasts were first set down in an *'aide-mémoire'* of an agreement reached between the BBC and the political parties in 1947. Effectively it limited the BBC's freedom of handling political affairs. For an account of the fourteen-day rule and the ministerial concern that broadcasters might bypass Parliament see Grace Wyndham Goldie's account of the origins and interpretations of the *'aide-mémoire'*.[13] The problem for the BBC was to decide when the opposition should have the right of reply and this came to a head with the Suez crisis. The redrafting of the *'aide-mémoire'* in 1969 reflected a new set of practices that had come to be accepted. The conflict that had occurred with Suez could not happen again.

The political parties' control over party political and election broadcasting had its roots in the working party established between the BBC and the parties in 1953. In the second of his two extracts Anthony Smith describes the subsequent formation of the quasi-constitutional Party Political Broadcast Committee (PPBC), and argues that its existence tilts the balance of power towards Parliament and the existing parties. This in turn provides the country with a picture of political discourse dominated by Parliament. Our extract from the 1977 Annan Committee on the future of broadcasting confirms Smith's analysis: its discussion of bias against individual politicians, as Raymond Williams points out, 'slips curiously into a defence of respect for government'.[14]

Broadcasting – further restrictions

Broadcasters are most vulnerable to political pressure when they report on controversial issues. The Prevention of Terrorism Act of 1974 has given rise to new areas of doubt and uncertainty in broadcasters' freedom to report on Northern Ireland and IRA activities, for the Act requires all those who obtain information which might assist in the arrest of a terrorist to disclose it to the police.

The first indication of the way that the Prevention of Terrorism Act could act as a threat to press freedom was Mrs Thatcher's suppression of the 'Panorama' episode on the Carrickmore road block. For a more detailed account of this incident and an analysis of the clauses in the Act that can inhibit or influence journalists' inquiries see Geoffrey Robertson's account in *The Guardian*.[15] (For Mrs Thatcher's own assurance that there was no question of the programme being transmitted see *Hansard*.[16])

Politicians' traditional suspicion of the broadcasting media surfaced in 1980 in a completely new legal constraint on investigations of both historical and contemporary issues for programmes. Tucked away in the 1980 Broadcasting Act is a set of clauses establishing a statutory Broadcasting Complaints Commission. The Commission, which completely replaces the existing complaints procedures, will be a quasi-judicial body whose task it is to establish a set of case law on complaints made by individuals and corporations about infringement of privacy of the dead and the living, and misrepresentation. The Commission has the power to call for people and papers. Broadcasters are concerned that the problems that this will involve will be a further disincentive to investigative reporting. For a more detailed discussion of the issues involved see the 'Look Here' programme on the Broadcasting Complaints Commission.[17]

REFERENCES

1. David Tribe, *Questions of censorship* (George Allen & Unwin, 1973) p. 70.
2. *Report of the broadcasting committee* (The Ullswater Report) (Cmnd 5091, HMSO, 1935).
3. *Report of the committee on the future of broadcasting* (The Annan Report) (Cmnd 6753, HMSO, 1977) ch. 2, pp. 8–9.
4. *Report of the broadcasting committee* (The Sykes Report) (Cmnd 1951, HMSO, 1923).
5. *Report of the broadcasting committee* (The Crawford Report) (Cmnd 2599, HMSO, 1926).
6. Tom Burns, 'The organization of public opinion', in J. Curran, M. Gurevitch and J. Woollacott (eds), *Mass communication and society* (Edward Arnold in association with OU Press, 1977), p. 53.
7. See Anthony Smith, *The shadow in the cave: the broadcaster, the audience, and the state* (Quartet, 1976) pp. 62–4.

8. For an account of the succession of confrontations between the BBC and the government over political reporting see Asa Briggs, *Governing the BBC* (BBC Publications, 1979) ch. 4.

9. Annan Report (1977); see Reference 3.

10. See *The Guardian*, 13 February 1981.

11. For a comparison between the IBA and the BBC in respect of government pressure, see Colin Munro, *Television, censorship and the law* (Saxon House, 1979).

12. For an account of the origins of the BBC's 'prescribing memoranda' see Lord Normanbrook's letter in Colin Munro (1979), pp. 10–11; see Reference 11.

13. Grace Wyndham-Goldie, *Facing the nation: television and politics 1936–76* (Bodley Head, 1977) pp. 122–8, 175–86 and 302–3.

14. Raymond Williams, 'Television and the mandarins', *New Society*, 31 March 1977, p. 652.

15. Geoffrey Robertson, '"Panorama" and Mrs Thatcher', *The Guardian*, 12 November 1979.

16. *Hansard,* HC Debs, 8 November 1979, Cols 607, 608.

17. 'Look Here: The Broadcasting Complaints Commission', London Weekend Television, 5 October 1980.

A field of forces*

ANTHONY SMITH

We have seen in the period since 1955 one important segment of the political communication of British society pass into the hands of professional television producers and managers. A considerable literature has developed, especially since 1968 when television began to play a really important role in political events, and much of it seeks to establish a working model of this new locus of media power. What has become clear is that it is no longer possible merely to ask questions about the extent of 'state control' or about the amount of 'censorship'. Political broadcasting in Britain is neither censored nor controlled invisibly from outside the institutions set up to perform the task; at least, it is no more subject to some form of habitual alien interference than is the press. But it is profoundly subject to constraints which belong peculiarly to its own institutional framework. The BBC and the IBA and all their component elements operate with a model of the political environment which is of their own making – it is a facsimile of an outer political world constructed out of precedents set in broadcasting's own history. Political television operates within a field of force, with lines of advice and pressure running right through the society. The 'controls' are built into the assumptions inside the minds of producers and management.

Professor Burns in his study of the BBC's managerial processes concludes, perhaps exaggeratedly, that if the enormous potential of the BBC as a source of political, cultural and social enlightenment is to be realised, 'some means have to be found of freeing it from its client relationship to government; above all, it has to be delivered from the paralysing threat contained in a licence which measures out its life-expectancy in ten-year doses'.[1] It is difficult to see how else the BBC could be found secure roots in British society, although the prescription is no doubt correct. An institution requires to hold some form of title deeds to its monopoly or hegemony over an area of social activity; the BBC operates according to a Tudor-style 'royal privilege' and the entire world picture which it contains and which it passes on to the society is shaped by that

*From *Television and political life: studies in six European countries* (Macmillan, 1979) pp. 36–40.

central fact. There is no other sector within economy or society available for a non-commercial organization wielding so much power. The sovereignty of broadcasting has to rest somewhere within political parties or industry or a national constitution. It has in practice to be held accountable to that source of sovereignty either at prescribed times, or according to statute or custom, otherwise it becomes subject to permanent demands for reorganization and reconstruction. New proposals exist in Britain for different forms of organization for the control of broadcasting, but they are all based upon the idea of a public 'authority', its controls resting upon the bedrock of 'public' individuals tested in 'public' life and representative in a general way of different segments of the society. These are held to mediate and diversify the power of the state (or, rather, the government of the day) but they are not a substitute for it.

Professor Burns' study has opened up a variety of wholly new considerations concerning the operations of British broadcasting, perhaps more profoundly than those of any of the three post-war official committees of inquiry. He shows how the BBC's original set of high purposes, the public service mission of its founder John Reith, have been supplanted by a 'miscellany of values and purposes compounded of individual commitments to professionalism, to careers, to managerial efficiency, to saving money or making money, which are the prevailing currency'.[2] Successive attempts to 'modernize' the operations of the BBC, in particular in response to the rise of its powerful rival and companion, the IBA, have amounted to the imposition of different managerial 'atmospheres' in which producers develop (partly illusory) loyalties to topical ideas of perfection, which tend to shift their attention from the central historic ideals of the BBC. In the 1970s, however, this dedication to efficient managerialism and professionalism has pervaded the whole of British broadcasting; the institutional worlds of the BBC and the commercial system have grown more and more alike, their personnel interchangeable, at the humblest production levels, at technical levels, and at the highest levels of management. One Chairman of the IBA has become Chairman of the BBC; one Vice-Chairman of the BBC has become Chairman of the IBA. The Chief Secretary of the BBC has become Director of Television at the IBA. Three BBC Channel Controllers since 1967 have accepted posts in senior management in various commercial programme companies. Managerial miscegenation has become almost complete and it is inevitable, therefore, that one convergent set of ideals and cultural purposes will come to be expressed by British broadcasting, despite the differences of structure and constitution within the double system. The commercial system, less deeply embedded in political life than the BBC, has always tended to be slightly more detached from politics, enjoying what appear to be better relationships with senior politicians while worrying less at times about offending them. Commercial television, in its documentary output in particular, has demonstrated a greater willingness to allow its producers individual independence, not appearing to mind when programmes have been publicly labelled as partisan. The difference is one of degree, and the BBC would argue that in the field of drama it has allowed producers to take a far more forward stand than their counterparts in commercial broadcasting. Certainly, each institution has areas of programmes which are less worried over, less picked at.

The paradox is that this loosening of the system has resulted partly from the growing convergence of its two halves; producers must be treated in one institution as well as they have come to expect from the other. Vexations produced by over-management have made producers increasingly aware of their own professionalism and its marketability. There is a growing tension, which is almost certain to become one of the main themes of the 1980s throughout the world of the electronic media, between institutions and creative workers, who more and more find themselves ready to face the open market-place, or who wish to work only for brief periods at a time, on stated projects, with one organization or another. This is not the place to examine all of the ramifications of the move towards freelance employment, and the pressures it generates within trade unions as well as employing bodies, but it is extremely relevant to our theme to point out that any significant increase in the number of producers who turn freelance will have considerable repercussions on institutional ability to control output *ideologically*. Freelance workers are far less susceptible to the conditioning of the 'private world', less accessible to the flow of unstated inhibitions, less manipulable by the promise of a place in a large and secure career structure. The growing power of freelance producers will also increase the power of staff producers, through the processes of convergence and compatibility. A profession can survive half staff and half freelance but the rights earned by the latter will affect the attitudes of the former. One must expect a new mood of independence on the part of producers towards management, as well as a growing *dependence* as producers compete piecemeal for jobs.

The BBC and the IBA both face the 1980s in a mood of great nervousness. It is inevitable that before another decade is out there will be some kind of major reorganization within broadcasting or perhaps in the shape of a third or fourth broadcasting authority (as proposed by the Annan Committee). No one expects the issue to be quickly resolved. It is more than forty years since Reith left the BBC which he had created to be a keeper of the nation's conscience, above the buzz of political parties and factions. Yet Britain has never been able to lose track of the idea that broadcasting was to operate according to the principle of a second Established Church, even though both parties have undermined the ideal. The Labour Party treated it as another large nationalized utility; the Conservatives have looked for appropriate bits of broadcasting to hand over to commercial operators. The system seems more and more riven. The broadcasting institutions themselves demand only more of what they have already, more channels, less change. For some observers – including the present writer – the only route back towards dedicated broadcasting is through a plurality of institutions, some large, some small, each with its own safe form of finance and its own section of electronic media. A low-key competition between parallel institutions should maintain whatever level of independence is possible from political interference in a society where politics has come to depend upon broadcasting. Caution has grown over broadcasting slowly like lichen over standing stones; it has also perhaps attacked British society as a whole. The BBC and IBA are hemmed in by their own accumulated rulings and procedures and need the helpful competition of a newly-founded broadcasting authority concerned with a new channel, or with cable or local sound radio or another of the new electronic media which are destined to arrive in the decade of the 1980s. Fresh impetus can come only from a new enterprise which has not yet acquired the accumulated inhibitions which accrue from operating over the course of decades within British society. That would perhaps dispel one real danger built into the system: broadcasting in Britain needs to be fearful of its own proneness to fear itself.

REFERENCES

1. Tom Burns, *The BBC: public institution and private world* (Macmillan, 1977) p. 296.
2. Ibid.

The power of the parties*

ANTHONY SMITH

In its internal document 'Principles and Practice in News and Current Affairs',[1] one of the main texts of broadcasting practice, the BBC maintains that it is its express duty to uphold parliamentary life. Interpreted in the context of the Northern Ireland conflict, for instance, this means that time can be found to represent all groups which participate in elections, but not the para-military groups, whatever their standing or degree of acceptance within their respective communities. In another document, 'Principles and Practice in Documentary Programmes',[2] the BBC makes it clear that the individual employee is not empowered to make any programme the expression of his own views or position; where a producer feels he wishes to make a statement on a subject of concern in his own name, he has a clear duty to resign and see if in due course, he is invited to make a programme as a member of the public, expressing his own view. There are slight exceptions to this, where a producer is in himself of sufficient stature 'to make a personal, visual or artistic statement on some subject in which wholly black and white views do not exist'. Television production has come to involve an ever more variegated set of skills; maintaining impartiality depends upon far more than decreeing who shall or shall not 'appear'. It entails the creation of a cadre of impartial people able to administer an impartial system, at the heart of which lies the promise to the politicians as a whole that their specific needs will be catered for.

Over the years the BBC and IBA have granted important 'hostages' to parliament, in the form of systems of ministerial broadcasts and party political broadcasts. The former date back to an *aide-mémoire* of 1947, redrawn in 1969.[3] [. . .] In practice a semi-formal Party Political Broadcast (PPB) Committee has come into being over the years in which the sharing out of time takes place between delegates of all the parties with representation in Parliament, of the BBC and IBA, of the party organizations, and under the chairmanship of the Lord President of the Council (a senior minister responsible for various matters including the organization of House of Commons business). The PPB Committee tends to operate on

*From *Television and political life: studies in six European countries* (Macmillan, 1979) pp. 15–16, 17–19, 21–2.

the basis of its own precedents; government and opposition are normally given equal time, the Liberals just over half of the time given to each of the major parties. Since the arrival in Parliament of the Welsh and Scottish Nationalist and Northern Irish parties in the 1970s, time is provided within their respective countries, according to their standing within those countries. Thus, for example, the Scottish Nationalists whose total voting strength when measured against the total for the United Kingdom is very small but which is very large when considered against the total for Scotland, are given a relatively large amount of time within Scotland alone.

The parties are permitted to use their time as they wish, and their allocation includes, of course, radio as well as television. The programmes are of varying lengths, sometimes as short as five minutes, sometimes fifteen. Although editorial control rests in practice with the parties, the BBC and the IBA are compliant publishers and are therefore bound in law for libel or other misde-meanours (for example, breaches of the laws of contempt of court or the Race Relations Act) which may occur within them. In the run-up to elections a special series of election broadcasts are transmitted within a three-week period which follow roughly the same rules as the party political broadcasts; their governance is controlled by the same semi-official PPB Committee.

The PPB Committee has thus acquired a novel role within British constitutional life. It was formed *ad hoc* and it continues to be recalled *ad hoc*. After each bout of activity it virtually ceases to exist. However, when the government decided to hold a referendum on membership of the Common Market, the enabling legislation included a clause which instructed the broadcasting authorities to make provision for the two sides (that is, the organized campaigns for and against continued membership of the EEC, which did not correspond with party lines) to have equal shares of broadcasting time. Almost immediately the broadcasting authorities were in touch with the Lord President of the Council's office which normally convenes the PPB Committee; (it is not precisely clear which side made the first contact). The Committee simply met, unilaterally as it were, asked representatives of the pro- and anti-Market campaigns to be present and proposed that they adopt the traditional format used in party and election broadcasting, which, being newcomers to the business, they instantly accepted. In retrospect several of those involved thought that a different system would have been appropriate to the referendum; perhaps many very short sloganized broadcasts, or just one or two very long explanatory programmes, or a combination of both. In practice the referendum campaign came to resemble in its broadcast aspect a general election fought between two parties. The two sides drew lots in the Lord

President of the Council's office to decide which would have the right to choose the order of the broadcasts. In the event the pro-Market campaign chose to have the last broadcast of all and therefore the 'antis' had the opening broadcast. Normally, in general elections, the government has the last broadcast which takes place not the night before polling (when the nation is given an evening without politics, to enable sober reflection to take place) but two nights before, with the opposition having the penultimate broadcast. What the experience of the referendum showed was that a new quasi-constitutional device has come into being in the era of broadcasting – the PPB Committee, self-constituted and confidential. It helps to tilt the balance of visible power towards Parliament and the existing parties. Whenever the Communist Party puts up a large group of candidates, it is normally given one small broadcast in non-peak time; it always protests vociferously at its exiguous share as does the National Front, the party from the extreme right.

The party and election broadcasts are produced under a dual editorial control. The broadcasting authorities continue to act as the publishers of the material; they reserve the right to intervene in the content of the programmes as planned and they provide the programme-makers with a producer, a studio and various other services and facilities. The producer tries to help the political group concerned make the most effective broadcast within the terms of the programme idea and the script provided by the party concerned. It is a difficult half-role for the producer. The party has to find its own means to obtain special effects or visual devices, including the cost of the actual film it uses, if any. The parties sometimes attempt whole programmes made at their own expense and simply hand them to the BBC to transmit or finish off. Usually, however, they use the time for a senior politician to address the public directly and as convincingly as possible. However, the view is increasingly widely held that some kind of reform of election broadcasting is necessary in Britain, in order to render the democratic system more credible in the minds of voters, and to make it better understood [. . .]

The broadcasting authorities [. . .] find themselves deeply involved in the minutiae of arrangements which are designed to support the parliamentary system and the parties currently represented within it. The broadcasting system emerges from Parliament and in turn provides the country with a picture of political discourse dominated by Parliament. Broadcasting is therefore not part of a 'fourth estate', if such there be, but rather operates impartial brokerage within a prevailing political system, to which new admissions are very difficult to achieve. In Scotland and Wales nationalist parties have fought their way via election struggles into the arena of regional politics, and via party political broadcasts onto the television screen. Small parties dealing in the political affairs of the whole country seldom qualify for their own broadcasting time, unless they put up a large number of candidates in a general election or make some other major manifestation of their would-be involvement in the affairs of Parliament. The 'social forces' or 'popular movements', like those of Germany or Sweden, simply have no place within day-to-day broadcasting, though they do frequently have a place in the governing bodies; there is nearly always a Governor of the BBC or Member of the IBA who is a prominent trade unionist and another who is a prominent industrialist – they appear not as the nominees of their respective constituencies (though nominations are often discussed between Home Office and the Trades Union Congress or the Confederation of British Industry) but as individuals who are expected to take up stances on relevant issues in a manner consistent with membership of their respective groups. However, apart from the major political parties (and, in slightly different ways, the major churches) no organized group has earned for itself a *statutory* section of broadcasting time. 'Community access' time is given out randomly, and seldom to the same group twice.

REFERENCES

1. Circulating internally since 1969.
2. *Principles and practice in documentary programmes* (BBC, April 1972).
3. The texts of both are published as Appendices to G. Wyndham-Goldie, *Facing the nation: television and politics 1936–76* (Bodley Head, 1977).

Bias against individuals*

Para. 17.24. Suggestions reached us that broadcasters give certain individuals in political life scant or unsympathetic coverage. In our view there is some truth in the argument that broadcasters give the impression that some politicians are political mavericks and hold unacceptable views. On the other hand, it is true that some politicians, by advertising their hostility to the medium, induce broadcasters to give them time on the air to prove that there is no bias against them. But broadcasters should not differentiate between parliamentarians whom they may regard as in the political mainstream and those swimming against the tide, and neither should be consistently excluded from broadcasting their views. It is for the electorate and not for the broadcasters to judge the statements of politicians. Nor should anyone who broadcasts use the air waves as an opportunity to smear and destroy the reputation of politicians. Hard-hitting criticism is one thing: but statements which in effect discredit, not merely the politician himself but the whole concept of government without which a society cannot exist, destroy public confidence in the nation in a peculiarly poisonous way.*

(*Making allowances for eighteenth century diction and political concepts, the words of Lord Chief Justice Camden in *Entick* v. *Carrington* (1765) still have force: 'All civilized governments have punished calumny with severity; and with reason; for these compositions debauch the manners of the people; they excite a spirit of disobedience, and enervate the authority of government; they provoke and excite the passions of the people against their rulers, and the rulers oftentimes against the people.')

*From *Report of the Committee on the future of broadcasting* (The Annan Report) (Cmnd 6753, HMSO, 1977) p. 275.

CHAPTER FIVE

The D Notice system

Introduction

In our view the system makes a valuable and effective contribution to protecting from disclosure 'military' information which needs to be concealed and which it would be useful to other powers to possess. By its operation Her Majesty's Government succeeds, year in and year out, in keeping out of newspapers, radio and television a great deal of material which, as far as we can see, could not be kept out in any other way.[1]

The D Notice system has no legal authority. It finds a place in this section on legislation because of its symbolic importance. The system is frequently discussed in conjunction with the Official Secrets Act of 1911. D Notices, it has been argued, provide a flexible middle ground between a rigid application of the Official Secrets Acts and a written code.[2] It is also claimed that D Notices protect the national interest. But it could equally be argued that the D Notice system serves to perpetuate the status quo in a traditionally authoritarian political culture. The defence journalist Chapman Pincher once remarked that if journalists continued to be intimidated by Whitehall D Notices, the D for Defence would soon be changed to a G for Government.[3] Only the British, claims Pincher, would call this system voluntary.[4]

The D Notice system is a uniquely British phenomenon. The only comparable practice, according to the Ministry of Defence, exists in Australia. In Britain, the system operates as a voluntary arrangement between government departments and the press and broadcasting organizations. A committee, made up of civil servants and representatives of the media (the Defence, Press and Broadcasting Committee), issues confidential D Notices to the media, *requesting* a ban on the publication of information about subjects that are considered to have a connection with national security. These notices have no legal force, but if they are deliberately breached there is always the possibility of a prosecution under the Official Secrets Acts.

The original D Notice Committee – known at first as the Admiralty, War Office and Press Committee – was set up in 1912, the year after the Official Secrets Act 1911 came into force. Except for the period from 1939 to 1945, when it was replaced by the Press

Censorship Department at the Ministry of Information, the Committee has been in existence ever since.

How important is the D Notice system in the context of contemporary political journalism? In the first paper in this section Duncan Campbell takes a critical look at the composition and status of the present Committee (in an article which precipitated a House of Commons Select Committee investigation). The system has now broken down, claims Campbell, and it is ultimately irrelevant. In the second extract Peter Hennessy, Whitehall correspondent of *The Times,* finds that it symbolizes a certain British journalistic tradition of deference to authority; the majority of journalists, he alleges, sadly continue to reflect the perspectives, slants and priorities set out by government departments.

Current D Notices
There are twelves D Notices currently in force. The following list gives the subjects that they cover:[5]

D Notice No. 1
Subject: Defence Plans, Operational Capability and State of Readiness
D Notice No. 2
Subject: Classified Military Weapons, Weapon Systems and Equipment
D Notice No. 3
Subject: Royal Navy – Warship Construction and Naval Equipment
D Notice No. 4
Subject: Aircraft and Aero Engines
D Notice No. 5
Subject: Nuclear Weapons and Equipment
D Notice No. 6
Subject: Photography
D Notice No. 7
Subject: Prisoners of War and Evaders
D Notice No. 8
Subject: National Defence – War Precautions and Civil Defence
D Notice No. 9
Subject: Radio and Radar Transmissions
D Notice No. 10
Subject: British Intelligence Services
D Notice No. 11
Subject: Cyphers and Communications
D Notice No. 12
Subject: Whereabouts of Mr and Mrs Vladimir Petrov

The Defence Committee (1980), and the D Notice system

The editors of the *Daily Telegraph*, the *Daily Mail*, the *Daily Mirror*, the *Sunday Telegraph* and the *Sunday Mirror* all approved, in their evidence to the Committee, of the D Notice system. The editor of the *Sunday Mirror* remarked that both he and his staff found it to be 'one of those quaintly British institutions which should be preserved as long as possible'. The editor of the *Financial Times* merely recalled that during eight years in his job he had never seen a D Notice.

Jacob Ecclestone, President of the NUJ, articulated a more critical view, declaring that he found the D Notice Committee to be a 'dangerous anachronism'. 'The D Notice system,' he wrote, 'is one way of encouraging bland acceptance of what civil servants want the public to believe.' And, he went on, 'it is the very existence of the system, and the knowledge of its existence in the recesses of their consciousness, which help to condition the way in which journalists work. . . . It is my view that immense damage is done, both to the quality of journalism in this country, and to the vigour and responsiveness of our democratic institutions, by the secrecy which permeates much of our society.'

The Defence Committee which examined the system in 1980 agreed that the D Notice system was failing to fulfil the role for which it had been created. But while conceding that its appearance of covert censorship provoked much criticism, the Committee found the main charge against the existing system to be that clearly it did not command the confidence of a significant part of the media. Despite this the Committee concluded that the D Notice Committee should be retained 'at least until there is a fundamental review of the operation of the Official Secrets Acts'.

REFERENCES

1. *Security procedures in the public service: report by the Radcliffe committee* (Cmnd 1681, HMSO, April 1962) p. 37, para. 133.
2. R. Callender-Smith, *Press law* (Sweet & Maxwell, 1978), p. 155.
3. Anthony Smith (ed.), *The British press since the war* (David & Charles, 1974), p. 179.
4. *Third report from the defence committee, session 1979–80, the D Notice system* (HC 773, 1980), p. 77.
5. Ibid., p. 3.

The D Notice quangette*

DUNCAN CAMPBELL

The D Notice system is one of the greater mysteries of British journalism. Many members of the public believe it to be a means for the government to suppress news of their favourite grievance. Even quite experienced journalists working on a 'sensitive' story fear – absurdly – that their efforts may be frustrated by the arrival of the D Notice carrier, despatched urgently from the Ministry of Defence. American and other foreign journalists regard the system of self-censorship it embodies as peculiarly British, a further example of placid press complacency.

Ironically, one reason the D Notice system has broken down is the deep secrecy with which it is surrounded. Few media employees have any idea of what D Notices say, or where in their respective organizations they might be found. If they did know what the D Notices said, they would be surprised by the all-embracing sweep of censorship which they suggest. D Notice No. 1 on 'Defence Plans', for example, would if obeyed prohibit the British public from hearing anything not 'released officially' or 'published in another country' on:

> Information relating to . . . defence policy or plans . . . actual Service manpower strengths by specialities, categories or trades . . . future movements or intended destinations of HM ships . . . current or projected tactics (or) trials. In cases of doubt, you are requested to seek advice through the appropriate government Department.

Quite clearly, the press does not in its daily work suppress all information on defence which has not been 'officially released'. It therefore comes as something of a surprise that a serious body can issue such a permanent proclamation and continue to expect to be taken seriously.

D Notice No. 1 is just one of twelve notices which have remained unaltered since their issue in August 1970. Contrary to popular myth they do not arrive by despatch rider, but lie gathering dust in an editor's drawer. Each set of notices is contained in a small green

*From *New Statesman*, 4 April 1980.

loose-leaf folder. The folder also contains an explanation of the system and a list of committee members. Each folder is numbered and stamped in gold lettering (the *New Statesman* is issued with no. 511).

The members of the D Notice Committee include four top civil servants and eleven 'press and broadcasting' representatives. Numerically, it would appear, the Committee is run by the press. The truth is clearer from a detailed examination of the membership list; the civil servants are all heavyweight permanent secretaries, while the press members are predominantly some distance from frontline news gathering. The civil service members are Sir Frank Cooper, Chairman (MOD Permanent Under-Secretary), Sir Robert Armstrong (Home Office), Sir Arthur Hockaday (also MOD), and Sir Anthony Duff (Deputy Under-Secretary at the Foreign Office). The press contingent is led by Windsor Clarke, the 'Group Editorial Consultant' of Westminster Press, who is the Vice-Chairman, and includes the following:

John Grant, Managing Editor, *The Times*; J. H. Donlan, News Editor, *The Sun*; J. H. Ramsden, Editor of *Flight* magazine; J. Bishop, Editor of the *Illustrated London News*; B. Vickers, Editor of the *Scottish Daily Record*; David Chipp, Editor-in-Chief of the Press Association;[1] T. Smith of the *Melbourne Herald* cable service; H. Whetstone, Editor of the *Coventry Evening Telegraph*; Richard Francis, BBC Editor of News and Current Affairs; and D. Horobin of ITN.

The Defence, Press and Broadcasting Committee might have greater credibility as an advisory body if their record was as anything other than a rubber stamp for the civil service view of affairs. The membership distinctly omits those sections of the press with a critical attitude to government secrecy. The Committee in fact seldom meets more than once a year, and then almost ceremonially. Since 1971, when the current set of Notices were issued, the Committee has met eleven times. All the work is done instead by the Committee secretary who is a salaried £15,000-a-year Ministry of Defence employee. The current holder of the position is Rear-Admiral W. N. Ash, who was appointed at the beginning of this year.

All twelve D Notices take the form of general please-do-not-publish-anything-new-concerned-with-certain-topics. On occasion 'some relaxation may be possible' from stiff censorship: the most widespread ban, as may be imagined, concerns intelligence activities. D Notice No. 10 calls for a complete secrecy on all details of intelligence or security activities. Its terms would specifically prohibit publication of any of the *New Statesman* stories on these subjects this February. In particular, telephone tapping cannot be discussed:

> You are requested not to publish anything about . . . details of the manner in which well-known intelligence methods (e.g. telephone tapping) are actually applied or of their target and purposes . . .

Our article on this subject, which was reported by almost every other publication, has breached D Notice No. 10 (and others). This did not matter in the slightest; the D Notice system bears no relationship to the Official Secrets Act and it was clear (not least from the Home Secretary's recent announcement on the subject) that telephone tapping was a matter of considerable public concern, particularly as it had got so out of hand.

Admiral Ash reflected official alarm over awakening public interest when he circulated a reminder to editors that D Notices were still 'in force' on 11 February. D Notices do not, however, have any 'force'. They merely operate by consent and are written to reflect a presumed consensus. But the system is now far behind the times, hopelessly immutable, and ultimately irrelevant. Neither the *New Statesman* nor any other responsible publication would wittingly publish information which endangers life or serious national interests. In these matters, however, neither we nor anyone else is usefully guided by the blanket ban on discussion contained in D Notices issued by a committee rubber stamping the views of the vested military and other civil service interests. In these circumstances the editor of the *New Statesman* has suggested to Admiral Ash that the disbandment of the Defence, Press and Broadcasting Committee would be a worthwhile contribution to the present government's crackdown on unnecessary quangos. The D Notice Committee is currently maintained at public expense on the Ministry of Defence budget.

Admiral Ash replied tersely (see correspondence). His letter arrived in true D Notice fashion, by despatch rider from the Ministry of Defence.

On critical occasions in the past, the D Notice Committee has ill served the press, and demonstrated who actually calls the shots. In 1961, the Committee cheerfully passed out a notice which ostensibly banned all unauthorized discussion of any military equipment whatsoever until 'officially announced'. An outcry by some alarmed newspapers resulted in the notice being withdrawn and rewritten; it then became (and now remains) meaningless. The current equivalent notice (No. 2) – 'Classified Military Weapons, Weapons Systems and Equipment' – is unhelpful, since it precludes discussion of 'classified' systems weapons but offers no guidance as to which are, and are not 'classified'.

Persons not known for their radicalism, such as Lord Shawcross and Chapman Pincher of the *Daily Express*, have observed that D Notices were to avoid embarrassment or to 'protect a department rather than national security'. The worst example of this was in 1967, when a new Notice was rushed out to prohibit any discussion of traitors living abroad (Philby, Burgess and Maclean). The Notice was aimed specifically at investigations into the full extent of Philby's treachery then being conducted by the *Sunday Times* and *The Observer*. Both papers, after some debate, completely ignored the attempt to suppress the Philby story.

Both the abortive censorship of the Philby affair, and the D Notice rumpus of 1967 involving the *Daily Express*, left their mark on the procedure. Subsequently, it has become clear that the system, besides its absurd generalities of censorship and irrelevance, has no value in one area where such a body might make a positive contribution to journalism and the public interest. That is the administration of the Official Secrets Act and the opening up of the processes and activities of government. Two cases under the Official Secrets Act have shown that obeying D Notices provides no protection whatsoever to journalists. In the 1970 *Sunday Telegraph* case, both the newspaper and journalist Jonathan Aitken had cleared their articles entirely (which made use of an alleged official report on British arms supplies to Nigeria at the time of Biafra) with the D Notice Committee. It was of no avail.

Similarly, in the 1977 ABC case, where the present author and another journalist interviewed a former soldier with intelligence experience, we were in obedience to the terms of D Notice No. 10, which is only concerned with the publication, not the *gathering*, of information. Once again, although the point was usefully taken in defence, it did not prevent a long and costly prosecution.

As far as opening up government is concerned, the Committee as presently constituted is clearly not interested. To raise these issues, the *New Statesman*'s editor Bruce Page responded to Admiral Ash's circular with a lengthy comment on the issues, and an invitation to debate the matter (see correspondence). Admiral Ash has replied that discussion would be 'tendentious'.

We do not suggest here that D Notices should be ignored and forgotten. For most of the major national media, that has already happened to a greater or lesser extent. (Minor publications may continue to be intimidated.) But formal recognition should be given to the actual ending of the system, through the disbandment of the Committee in its present form. It might ideally be replaced by a more genuinely representative interface between Fleet Street and Whitehall which sought to open up the government and not to close down press investigation. In the meantime, it clearly borders on the farcical to suggest, as Admiral Ash did in February, that a set of largely forgotten non-legal rules remain 'in force'.

Correspondence between the New Statesman *and the D Notice Committee*

Defence Press and Broadcasting Committee
Memorandum Ref **11 February 1980**
 DN/5009/DPBC &
 DN/5010/DPBC

D Notice on British Intelligence Services and Cyphers and Communications

Following the appearance in the press of recent articles on the subjects concerned, inquiries have been received from editors as to the continuing validity of D Notices Nos 10 and 11.

The need to protect the information on the intelligence services covered by these two Notices is unchanged and remains of the first importance in the interests of national security. Editors are requested to be continued to be guided by the advice contained in them. As is the case with all D Notices, the guidance in Notices Nos 10 and 11 is kept under review by the Defence, Press and Broadcasting Committee.

The Secretary of the Committee remains available to editors at all times for consultation and advice on any aspect of the D Notice system.

W. N. Ash, Secretary of the Committee

New Statesman **14 March 1980**

Dear Admiral Ash,

After some consideration, we feel that we should reply in some detail to your letter concerning D Notices 'in force'. It is unfortunate that the letter omits to refer to the General Introduction which is issued with D Notices, and in particular the observation therein that the 'D Notice system is entirely voluntary and has no legal authority'.

Your letter appears intended to answer inquiries from other editors who, following the recent publication of a number of articles on intelligence matters, are confused as to the role of D Notices. It is unfortunate that nothing in the letter seeks to balance the public interest in these matters with the blanket ban on discussion contained in the two Notices – Nos 10 and 11 – to which you refer. These Notices, it is worth observing, are unaltered since their issue on the 16 August 1971.

You will perhaps be aware from reading recent *New Statesman* articles and other reports that matters we have recently raised in the areas concerned are of deep public concern. This, we would suggest, is evident from the press, parliamentary and public response to our discussions of phone tapping, mail opening or the real cost of the intelligence services. The Home Secretary, for example, has recently seen fit to convene an inquiry into telephone tapping.

The D Notice system, the Introduction also notes, 'depends on goodwill and in effect very little else'. There is no reason not to extend all goodwill to yourself and your Committee members. There are many reasons not to extend the same silent goodwill to the matters and organizations covered in the D Notices you mention.

It has always been an open question whether an informal arrangement made in exceptional times could be legitimately extended and institutionalized. Today, it cannot be said that there is any simple unanimity about political issues. It must be stressed that during the 1970s the intelligence services in many western societies have, by their actions and attitudes, lost the confidence of large sections of the public. (The fact that there are other societies where such trust has never existed does not affect the point.)

If it is the case that these notices have been kept 'under review', then it is remarkable indeed that there has been no change in them to reflect the changes in public knowledge and public attitudes since 1971.

During the 1980s – in our argument at least – there are political and civil liberties which are directly threatened by many activities of the intelligence and security agencies (D Notice No. 10) and by those departments engaged in communications interception (D Notice No. 11). No doubt you would take a different view, but it would be hard to deny that this is a legitimate subject of debate. If the 'reviews' conducted by your colleagues and yourself lead to no discernible changes, then we would ask you to consider whether your organization still serves any useful purpose.

It must be plain to you and your Committee that many serious media organizations now give the system little or no credence. They apply instead their own best judgement on what may wisely be published and what may not. A set of D Notices attempting to suppress any real information in the areas concerned is of no value.

As a contribution to public understanding we propose to publish edited versions of your letter and our reply.

Yours sincerely, Bruce Page, Editor

Defence, Press and Broadcasting Committee

19 March 1980

Dear Mr Page,

(. . .) Your representation of the D Notice system is so tendentious and wide of the mark that I do not think that anything would be gained by joining issue on it.

You know, of course, that the Periodical Publishers Association, of which I understand the *New Statesman* is a member, is among those who represent the Press on the Defence, Press and Broadcasting Committee.

Yours sincerely, W. N. Ash

REFERENCE

1. David Chipp resigned from the D Notice Committee in October 1980, stating that he considered it to be 'irrelevant to the needs and practice of the 1980s' (*The Guardian*, 15 October 1980).

Public watchdogs and executive poodles*

PETER HENNESSY

Introduction

The D Notice system touches a strain of deep ambivalence in many journalists, including those who are convinced that Whitehall remains the citadel, the Monte Cassino, of excessive secrecy in the western world. For the areas covered by the twelve notices coincide with those subjects where even the most active proponents of open government acknowledge that departments have a legitimate right to try and preserve confidentiality.

There is something fundamentally unacceptable, however, to any journalist worth his salt, about a system of self-censorship operated jointly by the press and government in peacetime. For many on the press side, it is tantamount to a prisoner loving, even forging his chains. North American journalists are right to regard the arrangements as a uniquely British institution, a monument to genteel fixing by Whitehall and Fleet Street for the benefit of what both sides define as the national interest.

Its survival for sixty-eight years, with a six-year wartime interregnum when it was replaced by something worse, could only be sustained in a nation whose journalistic tradition rests more on deference to authority than 'whistleblowing'. The Westminster Lobby correspondents, and their ninety-six-year-old Lobby system, now, sadly, imitated by most other groups of specialist reporters, reflect the same, self-defeating impulse that has gelded the British press in the name of efficient news gathering and management. Given the mixed feelings the D Notice system arouses on the press side, perhaps the most illuminating method for judging its working is to draw up a balance sheet of advantages and disadvantages.

Advantages

1. Subjects covered by the notices are kept to areas with a genuine national security content, though not all discussion of the British

---

*From *Third report from the defence committee, session 1979–80, the D Notice system* (HC 773, 1980) Memorandum, Appendix 12 (D22), pp. 138–9. This is a statement of personal views. It commits only the author and not the newspaper that employs him.

Intelligence Services is contrary to the public interest. Indeed, the public interest requires that the work of MI6, MI5 and GCHQ are subject to some scrutiny, particularly by the press, as Parliament is prevented from developing a watchdog function in these areas as ministers, with rare exceptions, refuse to answer Parliamentary questions about them.

2. At least the press has some say in the formulation of D Notice policy, unlike information policy in general in Whitehall which is kept the preserve of ministers and the ludicrously mis-titled Government Information Officers, both groups having a vested interest in the carefully controlled and partial release of information to avoid government embarrassment and political controversy.

3. The quality of holders of the post of Secretary to the D Notice Committee has been a definite advantage. (I have personal knowledge of two secretaries, Rear-Admiral Kenneth Farnhill and Rear-Admiral William Ash.) The secretaries have tended genuinely to serve the interests of the press in trying to persuade the directors of MI6, MI5 and GCHQ not to take their customarily negative attitude to the disclosure of any information about the work of the secret agencies. This was particularly true in 1975–77, when Whitehall was arguing about the amount of information that should be released on the codebreaking successes of Bletchley Park in World War II. More generally, both secretaries have proved helpful, honest and robust in providing guidance on the genuine sensitivity of certain information, unlike again, many Government Information Officers who operate in a fog of ignorance and are masters of the misleading. Secretaries of the D Notice Committee have the great advantage of direct knowledge about the world of which they are paid to speak.

4. The system has been operated with great restraint since Sir Harold Wilson nearly destroyed it forever by ignoring the wisdom of the Radcliffe Report on the Pincher Affair in 1967.

5. It is entirely voluntary and has no bearing on the Attorney-General's powers to initiate prosecutions under Section 2 of the Official Secrets Act, 1911.

Disadvantages
1. The D Notice system goes against the grain of a free press in a free society. Permanent secretaries and working journalists should be like oil and water. The temperament, training and background of top officials in the Foreign and Commonwealth Office, the Ministry of Defence and the Home Office do not produce a strong impulse towards the disclosure of information. Open government is not a cause with which (with a few honourable exceptions who have to be kept secret for their own protection!) they sympathize. A leading

article in *The Times* expressed the contrast between Whitehall and
Fleet Street in a memorable and lapidary fashion in 1852:

> The first duty of the press is to obtain the earliest and most correct
> intelligence of the events of the time, and instantly, by disclosing
> them, to make them the common property of the nation. The
> statesman collects his information secretly and by secret means;
> he keeps back even the current intelligence of the day with
> ludicrous precautions. . . . The press lives by disclosures. . . .
> The duty of the one is to speak, the other to be silent.

There is no place for a D-Notice Committee in the world described by that leader writer.

2. There exists an abundance of what the *Times* man called
'ludicrous precautions' to protect Whitehall with or without the
safeguards of the D Notices. Britain has the most tightly drawn
secrecy statute ever to flow off the pen of a parliamentary drafts-
man. The framers of the civil service bible of do's and don'ts,
Estacode, surpassed themselves in devising a set of restrictive rules
on the disclosure of information by officials that is even more than
the Official Secrets Act, 1911. Government currently employs 171
press officers to massage Whitehall's conception of what is fit to
print into a form suitable for reproduction by journalists. The
Westminster Lobby correspondents, and their imitators in other
specialisms, ensure that, in the main, the context and content of
journalism reflects the perspectives, slants and priorities set for it by
government departments. The D Notice system is but a fifth wheel
on a Fleet Street/Whitehall relationship in which the balance of
advantage has long been tipped Whitehall's way, chiefly thanks to
the docility of those who should be the public's watchdogs and not
the poodles of the executive.

3. The D Notice Committee meets in private. It is not accountable to Parliament through the preparation of a regular annual
report. The press have no means of knowing that its representatives
on the Committee are fighting its corner.

4. The press representatives, by and large, are journalists in
managerial positions who have long since ceased to be active
personally in the process of prising information from a reluctant
Whitehall.

5. The system, though operated with admirable restraint in the
past thirteen years, is potentially open to abuse by a government, or
a trio of permanent secretaries, whose conception of 'national
security' is exaggerated, or self-serving, and a danger to free
expression and the public interest.

An American view of the D Notice system*

LEONARD DOWNIE

Americans find [the D Notice system] amazing and unusual. It is so clearly contrary to our experience and contrary to what one expects the British experience to be before one comes here. There are two or three reasons for that. One is this thing of having officials from the press recruited from the news media sitting with representatives of government on a quasi-governmental body and in effect, despite the fact that it is a voluntary system, carrying out some manner of regulation of press coverage. This is not only unheard of, there is no precedent for that in the United States, and in our particular case, with the press view of the American Bill of Rights and Constitution, it would be on our part entering into a voluntary relationship with government which we would find unconstitutional. Secondly, it does fall within a number of formalized practices of relationships between reporters and government officials, including the lobby system [. . .] which again have no counterpart in the United States, although I would hasten to add that individual reporters certainly have close relationships with individual officials in the American government and in their day-to-day work. Their habits may precisely resemble those of British reporters but it does not fall within a formal system, and the Lobby system, for instance, something which I am not allowed to be a party to as a foreign correspondent, is again a very strange system to me. The fact that it is formalized in that way as opposed to individual reporters establishing their own personal relationships with sources is very strange.

*From oral evidence in *Third report from the Defence Committee, session 1979–80, the D Notice system* (HC 773, 1980), p. 128.

PART TWO

Interpretations

The material in this part illustrates and analyses some of the different ways in which politicians, journalists, civil servants and academics have described and interpreted their roles in the process of information management in Britain. The extracts we have selected can be looked at in the context of the legislative framework set out in Part One: the formal versus the informal. They can equally well be read, and enjoyed, on their own. These illustrations are drawn from a variety of primary and secondary sources, including subjective first-hand accounts by politicians and civil servants, commentaries by political journalists and academic analyses. They express a variety of attitudes and assumptions about the British political system; they reflect a range of theoretical perspectives.

For the sake of organization, the material has been subdivided into four sections: The Prime Minister; The Cabinet; Parliament; and Whitehall. These divisions are necessarily somewhat arbitrary ones.

By way of an introduction, we have chosen an extract from Keith Middlemas's major analysis of the British political system since 1911. Middlemas argues that in Britain, one of the most secretive political societies in the western world, the management and manipulation of opinion has become a continuous process. The institutionalization of secrecy at all levels of the system, together with a closed political environment, has kept the British public politically illiterate. And in the sixties, claims Middlemas, the benefits of consensus politics came to be regarded simply as 'the lowest common denominator of policies designed to avoid trouble'.

The cult of equilibrium*

KEITH MIDDLEMAS

Symptoms of excessive formalism and lack of flexibility began to
appear in all the component parts of the [political] system during the
sixties. Enthusiasm for sheer size and economics of scale began,
sporadically, to be replaced by calls for devolution, disaggregation,
participation, albeit without the enthusiasm which lent colour to the
dramatic events in France and in Italy in 1968. In a very general way,
the supposed benefits of consensus came to be seen, not as high
aspirations as in 1940, but as the lowest common denominator of
policies designed to avoid trouble. The growing complexity of the
state apparatus, the real if unadmitted power of bureaucrats and
technocrats over government, and the heavy-handed attitude of
institutions towards dissent contrasted unfavourably with the actual
inability of the state (compared with its European competitors) to
accomplish its declared job of delivering a consistently better
future. There is no lack of evidence (though inevitably, in the
absence of official archives, it is superficial) to suggest that the
parties to the triangular system had become formal, professional
organizations to a degree unforeseen in the 1940s. Max Weber's
rule of 'universal bureaucratization' applied even to their consti-
tuent members, white-collar unions or industrial Federations. But
the secular constraints which had ensured compliance to government and governing institutions' authority became jaded – appeals
to the Dunkirk spirit succumbing, like patriotic calls of an earlier
period, to sheer over-use.

The area in which popular consent had to be upheld had widened
constantly since the 1930s, as matters such as supply of capital or
wage bargaining, once regarded as outside the scope of government, became politicized. But since governments' performance
could now be measured more easily against their own pretensions to
manage the economy, the returns from official propaganda in a
more sceptical, open society, steadily diminished. The trouble was
not that the demands of those excluded from rewards impinged too
harshly on the formulation of compromise, as Habermas forecast in
the late sixties,[1] but that very much larger and better organized

*From *Politics in industrial society: the experience of the British system since 1911*
(Deutsch, 1979) pp. 423–8.

groups than before had to be appeased. This demanded a constantly rising level of activity, deleterious to the larger balance – witness, for example, the difficulties of Conservative and Labour governments after 1961 in placating at one and the same time immigrants and the anti-immigration lobby, while attempting to keep the whole issue out of national political life.

According to analysts of public opinion, deference voting, the numbers of those consistently supporting one party, and the turn-out in general elections, declined after the mid-fifties.[2] Against a background of Liberal revival, a very widespread feeling accumulated that the parties were ceasing to be 'mass organizations' as that term had been understood in the uncomplicated post-war years, when youth and women's organizations attracted hordes of well-disciplined recruits. According to parliamentary party officials, the values of consensus politics made less impact, especially since politicians themselves seemed to sense, and at once appeal to, the lines of class cleavage which new age cohorts of voters imported as a prevailing characteristic of the sixties.[3] Yet the parties' mutual competitiveness, behind exaggerated election slogans based on a whole geography of market research and public relations work, brought them no nearer to discovering a golden key to unlock the public mind. It is quite possible that as early as the mid-sixties, electoral popularity had ceased to run concurrently with the economic cycle, though the supposed link between economic manipulation and voters' preferences remained part of conventional wisdom.

Several very general remarks can be made about the scepticism of this period when, for the first time in a century, a homogeneous, working-class, youthful culture broke out of the dreary confines of John Burns' pre-1914 truism – 'the tragedy of the working man is the poverty of his desires'. Changes in sexual habits, almost by definition, became a solvent of deferential attitudes. At a quite different level, the breach in the BBC's monopoly of radio and television altered the limits within which political variations and understandings had been aligned,[4] while the 1960 electorate 'more habituated to the printed medium than the electorate of any other large democracy' had, ten years later, turned to television as its prime source of political information.[5]

Cabinets had to readjust to the political implications of cultural change, as their predecessors had done after 1909. They still held substantial powers to inform and persuade; and the survival of continuous contract can be gauged, if only in a negative sense, from successive governments' control over information which they deemed should not become public. The fact that the Official Secrets Act was used no more than once a year on average[6] indicates conformity, not lax judgement – the stark truth about repatriation of the Russians who had fought in the war for Vlasov against Stalin, and the pitiful remnant of pre-1920 refugees, who were handed back, unrequested, to imprisonment or death, has only recently surfaced,[7] while in 1945–8 the Labour Party was allowed to know very little about development of the atom bomb or the preparations Attlee's Cabinet made to use troops for industrial emergencies like the winter of 1947 – which took a form not unlike that of the old Supply and Transport Committee.[8] Ten years later it was still as easy to conceal the fact of collusion with the French government at the time of Suez, and to restrain the dissenting Anthony Nutting from publication of some of the facts until a safe eleven years had passed.

Continuous contract is not a question of protecting top secrets like the decoding work at Bletchley Park, with its unpalatable evidence of spying on other nations' communications in peace-time, but of the institutionalization of secretiveness at all levels in the state apparatus. Of this, the extension of earlier conventions about Cabinet and civil service proceedings is a good instance. When the Select Committee of inquiry into the civil service in 1942 made far-reaching criticisms of bureaucratic rigidity, narrow, élitist composition, and Treasury inefficiency – much as Lord Fulton was to do twenty-six years later – the heads of departments met to concoct a reply; and not only rejected criticism outright, but warded off a dangerous proposal to keep the service under review by a House of Commons Committee. Sir Richard Hopkins, for the Treasury, suggested that 'it would be the thin end of the wedge for introducing a system of Congressional Committees for sharing in the work of the executive government'. Edward Bridges, the Cabinet Secretary, feared that 'Gestapo-like bands' of MPs, quite unqualified, might entrench on the work of the civil service, and noted with relief that 'the Estimates Committee before the war had been prevented from asking policy questions, and had worked satisfactorily'.[9]

Twenty years later, however, both Estimates and Nationalized Industries Committees had skilfully widened their terms of reference to include policy, even before Richard Crossman, apostle of 'open government', initiated more specialized Commons' committees of inquiry. Meanwhile, confronted with the absurdity of having no formal access to Cabinet documents since the Secretariat started work in 1916, government itself brought in the Public Records Act, 1958 and the 'fifty-year rule'. Historians ground forward year by year (while private collections and memoirs from the 'forbidden' period held a premium for serialization in Sunday newspapers) until rewarded with the prize of a thirty-year rule in 1967.

In itself, this amendment charted the shift in political climate: having pursued for years the lost private papers of ministers who had escaped the net in 1934, and harassed former civil servants like

Hankey and Thomas Jones,[10] the Cabinet Office suffered a series of reverses from the growing indiscretions of serving ministers. As late as 1952, Attlee could still castigate Bevan for claiming that Cabinet collective responsibility did not outlast the fall of a particular government.[11] The old tradition was followed in their memoirs by Eden and Macmillan. But after 1960, the pace of revelation quickened. Dalton's third volume of memoirs, *High Tide and After,* gave detailed instances of Cabinet and other private discussions and was followed by a number of lesser indiscretions, all breaking the old conventions.

A trend began in which ministers and civil service officials gave verbally the substance of Cabinet secrets, while avoiding open responsibility, to the authors of books like *The Battle of Downing Street*, and *Denis Healey and the Policies of Power*, and in 1965 Richard Crossman embarked on the diary in which he set out, quite openly, to challenge the whole corpus of information control.

The reaction of a prurient readership, avid for disclosures of personal foibles, vanities and betrayals, probably mattered less than the exposure of procedures and conventions created within a closed political environment to a public that had been kept politically illiterate. Crossman's 'revelations' about the role of the civil service may have done enormous harm not, as he intended, to stuffy, obstructive bureaucrats, but to the harmonious working of a finely calibrated machine whose values at first he simply failed to comprehend. However it was done, letting in the daylight on mystery – to use Bagehot's phrase – heightened rather than healed the breach between the real workings of the system and its formal presentation, weakening a major element in its coherence.

It is harder to discuss opinion manipulation in the very modern period. Looking at the fifties and sixties, Butler and Stokes commented on the increase in scepticism: 'A lengthening series of electoral studies might simply give repeated evidence of how very limited is the influence which political leaders are able to exercise over the mass electorate.'[12] It seems, on very limited evidence, that the post-war Labour government felt uneasy about using the propaganda machine which it had inherited,[13] and that this curious altruism contributed to the increasing detachment of government information services from party control; down at least to the mid-1950s. Labour responded to the anti-nationalization campaign mounted by the Iron and Steel Federation, Aims of Industry and Tate & Lyle, with diffidence and a reluctance to drum up a populist campaign, that can only be explained by its belief in the prior need the government had for employers' goodwill.

The constraints which bound the 1951 Conservative government in turn can be seen in their restraint from anti-union propaganda before the downturn in 1955 – the year in which Eden concluded: 'I knew that if we were to improve our position [in the election], I must in particular get my message to the better-paid, skilled industrial worker who could be expected to benefit from the kind of society we wanted to create.'[14] But circumstances and Nasser soon compelled him to revive the practice of manipulation to neutralize hostile comment in a manner reminiscent of Chamberlain at the time of Munich.[15]

This work, accompanied by evidence of governments' morbid sensitivity to public discussion of the briefing and lobby system,[16] suggest that possession of, and control of access to, technical and secret information continued to be a valuable weapon of control in political society. Indeed some of those who analysed the system in the sixties revived Ostrogorski's old fears in a new context, suggesting that access to the apparatus of advertising and opinion-testing would enable parties to manipulate mass opinion, causing it to demand rewards which, when in government, they could satisfy.[17] But a change was occurring even before 1964. For nearly five years of Wilson's administration, Downing Street was at loggerheads with Fleet Street, a condition only partly due to the suspicions of Wilson himself, a Prime Minister unnaturally preoccupied with his personal popularity. Macmillan and Home had already suffered similar exposure and, if the attacks were mild by American standards, and on the whole, superficial, they penetrated deeply enough to impair the appearance of magisterial authority of which, in his earlier years, Macmillan had been the outstanding exponent.

REFERENCES

1. Jürgen Habermas, *Legitimation crisis* (Boston, 1976).
2. D. H. E. Butler and D. E. Stokes, *Political Change in Britain: the evolution of electoral choice* (2nd ed., Macmillan, 1974) pp. 409–13.
3. Ibid., pp. 9–10, 409–11.
4. 'The structure of mass communications in Britain permits certain sorts of variations but they also contain the variations that are possible within quite narrow limits, set by the inconsistencies within a cluster of dominant interests.' P. Abrams, 'Mass communication', *Times Higher Educational Supplement,* 2 September 1977. See also Tom Burns, *The BBC: public institution and private world* (Macmillan, 1977).
5. D. H. E. Butler and D. E. Stokes (1974) p. 419; see Reference 2.
6. G. Drewry, 'The Official Secrets Act', *Political Quarterly,* January 1973, pp. 88–93.
7. N. Bethell, *The last secret: forcible repatriation to Russia 1944–7* (Futura, 1977). Nikolai Tolstoy, *Victims of Yalta* (Hodder & Stoughton, 1978) gives in detail the way Eden and Foreign Office officials concealed the truth even from Churchill.
8. Cabinet, 8 March 1946 *et seq.*
9. Note of a meeting, Treasury Papers, 11 November 1942.

10. Hankey's memoirs – *The supreme command 1914–18* – were ready in 1946 but their clearance was held up until, in the end, he published, without comment but in a bowdlerised form, in 1961. (S. W. Roskill, *Hankey: man of secrets Vol. 2 1919–31* (Collins, 1972) pp. 335, 532–4.) T. Jones was allowed only to publish *Diary with letters* in 1956 containing material after 1930 when he had already left government service, and his full *Whitehall diary* (R. K. Middlemas (ed.), Oxford University Press, 1969–71) did not appear until after 1969.
11. *The Times,* 20–21 August 1952.
12. D. H. E. Butler and D. E. Stokes (1974) p. 480; see Reference 2.
13. The Conservative Opposition and the press conducted a skilful campaign against 'excessive expenditure' in the information service to such effect that in 1948 cuts were made; the Central Office of Information remained careful to stay on neutral ground during the whole debate over nationalization.
14. A. Eden, *Memoirs,* 'Full circle', p. 299.
15. William Clark, Press Secretary at 10 Downing Street during the Suez crisis, recorded battering the parliamentary lobby, BBC and television with a 'well-orchestrated campaign of sabre-rattling', followed by the Prime Minister's off-the-record briefings with editors, not journalists, and Eden's preparations to control a hostile BBC, and to use secret funds to set up an alternative to its foreign news service – 'a ludicrous black propaganda station . . . to pour into Egypt the Goebbels-like stuff the BBC would not accept.' ('Ten Years after Suez', *The Observer,* 3 October 1966.)
16. As late as 1965 an *Observer* article, 'The Prime Minister and the Press', which revealed some of its workings, brought a peremptory demand from 10 Downing Street to the editor for assurances of future good conduct. One aspect of the departmental briefing industry which deserves notice was the activity of professional diplomats in the Foreign Service who, largely at journalists' own request, dictated the substance of many diplomatic correspondents' reports during the post-war years, wherever in the world they happened to be.
17. Samuel H. Beer, *Modern British politics* (Faber, 1976) pp. 347–8.

CHAPTER ONE

The Prime Minister

Introduction

We concentrate here on two recent Prime Ministers from the two main opposing political parties: Harold Wilson (Labour) and Edward Heath (Conservative). We begin with an account by the late John P. Mackintosh (MP and professor of politics) of the Prime Minister's power and ability to control the public relations of the government. This is followed by four short extracts from Richard Crossman's *Diaries*. Crossman was a member of the 1964–70 Wilson government, and he provides us with four glimpses of the Prime Minister's dealings with the media: Wilson ostracizing a member of the press; monitoring a ministerial interview on television; arranging for a favourable press briefing; arguing with his ministers about press relations. After Crossman we have Harold Wilson himself, agonizing – with hindsight – about the impact of his ministerial broadcast on devaluation. Next, Douglas Hurd, Edward Heath's Press Secretary, discusses the vital importance of broadcasting: for radio and television broadcasts, he feels, are now more important than speeches in Parliament. Then, the late James Margach, former political correspondent of the *Sunday Times,* gives a journalist's view of Heath's press relations. Finally, we end the section with an American comparison: an analysis by Colin Seymour-Ure of the crucial and individual role played by the US Press Secretary in relation to the American President.

The 'presidential prime minister' and the media*

JOHN P. MACKINTOSH

[One] source of strength to the Prime Minister is his opportunities to time and handle his initiatives on public affairs and their reception by the mass media. In fact, he controls, through his press aides, the public relations of the government. As Crossman puts it, the press are 'fed with the Prime Minister's interpretation of government policy and . . . present him as the champion and spokesman of the whole Cabinet'.¹ The press accept this relationship largely because of the value of No. 10 as a source of news so that many newspaper men wish to remain in good favour with the Prime Minister and his staff. Similarly, the Prime Minister can arrange his visits abroad, which usually draw considerable press and television coverage, as do his receptions for statesmen visiting Britain. Mr Wilson was always particularly conscious of the techniques of the mass media, so much so that the Conservatives came to suspect him of regularly contriving some exciting release on the opening day of their party's Annual Conference simply in order to blot it out of the headlines. But these techniques did not originate with Mr Wilson. Mr Macmillan also appreciated the importance of timing and of television coverage. The Prime Minister is the party's chief political strategist and the fact that the Premier can, to a large extent, choose when and how to act, confers a constant advantage over the Leader of the Opposition who has usually to be content with reacting. Only a Prime Minister who is caught in a position of acute unpopularity and finds power slipping away, falls into the position of having to react to the challenges of the opposition.

[. . .] Politicians often become familiar with the press and with journalists and become accustomed to their methods. They know that it is the unusual that is news and that there are fashions in journalism, that journalists are not necessarily more closely in touch with the public than politicians and that too much importance and influence need not be attributed to editorial opinion. Yet Prime Ministers know that if they are doing well, part of this will be reflected and intensified by a favourable press and that when they are doing badly, the position will be made worse by generally hostile treatment. Thus the press cannot, of itself, create a mood in the

*From *The government and politics of Britain* (Hutchinson, 1977) pp. 73–4, 109–11.

country but it acts as an accelerator and intensifier of feelings that are spreading for more objective reasons. When Mr Macmillan's policies were succeeding he was dubbed 'Wondermac' and 'Supermac' by the cartoonist Vicky and this tone permeated the press. When Mr Wilson had held the fort for eighteen months on an unbelievably slender majority, *The Economist* called him 'Britain's clever little man' and said that the 1966 election was a simple issue, 'Were you, or were you not for Mr Wilson?' Equally both leaders received severe treatment when their leadership encountered difficulties. Mr Heath always had a more neutral treatment by the press largely because neither they nor the public could easily grasp or characterize his personality and were left to concentrate on his policies. Great interest was taken in Mrs Thatcher as the first woman to be a potential Prime Minister. If she strikes a bad patch, some kinds of criticism may be ruled out because of her femininity but once again the press will both follow and lead opinion.

For a leader, attacks by some of the press are more indicative of public feeling or at least sound a greater note of danger than others. For the traditionally conservative *Daily Telegraph* to attack a Labour leader does him little or no harm but for the *Daily Mirror* to do so is most serious. It indicates that a paper which prides itself on being close to the people, and to pro-Labour people at that, detects a groundswell so strong that it feels it must register a protest. On the Conservative side it is similarly criticism from papers that normally aim to express conservative views that indicates something is wrong. It was the Northcliffe Press that turned on Baldwin in 1930 and made his life so difficult, while attacks on Sir Anthony Eden in the *Daily Telegraph* in early 1956 came from such a pillar of the Conservative establishment that the Prime Minister felt it necessary to issue a statement saying he did not intend to resign. Suggestions that a Conservative leader should resign would have little effect in Liberal or anti-Conservative papers such as *The Guardian* and *The Observer* but when a former Conservative candidate, Mr William Rees-Mogg (later the editor of *The Times*), wrote a feature in the pro-Conservative *Sunday Times,* 'Why Home Must Go', this appears to have been a major factor in making Sir Alec Douglas-Home decide to resign.

Television is less opinionated and a better medium for conveying information between the leadership and the public. The BBC and the ITV companies are by law obliged to give each party a fair share of political time and overall fairness can be enforced by the fact that the Prime Minister appoints the Chairmen and controlling boards in each case. This does not prevent disputes. Mr Wilson became convinced, during the 1966 election, in 1967–9 and again in the 1970 election, that the BBC was hostile. He felt that he was not treated

with proper respect and that the questioning in interview programmes he took part in was too hostile. Some of his staff went so far as to
attribute the Labour defeat in 1970 to the BBC but this showed an
element of obsession and a gross over-estimate of the effect of
television. On the other side, at certain periods in 1963 and 1964,
both Mr Macmillan and Sir Alec Douglas-Home were mercilessly
pilloried in satire and current affairs programmes and Mr Heath was
often hard pressed by questioners during his difficult period as a
leader who had not won an election and was trailing behind his party
in the popularity ratings. Prime Ministers can retaliate in these
cases. For many newspaper men, the report that they are out of
favour in No. 10 Downing Street, the source of so many good
stories, may cause serious alarm. A phone call to an editor from No.
10 complaining about an article or a news story tends to produce a
reprimand for the journalist rather than a rude rejoinder. A Prime
Minister or Cabinet minister who storms out of a BBC or ITV
programme or who writes to say he will never be interviewed by Mr
X again causes consternation among the television authorities.

REFERENCE

1. R. Crossman, *Inside view* (Jonathan Cape, 1972) p. 67.

Wilson and the media*

RICHARD CROSSMAN

Wilson and the Whitehall correspondent
22 February 1965
Cabinet went pretty well. It started with an item about the surcharge that we had imposed as one of our first actions on imported goods, which has caused the most appalling trouble with the EFTA countries.[1] Cabinet was now being asked for formal approval to a 5 per cent reduction in the surcharge at the very moment George Brown and Douglas Jay were announcing it at the EFTA conference! The only exciting part of this item was the lecture the Prime Minister gave us on the leaks which have been coming out of Cabinet recently, one of which anticipated the announcement on the surcharge. I chose my moment and went in to bat. I said I was heartily sick of leaks and I wanted to know how it was that the battle between Callaghan and Brown had been reported round by round in the papers. The reply I got from the PM was that there wasn't a word of truth in the story. So far, nothing had been discussed by ministers. The officials were still at work and he could say quite sincerely, with the support of the Chancellor, that the whole thing was the invention of the journalists.

Then Harold Wilson raised the issue of Anthony Howard. He has just been appointed by the *Sunday Times* to be the first Whitehall correspondent in history, looking into the secrets of the civil service rather than leaking the secrets of the politicians. His first article had been an analysis of the relationship between the DEA and the Treasury.[2] The PM said this was outrageous and he was going to accept the challenge of the *Sunday Times*. In order to kill Tony Howard's new job he forbade any of us to speak to him.

Wilson and George Brown's TV interview
30 September 1965
In the evening I went down to the BBC studios to watch George Brown being interviewed. The room was nearly full when the PM came in. George Brown was doing extremely well. He had had a long and tiring day but this didn't upset him until, right at the end, Robin Day[3] popped a question about his attitude to immigration

*From *The diaries of a Cabinet minister* (Hamish Hamilton and Jonathan Cape, 1975–6), *Vol 1*, pp. 165–6, 340; *Vol 2*, p. 108, pp. 349–500.

which he clearly hadn't expected. However, he recovered and responded well. I noticed that Harold took this very badly and told John Grist[4] before us all that it was an outrage to try and to trap a minister in that kind of way. He added ominously, 'We shall be watching throughout the Tory Conference to see if you treat them the same way as you treated us.'[5]

Wilson and Lobby briefings
4 November 1966
At morning prayers Burke Trend was listing the enormous number of subjects Cabinet had to deal with. When he'd finished Harold took me aside. He was deeply concerned to find that the morning papers were all blaming him for the blazing row with Heath at 3.30 yesterday and talking about his being rude and cruel and a bully. 'Was it really very harsh?' he asked me. 'Can you do anything about putting it right in the Sunday papers? Are you going to see any of them?' I told him I'd arranged to see Ian Waller of the *Telegraph* and Jimmy Margach of the *Sunday Times*. 'Brief them very carefully about the row with Heath,' he said. That's the second time he's asked me to do a job with the press and I spent part of the afternoon doing it. He had told me at Chequers that he is going to give up his Lobbies altogether and only see a group of journalists on Sunday evening. Everything else is to be left to my weekly Lobby on Thursdays. We'll see whether he really wants to hand over this much responsibility to his Lord President.

Wilson argues about press relations
11 May 1967
In cabinet we were supposed to discuss the South Arabian policy and the Aden crisis but as we sat down the PM began to talk about the press and we had a full hour of desultory discussion about press relations. Once again Harold started with his old complaint about colleagues who would go on talking to columnists and commentators who were hostile to us. Ian Trethowan and David Wood were quoted as the kind of person one shouldn't speak to. This started off a discussion in which ministers really began to answer back. I was glad of this because the one thing I find obsessional in Harold is his attitude to the press. After all, no one was more successful at handling the press than he in his first period as Prime Minister. Now he sees a few selected journalists on Sunday evenings at Chequers, condemns the press in general and suspects his colleagues of leaking. He's a voracious newspaper reader and each morning he's busy guessing which of us has given the particular piece of poison to which he takes objection and George Wigg feeds him in his hatred.

In addition there's a continuous row with the BBC which he

always compares unfavourably to ITN, with its friendly editor, Geoffrey Cox.[6] Yet last Monday evening I stayed behind in the Commons specially to see Harold give a superb forty-five-minute performance on BBC's 'Panorama'. He thinks he got this by being unpleasant to the BBC. Actually it was because he provided a superlatively good show. After the diatribe had finished Tony Crosland replied. 'Look here, PM, isn't that a recipe for disaster? If you tell us not to speak to the press at all or only to the correspondents you like, are we going to get the press we need?' He was followed by Patrick Gordon Walker who pointed out that in America LBJ was getting a terrible press because his attitude is exactly the same as the one Harold was recommending to us. Barbara then took up the discussion and said that he'd made accusations about members of Cabinet briefing the press against each other and it was high time he gave some concrete examples. I went on to say that I thought it was a mistake that he'd given up his press conferences. It seems to me essential he should hold at least one press conference a week in order to restore his relations. I hope the discussion did some good because we shall need it if we're to recover.

REFERENCES

1. The 15 per cent surcharge announced in the Statement on 26 October 1964 was reduced to 10 per cent on 27 April 1965, and finally abolished on 30 November 1966.
2. He wrote one more piece, on the Ministry of Technology and the Ministry of Aviation, before abandoning the attempt.
3. A former journalist who had gone into television in 1959 and acquired a reputation for provocative and determined interviewing, particularly in the field of current affairs.
4. Then Head of BBC Current Affairs.
5. By the end of Conference week it was public property that a major row had blown up between the Prime Minister and the BBC about their handling of Conference proceedings.
6. Editor and chief executive Independent Television News 1956–68, deputy chairman of Yorkshire TV 1968–71 and, since 1971, chairman of Tyne-Tees Television. He was knighted in 1966. [Subsequently, chairman of LBC, 1977–81.]

Devaluation
and misrepresentation*

HAROLD WILSON

There was every reason to feel that the operational stage of devaluation had gone successfully. The political consequences were still to follow. I was under no illusions about them.

My first task was the ministerial broadcast on both television channels on the Sunday night, 19 November. The draft I had prepared on the train back from Liverpool was sombre in tone; devaluation was a set-back, though this should not be allowed to detract from what we had achieved in ridding Britain of the £800 million deficit which we had inherited.

[. . .] At Friday night's meeting of ministers and my private office staff on the eve of devaluation I was pressed, above all by Dick Crossman, to alter the tone of the broadcast, and to drop the references to set-back and defeat, and almost to exult in our decision. I believe I was wrong to accept this advice and a comparison today of my original draft with the text of my Sunday broadcast suggests that I should have stuck to my first thoughts.

But this had nothing to do with the one sentence in that broadcast which was most seized on and used against me. In my original draft, under the heading 'What it means', I drew a distinction between what had happened to the pound internally, and externally. Recalling the devaluation of 1949, I was aware that there would be timid and frightened people thronging the post office and bank counters, pathetically believing that for every pound of their savings they had invested there, they could now draw only seventeen shillings. I was anxious to allay these fears.

[. . .] On returning to London I found a Treasury draft of my broadcast awaiting me. It was far too technical and jargonesque, though this was partly explained by the fact that the original decision had been that the actual announcement of devaluation was to be made in a television broadcast by me on the Saturday, before it was decided that an official announcement would be made by the Chancellor and myself, and that my broadcast would therefore follow on the Sunday evening. But, by pure coincidence, it made the same point about the fact that devaluation *had* not of itself reduced

*From *The Labour government 1964–1970: a personal record* (Penguin Books, 1974), pp. 588–90.

the cash value of savings and other bank deposits. The Treasury draft, quite coincidentally also, had a section headed 'What it means'. It went on, 'Devaluation does *not* mean that the value of the pound in the hands of the British consumer, the British housewife at her shopping, is cut correspondingly. It does not mean that the money in our pockets is worth 14 per cent less to us now than it was this (i.e. Saturday) morning.'

This was the only sentence of the Treasury draft I incorporated in the final version, replacing 'money in our pocket', by the more alliterative 'pound in the pocket'. Though I was cautioned by a civil service adviser, I was reinforced by the words of one of my own staff whose maiden aunt had telephoned to express concern that her Post Office Savings Bank holdings had been slashed by three shillings in the pound. As in my original draft, I kept in the fact in the same paragraph that '. . . the goods we buy from abroad *will be dearer* . . .' And again, '. . . I've said that *imports will cost more,* and *this means higher prices over a period for some of our imports, including some of our basic foods.* And it's vital that *price rises* are limited to those cases where increased import costs make this unavoidable.'

Though I referred to the cost value of savings, I made clear that prices would rise. Nothing could have been clearer, as my italics show. Equally, nothing said by any political leader has been more dishonestly or unscrupulously misrepresented and twisted for political purposes, by a hundred Tory speeches and a thousand press features.

The process began, the following evening, in a shrill broadcast by Mr Heath. Totally out of context he quoted the reference to the 'pound in your pocket', and interpreted it as a misleading pledge that prices would not rise as a result of devaluation.

He disdained to make any reference at all to my statements that prices would rise, or to the clear reason why I had made the point at all.

The Conservative press took up the point, with a degree of misrepresentation unworthy of them. And so it has continued to the present day. When, at question time in Parliament the quotation was explained, the references to rising prices cited, and the opposition silenced, unaccountably no report appeared in the newspapers which were running the 'pound in your pocket' campaign.

Some newspapers went further. The *Daily Express* began a series of weekly price-schedules each Saturday with an attribution to me twistedly headlined thus, 'The pound in your pocket *will not* be devalued'. They received little comfort in their statistics for some months, the only significant increases being a seasonal rise in the price of tomatoes and dearer beef, due to the most serious foot-and-mouth epidemic in our history.

To broadcast or not to broadcast*

DOUGLAS HURD

Speeches in and out of Parliament will always be important, but they are not now as important as broadcasts direct by radio or by television. Here the first and crucial decision for a Prime Minister on each important occasion is whether to broadcast at all. My diary is full of small wrangles on this question. When anything went wrong, or indeed right, the instinct of the party was usually that the Prime Minister should broadcast. We would then analyse the advantages and drawbacks of the different forms. He could do a ministerial broadcast as Prime Minister – but then under the rules the Leader of the Opposition would have the right of reply the following night. Or he could make a party political broadcast in a slot already reserved for the Conservatives – but that would make it a party not a national message. Or he could accept one of the pending invitations to take part in a current affairs programme – but much would depend on the competence or prejudice of the interviewer. While we argued over these pros and cons, the Prime Minister and his official advisers would stay cautious and uncommitted. Often the broadcast would be delayed or not take place at all. Often we on the party side would become extremely cross. Once I wrote: 'There are always excellent reasons for missing boats, and we are getting good at it.' Looking back I think that I was frequently wrong in this recurring argument. Prime Ministers should not broadcast too often. Each such broadcast should be an event. They should not, on the other hand, leave too long a gap between broadcasts, because broadcasting like cricket or tennis needs constant practice. They should broadcast when they have something positive and important to say, not whenever there is some sudden crisis which puts the government on the defensive.

Different arguments apply to other ministers and to the party as a whole. At a moment of real difficulty ministers are busy. The situation may be changing daily, and it will always be safer to stay silent than to broadcast and say the wrong thing. Junior ministers, who could be invaluable at such moments, are usually told to keep quiet, in pursuit of the silly but traditional policy of burying in the ground such political talents as they possess. Backbench Members

*From *An End to promises: Sketch of a government 1970–74* (Collins, 1979), pp. 79–83.

of Parliament cannot easily get the necessary briefing. So a government can drift dangerously until its output is less in quantity and quality at a critical moment than the output of its opponents. This is a particular danger for a Conservative government. Trade union leaders are usually ready to broadcast. At the national level they are well-briefed and articulate. The same cannot always be said of employers either in the public or private sector. Too often, poor innocents, they believe that silence is golden. Having kept silence for a few days they realize too late that they have been forced into a corner by public opinion based on the output of their adversaries. On industrial and economic matters the caution of ministers and the silence of employers were often during 1970–74 no match for the concerted effort of the Labour opposition and the trade union movement.

This was a recurring theme of my own notes to the Prime Minister. Here is a typical example from the spring of 1973.

> PM
> You may like to glance through this monitoring report of the week-end's radio and TV, with the immense coverage of the industrial and political situation.
> I think the position is:
> a) Ministers are broadcasting more often and better than before.
> b) Some of our backbenchers are good, others damaging: on average a good deal worse than Labour MPs.
> c) The TUs are *much* better than they used to be, as the monitor reports on Page 3.
> d) The nominal employers hardly ever appear and are bad when they do. This means that in the present situation we tend to be outnumbered; the need for continued exertion by ministers is correspondingly great.

As the situation in 1973 became more desperate this weakness persisted. Under the heading 'Miners – publicity' I wrote to the Prime Minister on 12 November. 'The party are still deeply worried about this. The press is good. But on radio/TV the National Union of Mineworkers have it mostly their own way. On Thursday Gormley appeared ten times, and was only matched once. Despite assurances the National Coal Board are almost silent. Ministerial appearances have been fitful – and not good.' I then went into the case of a minister whom 'the party thinks has an instinct for avoiding danger. Could you please have a personal word with him? A minister ought to appear each day on one aspect or another if we are not to lose ground.'

It was easy to understand why deeply tired and anxious men

should not want to broadcast. To broadcast successfully is almost as difficult for a minister as to speak in a foreign language. Some have the knack, others learn painfully or not at all. Indeed a different language *is* what is required. A minister reads paper after paper on his subject, bustles from meeting to meeting. He learns the jargon, the statistics are banged into his brain. He expresses himself in the language of that subject – and each subject quickly breeds its own language. After a particular meeting, say with the trade unions, he agrees to broadcast. He has an hour or two, perhaps only a few minutes, to think about the broadcast. He has to forget his detailed knowledge, forget the statistics, obliterate the jargon – and turn his thoughts and policies into the language of the living-room and the saloon bar. No doubt during those precious minutes of preparation some well-meaning lunatic of an adviser will peer round the door with a brief containing a fresh batch of statistics or a new refinement of jargon.

We tried to brief Mr Heath in the opposite direction, towards simplicity. On one occasion: 'words to avoid, because meaningless to the majority of audience: regressive, relativities, anomalies, unified tax system, productivity, threshold agreements, deflation, realignment.' These were of course all current jargon which we knew would trip all too easily off any minister's tongue once he was deep into argument with the interviewer. 'Also avoid percentages where possible . . . people do not understand references to Stage 1, 2, 3, unless explained.' And so on. I cannot pretend that we were brilliantly successful with this advice. We would have fared better with a man who had more time to think his way back into everyday language. In this respect we would have fared better with a superficial man who cared only for the politics of an argument and not for the facts and figures. Mr Heath believed that people deserved the evidence, and, by God, they were going to get it. It sometimes made for hard pounding. Most broadcasts on politics now take the form of an interview rather than a statement straight to camera or microphone. This has been one of the main shifts in methods of communication during recent years. The reason is fairly obvious. People are not used to hearing speeches in their living-room. The same voice talking continuously for more than a minute or two creates a strain. They are, however, used to conversation. They find it easier to absorb information and argument if it comes to them in the form of dialogue. They dislike violent disagreement because that too is unnatural in most living-rooms. The interviewer who picks a row with a politician, or a politician who picks a row on television with another politician, will soon find from his postbag that he has made a mistake.

The commonest criticism of political interviews is that the politician does not answer the question. Sometimes this is fair – though politicians probably give as straight an answer to an awkward question as, say, a professional footballer or club manager. But there is a previous point: what right has the interviewer to insist on his particular set of questions? On what principle have these questions been asked and others not asked? Anyone can find out the qualifications and the prejudices of a particular politician. What are the qualifications and prejudices of a particular interviewer? They are not so easily discovered. A politician can justly, it seems to me, use an interview to put across the arguments which he thinks are important on the subject being discussed. If he is skilful he can bring these in as part of an answer to a question which is put. But in any case he has the right when he leaves the studio to feel that he has said what he wanted to say, so that people can judge. The divine right of interviewers to govern a discussion is not absolute.

Of course there are occasions when a straight broadcast is best. At a moment of major crisis there is a general instinct that the Prime Minister should speak direct to the nation. A Prime Minister must first speak direct to Parliament, for that is a necessary convention of the constitution. Now that Parliament has finally allowed itself to be broadcast, a statement to Parliament is also a statement to the nation, and Parliament will be the main beneficiary. But in 1970–74 Parliament was still in purdah. A new device was needed if the Prime Minister was to dispense with interviewers and journalists and speak simultaneously through the media to the people.

That was the justification for Mr Heath's exceptional press conferences at Lancaster House. There was one already mentioned on Europe and another on the second stage of the incomes policy. 17 January 1973 – 'Quite a day. Briefing 10.30. Robert and William Armstrong and a mass of detail on the Stage 2 White Paper, coffee and biscuits. I try to guide it on to crude politics, and am rebuked. Redraft opening statement . . . To Lancaster House where in splendid white and gold room before a throng from around the world, EH performs admirably for an hour. Opening statement over-long, but the whole tone firm and calm.'

But whatever the techniques he uses, a Prime Minister will not communicate well unless he has a reasonable relationship with the communicators. There seems to be a regular cycle in the life of most politicians. The aspiring politician loves to communicate, and he likes journalists and broadcasters. At the next stage the politician still enjoys communicating, but he is enraged because what he says is not used and what he does not say gets banner headlines. He abuses editors to their face or rings up proprietors behind their back. He is above all anxious to put the record straight. Many politicians do not progress beyond this second stage. The third stage is weary disillusionment. Since the newspapers always get it wrong, since journalists and interviewers are mere butterflies of the moment, trivial or malevolent beyond cure, it is not really worth bothering a great deal about them. Only history will put the record straight. Mr Heath was not quite in this third stage, but sometimes not far off. He was rarely angry with the media, certainly much less so than some advisers, but he rarely warmed towards them. There were individuals of course whom he trusted and whose company he relished. There were occasions when he unexpectedly shone. The BBC knew a thing or two when they staged a 'Panorama' programme with him on Europe in the Metropole Hotel at Brussels. It was perhaps the best broadcast he did as Prime Minister. He was often at his best with European or American journalists, for he carried no scars from them, and they came from outside the intimate world of British newsgathering.

Somehow it should be possible to get these relationships right, or, if not right, better. The component parts are really not too bad. We have a set of journalists and broadcasters who, though often sensitive about any criticism of themselves, are on the whole talented and honourable. We have a set of politicians of whom exactly the same can be said. We have a general public which is better equipped to digest information than ever before. Yet politicians and communicators scratch and scrawl unnecessarily against each other's profession. They neglect the obvious fact that each profession is necessary to the other. When that relationship improves the public will be better served.

Heath's short press honeymoon*

JAMES MARGACH

During his days in opposition a pledge of an open administration and frank press relations lay at the heart of his proposed 'New Style of Government': everyone would share in the decision-making through constant disclosure of what was going on inside Whitehall. Was it not Heath who said in 1966: 'It is only when the opaque windows of Whitehall and around our working lives are opened that we shall find ourselves braced to make the immense efforts which are required in Britain today.' After the tantrums, bitter arguments and high tensions of Wilson's Mark-1 government there was therefore a sense of optimism as Heath moved in to No. 10. Perhaps at long last, the great ideal would be realized: access to Whitehall secrets, a genuine share in the great national debate; the door of Downing Street flung open wide, a welcome on the mat, come on in, so pleased to see you.

Alas, power, which has the ability to mellow some of those who achieve it, adding greatness where none was suspected, in Heath's case changed his personality almost overnight. When Prime Minister he became authoritarian and intolerant. The opaque windows and the front door were not open for long. The shutters were fastened and the door opened only to a select few by a government which was the most secrecy-conscious since the war. Downing Street became the most closed society in all my experience.

Heath had the shortest honeymoon of all with the political correspondents. Within months he dismissed them as an unfriendly lot, not simply because he identified them as dupes of Harold Wilson. Within three months of his becoming PM he decided to banish them to outer darkness. In the autumn of 1970 he released Leila Khaled, a Palestinian Arab terrorist, who had attempted to hijack an El Al Boeing plane flying to London. As she was a guerrilla he ordered her release in exchange for the terrorists' freeing hostages in other hijacked planes. The Lobbymen duly reported that many leading Conservatives, notably Enoch Powell and Duncan Sandys, regarded his action as surrender to terrorism, and showing lack of courage on his part. From that moment

*From *The abuse of power* (Allen, 1978), pp. 160–1.

onwards he more or less broke off relations with the political corps for their lack of cooperation and understanding. Things were never the same again. He and his PRO, Sir Donald Maitland, opted instead to operate through the diplomatic corps. In the end this encompassed his downfall. By the time of his defeat in 1974 he had cut himself off from political reality, and his base of political power, without the crucial daily contacts with the world outside, by his misguided decision to ostracize the media at Westminster.

Heath made no attempt to model himself on any of the Prime Ministers with whom he had worked closely. Instead he modelled his administration on the autocratic presidential style of de Gaulle, even adopting the Gaullist fashion of holding press conferences which really became TV spectaculars – with press men used as extras – during which the leader could expatiate on national and world affairs without the necessity of answering tiresome questions. Heath was so encouraged by his own Lancaster House experiments along these lines that he urged his advisers to plan a series of fireside chat shows to be broadcast simultaneously on both TV channels – thus enabling him to reach the carpet-slippered nation while by-passing Parliament, Fleet Street and the Lobby. 'Sunday Night at No. 10' was seen as a rival to 'Sunday Night at the Palladium'. Obviously the initial idea had come from officials who had spent too much time in Paris and Washington where Presidents do not customarily go through the Parliamentary-question hoop twice a week at the hands of people somewhat more motivated than television cameras. But as a new channel of power and communication it clearly carried attractive opportunities for news management, since the format, the issues, and even the choice of question, would be firmly in the hands of No. 10.

The presidential press secretary*

COLIN SEYMOUR-URE

Unlike British Prime Ministers', Presidents' actions tend to have a
deliberate latent (or implicit) meaning. For instance, they use travel
far more often than Prime Ministers do for the purpose of saying
something rather than for the sole purpose of going from A to B.[1]
Harold Wilson occasionally used travel in this way, but he was
unusual in this respect. Hagerty once persuaded Eisenhower unnecessarily to attend an OAS conference in Panama three weeks
after his operation for ileitis in 1956, to show that he was fit and in
control. Such travel has a more substantial purpose than travel
aimed simply at capturing headlines, such as Johnson was wont to
undertake. Presidential appointments (jobs not engagements) are
another means of conveying symbols. British journalists ask *why*
particular appointments are made by the Prime Minister. Less
often, perhaps, do they ask what the appointment is supposed to
mean.

The President deals in symbols, and his Press Secretary is slap in
the middle of the tricky business of interpreting them – which means
a kind of comment. He cannot just be a reporter, relaying to the
press what the President says and does. For it all means something
beyond its manifest content, and if he says 'No comment' his words
themselves are a comment. Interpretation, moreover, shades off
into the dangers of 'management' and deception.[2] The (often
adjustable) timing of a communication can make a big difference to
its symbolic meaning. The decision what to say and what not to say
can lead to 'deception'. Gerald Ford's Secretary Ron Nessen did not
like to interpolate items, about which he was briefed but not asked,
into his press conferences, for fear that they would be thought
'plants'. Some legitimate news was therefore missed.[3]

The risk of people attributing the wrong meaning to a symbol is
thus another threat to the Press Secretary's ability to make himself
understood. So is the attachment of an unintended meaning. 'Ford
the stumbler' was an image the White House did not quite succeed
in defusing even with humour, despite Nessen's efforts. Symbolic
communication is perilous because by definition symbols represent
the character not the substance of presidential policy. Their potency

*From 'Presidential power, press secretaries and communication', *Political
Studies*, Vol. 28, No. 2, 1980, pp. 260–5. See also the author's book, *The American
President: Power and communication* (Macmillan, 1982).

depends on the people's willingness to take substance on trust.

The President's tendency to communicate attitudes and symbols is reinforced by his combination of the offices of Head of State and chief executive. This produces contradictions (or at least inconsistencies and ambiguities) that again put the Press Secretary's credibility at risk. The office of Head of State tends to confer an 'expletives-deleted' quality upon presidential communication. It is nicely illustrated by the confusion or embarrassment momentarily felt when old associates address a newly incumbent President. On Eisenhower's first day in office General Omar Bradley phoned him. 'For years we had been "Ike" and "Brad" to each other', Eisenhower reflected later. 'But now, in the course of our conversation, he addressed me as "Mr President". Somehow this little incident rocked me back on my heels.'[4] 'Jordan, Jack Watson and the other young White House aides are obviously having a little trouble about how to address the new skipper,' reported James Reston during the Carter transition. '"Mr President" seems too formal. "The Governor" is out of date and a little confusing. And "Jimmy" sounds disrespectful if not downright cheeky.'[5]

Taken further, the dignity of Head of State can be elevated to mythology – Eisenhower as military hero (*Time* thought its readers were not ready for criticism of him in 1953); Kennedy and the Camelot myth (busily being punctured in recent literature).[6] Johnson, in an engaging incident, is said to have misled people about his birthplace. He pointed out a ramshackle cabin on his Texas ranch. 'Why, Lyndon, you know you were born in a much better house closer to town,' his mother remonstrated. Johnson replied, 'I know, Mama, but everybody has to have a birthplace.'[7] Nixon added flummery to his office. Ford, admittedly in an election campaign, said it would be undignified in a President to give a *Playboy* interview. The point about dignity and mythology is the little lies: they require the suspension of disbelief, which means hearing the truth but not the whole truth, plus a little bit extra. The Press Corps presumably accept the inevitability of some of it. Part, however, must induce scepticism or cynicism, since they see Downstairs as well as Upstairs at the White House and observe the political exploitation of the Head of State role.

[. . .] Another source of risk to the Press Secretary's control over his communication is the need forced on the President by the separation of powers to make his own opportunities for communication. His ease of doing so increases, rather than reduces, his need for choice. Congress and the Supreme Court are their own forum. Prime Ministers have Parliaments. Presidents broadly have to make their occasions (one curious by-product of which is that American universities are thick with sites marking the delivery of some historic address.)[8] Although the Press Secretary may be the main routine outlet of public presidential communication, he is never without competition (even if he is a Hagerty). Journalists will test his information against that of other sources, inside the White House and out. Some Presidents, like Eisenhower and Nixon, have sought to centralize communication. Others have not bothered or have failed hopelessly. The Johnson White House was 'one vast sieve' according to the historian Eric Goldman, a sometime strand in the mesh.[9] A Press Secretary will naturally find his credibility at risk from the usefulness to the press of other sources – including the President himself.

The President's style and conception of his job (its goals and powers) can affect his Press Secretary's credibility in a variety of ways. The conventional distinction between 'strong' and 'weak' Presidents can make a difference for a start. F. D. Roosevelt and Dwight Eisenhower, for example, both believed deeply in the presidency as a place of moral leadership. But their views of what this actually involved were quite distinct. The language in which they described them illustrates the difference. Where Eisenhower talked, in one exposition, of '*standing* for what is right and decent', Roosevelt talked of *reapplying* 'the simple rules of human conduct we always go back to'. The one chose static language, the other active. Eisenhower's idea was much the easier to communicate. Everyone could decide for himself what 'right and decent' meant, regardless of what Eisenhower might intend. Roosevelt, with a more dynamic idea of leadership, set himself – and his Press Secretary – educative tasks with a high risk of popular misunderstanding and controversy.[10]

The kinds of problem Presidents focus on can have greater or less communication risks. Foreign policy preoccupations, such as those of Presidents Kennedy, Johnson (as the Vietnam War built up) and Nixon, involve command powers and legitimate secrecy, which perhaps simplify a Press Secretary's tasks. On the other hand, the experience of Johnson and Nixon suggests that the problem of securing public support can be formidable and rebound on the Press Secretary. Johnson is the only President to have had four Press Secretaries in one term – or indeed to have switched Secretaries at all for reasons other than their death in office.[11]

A President's attitude to communication as a factor in his power is a crucial element in his Press Secretary's credibility. So sensitive was F. D. Roosevelt to communication that he had an aide spread papers all over his desk to impress Wendell Wilkie on a private visit. This might make a good test: which of his successors can one see doing the same? Kennedy? Johnson? Carter? Presidents might be located crudely on a scale. At one end are those who seem to have assumed the existence of an objective reality in the work of the President, which simply has to be relayed – 'the facts speak for themselves' – in order to keep the people informed. Truman, Eisenhower and Ford leant in this direction. Hagerty, of course, was under no such illusion, as the examples of his 'woodworking' have already shown; but his boss was. ('Woodworking' was named for Hagerty's remark that 'Boy, I sure had to dig into the woodwork for that one'.)[12] Ford's attitude is shown by his immediate decision to dismantle the Nixon news-management machinery and centralize the routine bits under Jerry ter Horst, his first Press Secretary. At the opposite end of the scale come the news managers – those Presidents with an instinctive feeling that most facts are really 'factoids', particular ways of looking at or describing things. (When does inflation become 'rampant', an energy shortage a 'crisis', a cold spell an 'emergency'?) Such Presidents – F. D. Roosevelt, Johnson, Nixon (and Kennedy?) – have sought by a more active and manipulative operation to create in people the reality they wish to be perceived. The other Presidents have certainly sought to manage the news, in the weak sense of trying to optimize its consequences, and they have done so through such tried techniques as timing, leaking, headline-catching. That is quite different, however, from deliberate efforts to procure a particular understanding of what the news actually is – separately, that is, from trying to optimize its consequences.

With Eisenhower freely admitting his ignorance of topics raised at his press conference,[13] Hagerty must have had a simple task compared with the Secretaries of Presidents aiming to demonstrate an (inevitably spurious) overall grasp. The role of Press Secretary under the 'strong' news managers must be incomparably more difficult and risky – not to say adrenal. Under these the Secretary is firstly at risk quite simply from the heightened awareness of news men that they are being got at. Secondly, he is vulnerable to the probably superior status and authority of communication experts elsewhere in the White House. Jack Valenti, for example, at one time had the job of Johnson's 'news creator', which he seems to have done very well;[14] and George Reedy talks of 'a long succession of PR specialists', most of whom departed in disillusion or frustration.[15] Ron Ziegler, as Press Secretary, was at first limited to a tactical role in the Nixon communications set-up, with Herb Klein, styled Director of Communications, operating at a strategic level.[16] Klein departed, and manipulative operations, of course, grew apace. Ziegler's importance – though not his credibility – grew eventually with awareness of his increasing closeness to the President.

Last among the risks to the Press Secretary's credibility may be mentioned the professional values of the White House press corps and the general political orientation of the United States press. The latter is epitomized in the kneejerk reaction of publishers against Kennedy's idea of introducing something like the British D Notice system of voluntary press self-censorship after the Bay of Pigs invasion.[17] This deep-rooted determination of the press to keep at arm's length from government owes something, presumably, to the tradition of separation of powers; but also, no doubt, to the absence in modern times of a strong party press, which in Europe has normally made the principle of independence from government coexist with that of loyalty to party – and hence, for some papers, of loyalty to the party in power.

The adversary stance among individual journalists (to be distinguished, obviously, from remorseless hostility) is a reflection of this culture. The Press Secretary may succeed in keeping relations good on a personal level. But, as the NBC broadcaster Edward Newman said on the appointment of his colleague Ron Nessen as Ford's Press Secretary, 'It ought to be understood by everyone that he's on the other side.'[18] The Press Secretary cannot sit on the fence for long. If he comes down on the side of the press, his credibility is threatened by journalists' suspicion that he may lose access to the President – or at least no longer have the President's full confidence. If, as is more likely, he comes down on the President's side, he is naturally suspect to the press corps.

REFERENCES

1. The Queen, more than the Prime Minister, says things a good deal by travelling. But then she is not allowed to talk very much in public. Travelling provides endless opportunities for symbolism on every scale. For example, Ben Bradlee: 'The President arrived thirteen minutes late, timidly carrying a felt hat. I had never seen him wear a hat, but he told us, "I've got to carry one for a while . . . they tell me I'm killing the industry."' From *Conversations with Kennedy* (New York Pocket Books, 1976) p. 197.
2. For Hagerty's fascinating news management after Eisenhower's heart attack in 1955 see P. Anderson, *The President's men* (New York, Anchor, 1969) pp. 222 ff.
3. *The Times,* 20 June 1975.
4. 'Some thoughts on the presidency', *Reader's Digest,* November 1968. Quoted R. S. Hirschfield (ed.), *The power of the presidency* (New York, Aldine, 1973) p. 118.
5. *New York Times,* 2 February 1977. See her Press Secretary's 'difficult adjustment' to calling Rosalynn Carter 'Mrs Carter'. Eric Goldman noted that Mrs Johnson's Press Secretary, Liz Carpenter, who had known Lady Bird Johnson for years as "Bird" now called her Mrs Johnson with complete naturalness. E. F. Goldman, *The tragedy of Lyndon Johnson* (New York, Laurel Books, 1974) p. 430.

6. For example C. and J. Blair, *The Search for JFK* (New York, Putnam, 1976).

7. J. D. Barber, *Presidential character* (Englewood Cliffs, New Jersey, Prentice-Hall, 1972) p. 54 quoting H. Sidey, *A very personal presidency* (New York, Atheneum, 1968) p. 167.

8. Winston Churchill's 'iron curtain' speech was made in just such a setting at Fulton, Missouri. As one more Churchillian speech in the House of Commons, might the impact of the phrase have been lost?

9. E. F. Goldman (1974) p. 142; see Reference 5.

10. Eisenhower 'believed deeply' that the President has 'one profound duty to the nation: to exert moral leadership'. Quoted in Hirschfield (1973) p. 123; see Reference 4. F. D. Roosevelt's famous 'preeminently-a-place-of-moral-leadership' remark was in a campaign interview in the *New York Times Magazine,* 11 September 1932. 'All of our great Presidents were leaders of thought at times when certain historic ideas in the life of the nation had to be clarified,' he said.

11. There are two exceptions who held office for very short periods. Jonathan Daniels served F. D. Roosevelt for some months after Early shifted jobs in 1944. J. F. ter Horst served Gerald Ford for one month.

12. P. Anderson (1969) p. 219; see Reference 2.

13. W. L. Rivers, *The opinion makers* (Boston, Beacon Press, 1965) p. 145.

14. E. Goldman (1974) pp. 135–9; see Reference 5. P. Anderson (1969) pp. 378–86; see Reference 2.

15. G. Reedy, 'The President and the press: struggle for dominance', *Annals of the American Academy of Political and Social Sciences,* September 1976, p. 68.

16. For details, see W. E. Porter, *Assault on the media* (Ann Arbor, University of Michigan Press, 1976) pp. 23 ff.

17. P. Salinger, *With Kennedy* (New York, Avon Books, 1967) Ch. 9.

18. *New York Times,* 21 September 1974.

CHAPTER TWO

The Cabinet

Introduction

This section begins with John P. Mackintosh's account of the Prime Minister's strong position in relation to his or her ministers; in Cabinet, it appears, some ministers are more equal than others. On 3 May 1973, *The Times* published a leader with the title 'Whitehall's Needless Secrecy'. It was the first comprehensive account published of the elaborate system of Cabinet committees. At the time of writing there were sixteen, and all of them had the authority to act on behalf of the Cabinet as a whole. There was a public right to know, argued *The Times,* which ministers were concerned with which policies. This right was more important than administrative convenience. In a parliamentary democracy, the leader concluded, the selection of ministers to make key decisions and recommendations should be open to public scrutiny. Our second extract is a detailed account by the editor of the *New Statesman*, Bruce Page, of the operation of the Cabinet committee system under Jim Callaghan. The dangers of this system, Page believes, lie both in its secrecy and in its personal, autocratic nature. Following Page, we have two anecdotes from the Crossman *Diaries.* The first is about ministers and the media; the second concerns the fine distinction between 'leaking' and 'briefing' in Harold Wilson's government. Next, Sir Burke Trend (now Lord Trend), a former Secretary to the Cabinet, argues that because of collective responsibility, Cabinet secrecy must be upheld: 'privacy' must be preserved in relations between ministers. Tony Benn then describes the relationship between ministers and the powerful senior civil servants. Ministers, he claims, can all too easily be manipulated by Whitehall. In the next extract, Professor Ronald Dworkin discusses the argument that secrecy can weaken representative democracy. David Curzon, an economist, takes up this theme and provides some telling examples of the implications of secret decision-making in recent US administrations.

The prime minister and the Cabinet*

JOHN P. MACKINTOSH

A more normal and regular limitation on a Prime Minister than the very remote possibility of a breakdown of party loyalty lies in the relationship with ministerial colleagues inside and outside the Cabinet. The limitations arise in several situations. When a Prime Minister is chosen or wins an election, greater power is conferred upon him, but the immediate objective is to end any old party feuds and to draw everyone round the new leadership. So most new Prime Ministers are inclined to include in their Cabinets or other ministerial posts those men whom they have just beaten in the contest for leadership or their chief lieutenants when in opposition. Thus it would be unwise to omit certain individuals and better if places could be found for a whole series of groups whom the Prime Minister, on purely personal grounds, might have preferred to exclude.

[. . .] Within this framework, the more normal limitations arise from the day-to-day operation of the Cabinet system. Here the Prime Minister has the advantages already listed of choosing the men, passing the agenda, chairing the main committees and preparing the ground with preliminary talks; he or she can decide if and when to intervene during the discussions, whether to allow the argument to continue by postponing a decision or when to halt and sum up the sense of the meeting. Yet, in almost every government, the Prime Minister has been over-ruled on certain issues, though most ministers agree that when this happens, it is a little surprising and a sign of misjudgement in one form or another. Mr Gordon Walker in his book, *The Cabinet*,[1] gets the emphasis exactly right when he announces in somewhat surprised tones that 'Mr Harold Wilson and his Foreign Secretary were once over-ruled by the Cabinet on a matter of great importance'. If this happens frequently, confidence in the Prime Minister will wane.

The purpose of Cabinet meetings is to keep members informed of major policy developments (the Foreign Secretary regularly reports on what he has been doing), to settle inter-departmental conflicts and to test opinion on the larger policy issues that are facing the

*From *The government and politics of Britain* (Hutchinson, 1977) pp. 76–9.

government. Often, on these questions, the Prime Minister may not have a clear view. He may be waiting to see how a situation is developing and how opinion is forming among the public, in his party and among his colleagues. But once the Prime Minister has formed a view and wants to ensure its acceptance, the odds are heavily in his favour. For instance, if the division of opinion is serious and opposed to him, the Premier can see those who may be likely to disagree with him one by one, as Mr Wilson did in the sterling crisis of July 1966, when he tackled each devaluer in turn until the opposition crumbled, leaving only George Brown to threaten and then to withdraw his resignation.

The seats around the Cabinet table are arranged in order of importance, the most influential posts carrying places opposite or close beside the Prime Minister. He will invite the senior ministers, especially those with such important or wide-ranging responsibilities as the Treasury, Foreign Affairs or the Leadership of the House, to contribute and it is a brave junior Cabinet minister (already overburdened by a heavy departmental load) who will challenge these more experienced, senior men. Also the circulation of information is selective, only a few of the Cabinet receiving the bulk of Foreign Office telegrams. Moreover the burden of their own work usually prevents the departmental ministers from reading even those telegrams of major importance which are circulated to the whole Cabinet. Richard Crossman, when Minister of Housing, once told the author that he had never said a word on Vietnam, but he had become so worried that (in 1967), he decided for once 'to be a Cabinet minister'. This meant that he deliberately neglected his own work and waded through the mass of paper on Vietnam so that he was in a position to put his own views. Thus, though there is an element of discussion and decision-making in the Cabinet, the Prime Minister and those he has chosen to be his principal lieutenants are in a strong position.

REFERENCE

1. Patrick Gordon Walker, *The Cabinet* (Jonathan Cape, 1972).

The secret constitution: the Cabinet committee system under James Callaghan*

BRUCE PAGE

The Cabinet, like any other large administrative body, must always delegate a great deal of work to smaller groups. But in less exalted structures – the boards of industrial companies, the management committees of local Labour parties – the membership of any sub-committee is normally a matter of record.

Not so with Cabinet committees. They are shadowy sub-divisions of a body which, for all its national importance, has only a shadowy existence itself. The formal position in Whitehall is that Cabinet meetings 'do not occur', even though their rather sketchy minutes turn up thirty years later in the Public Record Office. In humbler life, the personnel of a sub-committee will normally be voted by the larger committee of which it is a part. But a Cabinet committee consists simply of those persons whose names the Prime Minister chooses to approve. Generally, even Cabinet ministers have very little knowledge of the make-up of committees on which they do not serve themselves.

They know, however, that what usually matters about a committee is who is missing from it, rather than who is on it – and the list which the Home Office suggested for the broadcasting committee was exactly a case in point. Certain Cabinet ministers would have to be on such a committee for purely organizational reasons: the Home Secretary himself; the Foreign Secretary, David Owen (because of the BBC's overseas broadcasts); the Secretaries of State for Wales and Scotland (because of regional implications); and the Chief Secretary to the Treasury, Joel Barnett (because of the public-expenditure implications).

Organizationally indispensable they might be. But there was not a minister on the list known to have taken any detailed interest in broadcasting affairs. And the one 'outsider' nominated, Mrs Shirley Williams from Education and Science, was equally innocent of any such connection. Carefully *excluded* were the names of three minis-

*From the *New Statesman*, 21 July 1978.

ters known to be interested in broadcasting reform: Tony Benn, Roy Hattersley and William Rodgers.

Had the Prime Minister let this carefully-packed list go through, then the Annan Report would have been effectively sterilized. But on broadcasting – unlike Official Secrets – Mr Callaghan is motivated by something akin to radicalism: specifically, a hearty dislike of the BBC and ITV hierarchies, whom he believes to be guilty of undue arrogance, and cruelty to politicians.

Therefore he rejected the draft White Paper, and, more important, the proposed Cabinet committee list. He brought in Hattersley, Rodgers and Benn to the committee, and put himself in the chair. The committee was now packed in the opposite sense: at its January meeting Mr Rees attempted to defend the conservative paper that his advisers had produced, and in the words of one interested witness 'he got his balls chewed off.'

The membership of the committee now became known – not publicly, but on the grapevine to most broadcasters with an active interest in the fate of the Annan Report. Throughout the spring, its members were energetically lobbied by television producers objecting to the idea that the powers of the BBC and ITV should be re-established without modification. During March and May the 'radical' side in the committee won most of the arguments. They were better briefed, and they were encouraged by the Prime Minister, who got his personal advisers Bernard Donoghue and David Lipsey to draw up an 'anti-White Paper'.

Recently, the Secretary to the Cabinet, Sir John Hunt, was asked to justify the practice of keeping the membership of Cabinet committees secret. He replied that if members' identities were known, they might be 'subjected to pressure', and the story of the broadcasting committee is plainly a case in point. There is no evidence that the pressures applied to its members were unwelcome: but they resulted last week in the full Cabinet's decision, endorsing the committee's finding, to send to the printers a White Paper which adopts many of the 'impractical' reforms which the civil servants were determined to suppress; notably, the 'pluralist' fourth channel, to be operated by a new Open Broadcasting Authority. Some people may think this a bad result. Others, perhaps, will think that a society in which pressure cannot be applied to office-holders is not a democracy, but a bureaucracy tempered by plebiscites.

If, however, one does read this story as a triumph of democracy, it remains a triumph of a strictly limited kind. Exactly the same system has produced the opposite effect in the case of Official Secrets reform.

Labour's commitment to open government was a manifesto pledge in 1974. Not only were the notorious Section 2 provisions of the Official Secrets Act to be repealed: there was to be a new measure which would 'put the burden on public authorities to justify withholding information'. Whatever may be said about interpretation, there can be no doubt that this represented a pledge on official secrecy far more comprehensive than anything promised to the voters about reform of television.

The White Paper which was produced on Wednesday [19 July 1978] scarcely pretends to redeem the pledge. The catch-all nature of the present Official Secrets Act is abolished – so that not all unauthorized disclosures are automatically criminal. There is no right-to-know clause: chiefly, the proposed 'reform' merely defines more closely those classes of information which supposedly require the protection of criminal sanctions, leaving civil servants to face internal disciplines if they disclose without authority much information which would be automatically public in other systems of government.

On this question the views – or prejudices – of the Prime Minister accord entirely with those of the civil service: that is, he regards information as an insider's prerogative, one of the necessary advantages that he or she brings to the conduct of business. Under the Callaghan regime, 'leak inquiries' have been pursued with extreme rigour.

And these views of Mr Callaghan's were made flesh in the personnel of the Cabinet Committee which supervised the drafting of the White Paper. Known (under the curious classification system, of which more later) as GEN 29, it was chaired by Mr Callaghan himself, and contained:

Merlyn Rees (Home Secretary), Denis Healey (Chancellor), David Owen (Foreign Secretary), Lord Peart (Lord Privy Seal), Michael Foot (Lord President), Fred Mulley (Defence Secretary), Elwyn Jones (Lord Chancellor), Shirley Williams (Education & Science), Edmund Dell (Secretary of State for Trade) and Sam Silkin (Attorney-General).

Again, the unavoidable administrative needs come through: plainly, such a committee must include the heads of 'sensitive' departments like the Treasury, Ministry of Defence and Foreign Office, together with Lord Peart, whose Civil Service Department was responsible for drafting papers on official attitudes to information-dispensing (a case, one might say, of gamekeeper turned gamekeeper). Equally plainly, such ministers would not find it easy to take their officials along in support of a radical view on official secrecy – even if, like Dr Owen, they might find their party following enhanced by such a stand.

But the critical point is the absence, this time, of Hattersley and Benn: seen, by the Labour Party at large as contenders, from right and left, for the inheritance of its radical tradition. There is no administrative reason, of course, why the Secretary of State for Prices and Consumer Protection and the Secretary of State for Energy should be on the Official Secrets committee. But then there is no administrative reason why they should be on the broadcasting committee. The truth is simply that the Prime Minister thought their radical commitments would be useful in one case, and a regrettable nuisance in the other.

A significant aspect of the Cabinet committee system is that it is virtually impossible for anyone outside the Cabinet Office to have a complete, up-to-date knowledge of its structure. Given that there are always certain parameters to be observed (some ministers are unsackable, some jobs have got to be discharged) the system is capable of instantaneous and covert manipulation at the whim of the Prime Minister and his advisers. *Organization of Cabinet Committees,* the book which describes the system (and is classified as 'confidential') is issued to ministerial departments, but it is usually six months or more out of date.

Knowledge is power, said Hobbes, coining the maxim which all Whitehall life observes: and the fact that the Prime Minister is the only politician with access to all the intricacies of the system is central to its nature. It is part of the Faustian bargain which the Prime Minister of the day makes with the central bureaucracy: they operate on his behalf a highly personal power-machine which makes it difficult for ministers to challenge his will on specific issues; the consequence, however, is that the Prime Minister is apt to become more dependent upon his officials than upon his colleagues. The effect was seen in extreme form in the last days of the Heath administration, when the Head of the Civil Service, William Armstrong, became on his own admission something close to deputy prime minister.

Naturally, very few Cabinet ministers or senior civil servants would admit the truth of such an indictment – nor should such an indictment suggest that de-mystifying the committee systems would neutralize all our political woes. But before exploring the mandarin subtleties of the argument, it is necessary to give an anatomy of the system as it stands, in so far as its shape can be made out through the mist of initials and quasi-acronyms in which it is clothed.

In doing so, there is a general principle to observe, which is that most of the structure represents nothing more than ordinary, rational delegation; just as the anatomy of a Mafia syndicate, once disclosed, turns out to resemble for the most part that of any orthodox business concern. As one Cabinet Office veteran explains, what one looks for in the Cabinet committee system is the occasional, critical divergence from rationality – and always, for the contrast between what is there, and what might be there but has been omitted.

As one might expect, there are two types of committees: *standing committees*, which fulfil regular or anyway slowly-evolving functions, and *ad hoc committees*, which are set up to deal with issues of the moment. For both types bear classifications that are peculiar to the Prime Minister of the day, a feature which emphasises the personal idiosyncratic nature of the system. At any one time there are usually 20–25 standing committees doing business, of which about half really matter. These are identified by letter-combinations.

Ad hoc committees are numbered as they are set up, with an overall tag for the Prime Minister who creates them: the whole system being started afresh with a change of Prime Minister. That is to say, all *ad hoc* committees under Callaghan are tagged GEN (for 'general'), with a number: GEN 38, for instance, having been a committee of junior ministers, assembled under Peter Shore, the Environment Secretary, to examine the problems of the inner cities. Since Mr Callaghan's advent as Premier, the GEN numbers have risen to about 130 – though most of the groups have served their *ad hoc* purpose, and become inactive. (A GEN which was set up to examine relationships between the Parliamentary Labour Party and the Cabinet met once, agreed, and was disbanded.)

Under both Wilson administrations, *ad hoc* committees were labelled as MISC (for 'miscellaneous'). This is not a reflection of the Wilsonian style of government: it is simply that the label alternates with change of Premier between GEN and MISC, so that Edward Heath's *ad hoc* committees were numbered as GENs.

The code-names of the standing committees also change with a change of premiership. Sometimes, this is due to real administrative evolution, but mostly it reflects nothing more than Whitehall's penchant for a swift turnover of jargon. 'In conversation, it helps civil servants to separate the ins from the outs' is the way one former economic adviser puts it. 'If I happen to quote the wrong name for the principal economic committee, then it shows I'm not an important fellow any more.'

The present name for this committee is EY, derived loosely from 'economic strategy'. It is not, however, significantly different from what was known variously under Harold Wilson as the Steering Committee on Economic Policy (SEP) and the Ministerial Committee on Economic Strategy (abbreviated less happily to MES). It is chaired by the Prime Minister, and it includes Denis Healey (Chancellor), Merlyn Rees (Home Secretary), David Owen (Foreign

Secretary), Michael Foot (Lord President), Eric Varley (Industry), Tony Benn (Energy), Roy Hattersley (Prices), Albert Booth (Employment), Peter Shore (Environment), Edmund Dell (Trade), Shirley Williams (Education), Harold Lever (Chancellor of the Duchy of Lancaster) and Joel Barnett (Chief Secretary to the Treasury).

The membership of EY, which meets at least fortnightly and usually more often, defines the Cabinet's 'first team'. There is then a companion economic committee, code-named EI and chaired by Eric Varley, which is supposed to deal with the industrial implementation of the economics strategies determined by EY: although this includes the senior figures of Booth, Dell, Hattersley and Lever, it also takes in the 'territorial' Ministers for Scotland and Wales (Bruce Millan and John Morris) and two non-Cabinet members in Gerald Kaufman and Alan Williams, Ministers of State for Industry.

The convention of having separate committees to deal with the strategy and tactics of economic management has been established for some time: EI is plainly the descendant of what was called IDV under Wilson. But the real difference between them is to do with political seniority, rather than specialization of task. Any matter of industrial development, if it excites the interest of political heavyweights, will be taken over by EY or by the full Cabinet – as happened with the recent argument over the National Enterprise Board plan to allow lucrative private shareholdings in its proposed micro-electronics investment, which was a case of a tactical question which roused larger political passions.

EY has an offshoot called EY(P) which has often been much busier than its parent: the brackets denote a sub-committee, and the P is for 'pay'. This committee, which is chaired by Roy Hattersley, and contains Michael Foot, Eric Varley, Albert Booth and Merlyn Rees, is concerned with pay settlements, and it takes an active, negotiating role – unlike the monitoring work of its Wilsonian predecessor, known as EC(P). During the recent pay round EY(P) met almost weekly, and covered much extra ground by circulation of paperwork.

Constitutionally, it is something of a development for a regular piece of Cabinet machinery to be part of the daily detail of pay negotiations. But a larger point is made by contrasting the busy presence of EY(P) with a striking *absence* from the structure: there is no Cabinet committee to oversee monetary policy. Monetary questions are, of course, discussed in EY, but the full committee is far too cumbersome to give the workings of the financial system the attention that EY(P) gives to wages. Monetary decisions are made quite informally by the Prime Minister, the Chancellor and their officials, being announced to EY as accomplished fact. (Generally, EY members learn of a change in interest rates by reading their newspapers.) Much useful work might be done by a monetary sub-committee of EY, but it seems that Premiers, Chancellors and Treasury officials have found daily autonomy more tempting.

EY occasionally takes energy questions, but their normal home is the energy committee, ENM. This includes Joel Barnett, Roy Hattersley, Shirley Williams, David Owen and Bruce Millan (Scotland). One would expect the Energy Secretary, Tony Benn, to be included, which he is. But one would also expect him to be in the chair, which is actually taken by Eric Varley. Here is a subtle refinement of the system: given Benn's following, there could be no question of his exclusion from the publicly-appointed Cabinet, but within the secret system of committees the Premier can register disfavour by excluding Benn from chairmanships, which are reserved for trusties like Varley and Rees.

Merlyn Rees chairs HS, which is the largest committee because Callaghan has brought together into it the ministers for education and social services, who had their own committee under Wilson, separate from the Home Secretary. But this, like all phenomena in the system, is a political and not an administrative grouping: every position in a Cabinet committee is personal to the person concerned; at major committees, deputies are not accepted, and there is no concept of vice-chairmanship. Lacking its chairman, a committee simply does not meet.

As well as being home affairs, education, social services, HS takes most housing matters, dealing with much business which never goes to Cabinet. (Transport questions generally go to EI.)

At the other end of the size range is DOP, which brings together defence and foreign affairs under the Prime Minister's chairmanship, and is the oldest committee, in that it goes recognisably back to the Committee of Imperial Defence of 1904. It includes, naturally, the Foreign Secretary, together with the Home Secretary and the Chancellor: its curiosity is that the Chief of the Defence Staff is normally present, whereas in other committees departmental officials are merely on call outside. The reason advanced is the technical nature of the problems discussed in DOP: it appears, however, to present the military with something of an advantage when public spending cuts are in question.

Of course, some standing committees have only slight, or transient importance, such as QF, which dealt with the Queen's Speech. (RJ, which dealt with the Jubilee, has been disbanded: it was perhaps felt that an *ad hoc* approach would be inappropriate.) But LG, which organises the legislative programme, is always crucially important. This is chaired by Michael Foot, and contains the

Attorney-General, Sam Silkin, together with the Lord Advocate for Scottish legalisms, the Chief Whip, Michael Cocks and his House of Lords equivalent (the Captain of the Gentlemen at Arms, Lady Llewellyn-Davies).

Certain committees seem to be in quiet phases, after periods of intense activity: CQM, which deals with Common Market questions; CFM, dealing with overseas fisheries; and the two devolution committees DVY (formerly DP) and DVP (formerly DS), which bear roughly the same relationship to each other as EY bears to EI. Despite left wing suspicions that there is a security and intelligence committee, this does not seem to be the case: possibly, however, a committee would provide better supervision than the present system in which MI5 reports to the Home Secretary individually, and MI6 to the Foreign Secretary. There is, however, a committee on terrorism called TRM, which may be one of the few cases where secrecy over membership has an obvious justification.

It is a relatively minor committee called RD, under David Owen, which provides one of the neater examples of the absurdities which secrecy can generate. As the business of RD is to co-ordinate overseas aid, it includes Judith Hart, the Minister for Overseas Development. Recently, Mrs Hart was questioned by a sub-section of the Commons Expenditure Committee, and was asked persistently to agree that there ought to be some organization to co-ordinate overseas aid. Her answer became more and more contorted as she tried to answer truthfully without breaking the rules which disallow the simple answer: 'There is such a body, and I am on it.'

Inevitably, there is no hard-and-fast way of deciding which issues justify a standing committee, and which should remain *ad hoc*. Under Edward Heath, Irish policy was handled by GEN 29: in 1974 under Labour it graduated to a standing committee coded IN. On the other hand, Southern African affairs in this government are handled by GEN 12, which is a committee that meets rather rarely, but receives a great deal of paperwork from the Foreign Secretary.

But GEN/MISCs can obviously provide more opportunity for discreet manipulation than do standing committees, which must to some extent recognize on-going bureaucratic structures. There is, for instance, a GEN 91 to deal with the press, chaired by Peter Shore. At present, it is not doing business, but it might become very busy if Mr Callaghan could get a successful election behind him: whereupon the development of its membership will become an interesting study, as was the case with broadcasting and Official Secrets. (*Ad hoc* committees tend to be assembled in the flare of crisis. They fade into inactivity if the crisis dies down, or if nobody can think what to do about it. A case in point is GEN 112 on British Steel, now baffled and inactive.)

Suggestions were made early this year that, by way of a commitment to openness, the government might publish the list of Cabinet committees. There was a frosty response from the Prime Minister. Many wondrous casuistries are advanced to justify the preservation of secrecy: the finest, perhaps, being one ascribed to Michael Foot, which argues that if committees were not secret, then ministers would arrange their own ultra-private cabals, and not even the Cabinet secretariat would know what they were up to. But no realistic insider doubts the truth, which one Cabinet minister puts very bluntly: 'It's just very handy for Jim when he puts me on a committee, that I don't necessarily know what committee he's putting one of my competitors on.'

The committee system is of course not new: after its modest origins in 1904, it received its first massive expansion from Lloyd George, and its complexity appears to have increased greatly with the last ten years, which have seen the government's operations extend into more and more areas of national life. It has been stoutly defended by Robert Blake, Patrick Gordon Walker and Harold Wilson: all with variants of the same argument, which is that it strengthens Cabinet government by keeping the principal meetings clear of over-elaborate detail.

But none of these administrative arguments justify the two most conspicuous features of the system: its secrecy, and its entirely personal, autocratic nature. The ability to shuffle the pack of his colleagues without, for the most part, any effective scrutiny from party or public is obviously highly convenient for the Prime Minister and his official advisers. But amid the fantastic complexities of modern government – once again, his is the only machine which knows all that is going on – it makes him far more than the 'first among equals' of complacent constitutional history.

It exacerbates one of the natural dangers of our Cabinet system, which is that because the Prime Minister is the fount of all specific power, there is a tendency for the Cabinet to become a façade for one-man rule. And there is an awkward corollary to this: the less independence individual ministers have, and the less they have secure, acknowledged power bases of their own, the less strength they can bring to the Prime Minister's aid if he happens to need it. But there is a simpler point which goes beyond this: today's Cabinet is a social and economic executive such as Gladstone never dreamed of. It can scarcely be acceptable for a body with such aspirations to keep the nature of its organization secret.

The Cabinet and the media*

RICHARD CROSSMAN

Ministers on the media
16 September 1965
What we need now to complete our satisfaction is the successful launching of George Brown's National Plan this evening, and that is what we are all waiting for. Since I have only just been made chairman of the liaison committee it was far too late for me to take over from George Wigg, who has done a tremendous job in making sure that the First Secretary appears on the greatest possible number of TV and radio programmes as well as making a ministerial broadcast. Earlier on, Transport House had decided that he must go on 'This Week' (the Thames TV current affairs programme) because the BBC had turned down a ministerial broadcast as unsuitable. (The BBC were anxious to pare down the number of ministerial broadcasts as they required replies and comment from the other parties and so disrupted television schedules.) Thank heavens, George Wigg got this decision reversed. As a result he had caused maximum irritation in the BBC but he has got George a jolly good showing on all the media.

Leaking and briefing
11 November 1966
Our morning prayers developed into a long discussion because I found the Prime Minister obsessed with the problem of leaks. He was very upset by a leak which appeared in *The Sun* about the Common Market discussions in the Cabinet, and Burke Trend tells me there was a leak which was much nearer the commercial, profitable zone, about North Sea Gas, in the *Daily Mail*. Before coming over for morning prayers I myself had noticed in this morning's *Daily Express* a front-page story stating that George Wigg was handing control of the information services over to Dick Crossman whose job it was to clean up the party image. I'm afraid I assumed that George himself put it in and now that I've made some inquiries I am still suspicious because both Gerald Kaufman and Tam Dalyell saw him talking at length to the *Daily Express* man who wrote the story. Of course, when I put it to George he indignantly

*From *The diaries of a Cabinet minister* (Hamish Hamilton and Jonathan Cape, 1975–6) Vol 1, pp. 328–9, Vol 2, p. 120.

denied responsibility. In the course of our discussion I mentioned this leak to Harold as an example of the problem we face. Harold himself is constantly briefing the press and encouraging me to do a great deal of briefing too. I now have my own Lobby and my own regular individual contacts and I feed them regularly and, of course, I'm aware that other ministers are feeding and guiding their regular contacts, including George Wigg. I suggested that if we were to discuss it in Cabinet there would merely be a lot of accusation and counter-accusation and nothing would be achieved. I also told him that one way to reduce the number of leaks is to reduce the membership of the Cabinet from twenty-three to sixteen or seventeen. But as long as Harold himself feels that anything he tells a journalist is briefing and anything any other Minister does is leaking, we're not going to have a very constructive discussion.

Cabinet confidentiality – an extract from the evidence to the Franks Committee*

Question In paragraph 5 on page 3 of your statement you say 'No government discloses the list of its committees, their membership or scope . . .' I must say I do not see why it should be necessary to guard with a criminal sanction knowledge of how the Cabinet organizes committees of itself. To reminisce a little, I can remember asking once at the same time for a list of Cabinet committees and information about D-day; I got the information about D-day, but I could not get the list of Cabinet committees. It seems peculiar. Why should this information about Cabinet committees be withheld? I can see it may be a little more difficult if you are going to say 'and the members of the committee are so-and-so', because then you are exposing those ministers to nobbling from outside, though they should be able to stand up to that, but I do not see that we should be denied knowledge of how the government is organizing its business.

Sir Burke Trend It may lead on to who are the members of the committee. Would you give way to that, and expose the members?

Question I think I would. But I do not see why, if you wanted to, you could not say, 'These committees are the way the government is nowadays organized', and leave it at that. I cannot see why you should not let it be known that the Chancellor of the Exchequer is serving on that one and the Foreign Secretary is serving on this one; I do not see how that can damage the confidential nature of the Cabinet's proceedings, because we all know they must have sub-committees.

Sir Burke Trend One can only say that all governments, or at least all governments I have known, have always taken this line, and I think they take it almost by instinct. This is their affair how they choose to organize their business, whom they entrust what business

*From *Report and evidence of the departmental committee on Section 2 of the Official Secrets Act 1911* (The Franks Report) (Cmnd 5104, HMSO, 1972) Vol. 3, pp. 324–5.

to, how they organize themselves internally for dealing with any matter. At the bottom of it all is this feeling of collective responsibility. They may very well delegate X to three or four of their members in a committee, but whatever that committee may decide binds them all, and they know that. Why should they have to disclose how they have organized the treatment of that particular subject?

Question I can give one reason. If I had the list of the Cabinet committees in front of me, without necessarily the membership, and I saw they had a special committee of the Cabinet dealing with, say, air policy, and another one dealing with pollution problems, but they had not got one on some special economic problem and I thought they ought to have one on this subject, it would then be open to me to say, 'What a rotten government it is for not giving Cabinet attention to this pressing problem.' This gets me back to my original point: If you keep it so wrapped up how can you have any pressure on governments before decisions are made for good or ill?

Sir Burke Trend There is nothing to prevent you from pressing the government to give attention to that problem – you have a Member of Parliament, you can agitate, you can do whatever you like.

Question You say that all governments have taken this point of view, by which I understand you to mean all British governments?

Sir Burke Trend Yes, all British governments.

Question It certainly is not the point of view taken by foreign governments. I think a strong case could be made that the public should have this information, that the government ought not to conceal the way in which they organize their business. This is getting rather close to secrecy for secrecy's sake. How would you respond to that?

Sir Burke Trend I would simply say that I am afraid I could not agree.

Question Is not a vulnerable area, when we are talking about secrecy, the fact that those who are most critical of the Official Secrets Act know probably more than any member of the committee about the arrangements which have been built up over the years, and which have steadily increased, for briefing and informing at both an official and ministerial level? This brings us to another range of official secrets, who meets who and why; their knowledge of this system undermines a great deal the position of Cabinet secrecy. Would you agree this is vulnerable? If the Cabinet has a spokesman to brief certain people, albeit discreetly, does that not undermine a great deal of what in this discussion you are seeking to uphold?

Sir Burke Trend Yes of course it does. The whole area is vulnerable. A great deal of this arises from a misconception about what one means by open government. We all subscribe to the concept that government ought to be more open than it is, but do people mean different things in their use of that expression? It is one thing to say that once a government has made up its mind and has embarked on a particular policy, has taken a certain decision, the public are entitled to the maximum information about that decision which will enable them to form a critical judgement about it. In my personal view any government which knows its business will take trouble to see that its policies and decisions are properly and fully explained; and, if it is in doubt, it will adopt the Green Paper rather than the White Paper technique – it will publish an exploratory document or a document as a basis for discussion – it will test people's reaction. In all of that it will be, I suppose, technically in breach of the Official Secrets Act, but since it has authorized itself to do so, it will not. So I do not think the Official Secrets Act stands in the way of that very salutory and desirable process one atom. But before the point when it formulates its policy – again this is merely a personal view – governments do best if they are allowed to preserve a reasonable degree of confidentiality for their discussions, not merely for the sake of the nature of the subject on any particular occasion but for the sake of their own relations among themselves, how they choose to conduct and organize their business, the terms that one minister is on with another, the exchanges between them. These are a composite whole, and you cannot split them off in bits and say, 'You can disclose this to the public, but you must not disclose the rest.' Once you embark on the business of striptease of a government where do you stop? I do think, as with any other body of men who have to share collective responsibility, they are entitled to their own privacy. It is a difficult question whether you need a criminal sanction to protect that privacy. But, as I have said, please show me the alternative before you ask me to abandon the criminal sanction. It will have to be a pretty good alternative because I attach great importance to the mere fact of the confidentiality of a government's own relations within itself.

Question To revert to your analogy of striptease, do you not think that instead of the seven veils there are about seventy-seven? Are you frightened of trying to get a few off?

Sir Burke Trend I do not think the number of veils is obligatory, it is open to choice. But I think I want some veils.

Question Oh yes, I agree.

Sir Burke Trend And if you take away my omnibus veil, please give me something else pretty effective for the purpose I have in mind.

Question I do not see why you draw the line in that particular way. A great deal of what you have said can be extended towards further secrecy. I could make a case for the view that if the government disclosed even less than it does at the moment it would be better for the government. But how the government organizes its own sub-committees you do regard as a sticking point. In many other countries they do not. I am interested in why you feel we are right in our system on this and they are wrong.

Sir Burke Trend This is not just one personal view but a view that all governments in this country have always taken up to this time. They have not been prepared to disclose it until long afterwards, currently they have not been prepared to say how they organize themselves. If I may be permitted to ask you a question, why do you think that is so?

Question I think it is the force of tradition, always having done it that way, we think it is not only the best way but the only way. I am suggesting it is not the only way, and not even a very good way, it is the force of inertia that leads us to do it like that.

Sir Burke Trend I think it is an almost instinctive desire to preserve a reasonable degree of privacy about the relations between ministers.

Manifestos and mandarins*

TONY BENN

Ministerial relationships with officials
[. . .] There is [one] relationship which has received far less public attention, except in ministerial memoirs and some specialized writing, than its importance justifies. That is, the actual working relationship and the balance of real power as it exists between ministers, who have been elected to Parliament to implement the policy espoused by the majority, and the most senior permanent government officials within government departments, who have the major responsibility for public administration.

How the civil service gets its way
[. . .] They are strongly organized within Whitehall through a network of official committees, co-ordinated by the Cabinet Office under the general direction of the Secretary of the Cabinet, the most powerful figure of them all. The minutes of these committees are not circulated to ministers who are in general wholly ignorant about what is discussed, when, by whom, and with what effect. The civil service as a whole accept this process as very natural; and since their own promotion depends upon the approval of their most senior colleagues, they tend to follow the lead given from above. [. . .]

Determined mandarins have the power, and sometimes use it, to adopt some or all of the following methods:

a By briefing ministers
The document prepared by officials for presentation to incoming ministers after a general election comes in two versions, one for each major party. A similar document is produced after a reshuffle. It is a very important document that has attracted no public interest, and it is presented to a minister at the busiest moment of his life – when he enters his department and is at once bombarded by decisions to be made, the significance of which he cannot at that moment appreciate.

The brief may thus be rapidly scanned and put aside for a proper reading when the pressure eases, which it rarely does. In fact this brief repays the most careful scrutiny because from it can be

*From *Policy in practice: the experience of government* (Royal Institute of Public Administration, 1980) pp. 58, 65–72.

deduced the real policy of the department which officials hope the new minister will follow. It may be dressed up to look like a range of options for implementing his manifesto, but beneath that presentational language it reveals the departmental view.

b By setting the framework of policy

The key to civil service influence lies in its power to set the framework of policy. Lord Armstrong wrote very frankly about this power, as quoted in *The Times*:

> Obviously I had a great deal of influence. The biggest and most pervasive influence is in setting the framework within which questions of policy are raised. We, while I was at the Treasury, had a framework of the economy basically neo-Keynesian. We set the questions which we asked ministers to decide arising out of that framework and it would have been enormously difficult for any minister to change the framework, so to that extent we had great power.

Thus ministers are continually guided to reach their decisions within that framework. Those ministers who seek to open up options beyond that framework are usually unable to get their proposals seriously considered.

c By the control of information

The flow of necessary information to a minister on a certain subject can be made selective, in other ways restricted, delayed until it is too late or stopped altogether.

Sir William Hayter, a distinguished former ambassador, wrote this in a letter to *The Times* of 14 January this year:

> The temptation to conceal from an unreasonable minister facts which might tempt to confirm him in his unreason must have been very strong.

Geoffrey Moorhouse in *The Diplomats*,[1] his recent book on the Foreign Office, was even more explicit in describing the renegotiations that preceded the EEC referendum:

> Some of the home civil servants in the delegation from time to time quite deliberately kept their own Departments in London ignorant of what was going on in Brussels for a delicately balanced day or two, or even for a few vital hours. This was not a

betrayal of Whitehall; it simply meant that what Whitehall did not know Whitehall could not pass on.

I can confirm all that from my own experience in relation to a number of critical issues involving foreign policy, economic and industrial policy and civil nuclear policy. The breaking of the oil sanctions on Rhodesia, the use of movements against sterling, the protection of Treasury control of BP, the campaign for pressurized water reactors and many other issues were dealt with in this way. [. . .]

d By the mobilization of Whitehall

It is also easy for the civil service to stop a minister by mobilizing a whole range of internal forces against his policy.

The attempt by the then Foreign Secretary in 1975 to secure a separate seat for Britain at the North-South dialogue on energy was systematically undermined by the Foreign Office which made no secret of its hostility to any move which might weaken its support for a common EEC stance.

The normal method of mobilizing Whitehall opposition is for officials to telephone their colleagues in other departments to report what a minister is proposing to do, thus stimulating a flow of letters from other ministers (drafted for them by their officials) asking to be consulted, calling for inter-departmental committees to be set up, all in the hope that an unwelcome initiative can be nipped in the bud or transferred to the safety of an official examination. [. . .]

e By the mobilization of external pressure

If ministers require more pressure than can be generated internally then other resources may have to be brought into play.

A telegram from an embassy abroad can be elicited to give a warning of the consequences that would flow from the pursuit of a certain course of action. NATO, the EEC or even the views of multi-national companies or international bankers may be cited in support of a line of policy.

The IMF may actually have been informally encouraged to put pressure for public expenditure cuts upon the last Labour Cabinet, and I believe it was.

And these techniques can easily be reinforced by domestic pressures through the press. I am certainly not suggesting anything as crude as a direct appeal to the editor of *The Times*, the *Daily Telegraph* or *The Economist*. But such an appeal would not be necessary since the mandarins and the media proprietors share the same analysis and the same social values and the same interests which at certain critical junctures can be very useful.

f By the use of expertise

Most of my life has been in the departments which have a high
technical content – Post Office, Technology, Power, Industry and
Energy. It is the task of ministers in such departments to interrogate
their officials and the experts responsible until the political issues
can be disentangled from the technical one.

Any lay minister will start at a disadvantage in dealing with such
matters. It would be a mistake to suppose that senior officials are
any more expert than an experienced minister. They may, however,
seek to persuade a minister that the experts must be right and that
such technical decisions are non-political. [. . .]

g By the use of the CPRS

One important innovation in Whitehall was the establishment of the
CPRS which was intended to provide the focus for a broader, longer
and more detached view of policy than could be obtained from
departmental ministers or officials heavily pressed by the burden of
on-going business.

Though this idea of a think-tank has certain superficial attrac-
tions, it has in the event turned out to be a very different body.
Those recruited into it include both civil servants and outsiders, and
it has in practice become a powerful lobby for the Cabinet Secretary
himself to whom it is responsible. The quality of its work reflects its
small staffing. It is much more avowedly political in its opinions and
the head of it sits in Cabinet committees with the status of a Cabinet
minister able to circulate papers and to speak. [. . .]

h By the use of patronage

One extra source of power available to the civil service lies in its
strategic command of patronage.

Most public attention is focused upon the mere handful of
appointments that are specifically in ministerial control. The use, or
abuse, of the Honours List, or the charge of 'jobs for the boys' when
a party colleague is given a major post, attracts a great deal of press
attention. But thousands of run-of-the-mill appointments to
nationalized industries and quangos of one kind or another come
from civil service lists and reflect civil service preferences, even if
only because ministers are too busy to concern themselves with such
appointments.

Thus the civil service exercises an influence far beyond the
confines of Whitehall, and can call upon the resources of its own
appointees when it is necessary to do so.

i By the use of national security
Another power available to the civil service is the use of security arrangements. MI5 reports to the Home Secretary and MI6 to the Foreign Secretary, and the Prime Minister exercises supreme responsibilities.

REFERENCE

1. Geoffrey Moorhouse, *The diplomats: the Foreign Office today* (Jonathan Cape, 1977).

Open government – or closed?*

RONALD DWORKIN

Should cabinet deliberations and minutes be protected, as they now are, by the Official Secrets Act? [. . .] Discussion of that question is often ruined by a strange, polarizing presumption, which assumes that if Cabinet discussions are not protected by the full force of the criminal law, then they will inevitably be conducted as if Roger Graef and his 'Space Between Words' television cameras were there in the Cabinet room.

But in fact there are three, not just two, attitudes that government can take towards the security of this, or any other of its processes. It may continue to treat Cabinet meetings like military secrets, or like jury deliberations that must be kept secret at all costs. Or it may swing to the opposite extreme, and treat Cabinet meetings like meetings of Parliament itself, which must be thrown open to full and convenient public scrutiny.

But in most democracies the normal business of government is carried on under conditions that fall between these two extremes of compulsory secrecy and compulsory publicity. Government and the press deal with one another at arm's length. Officials may keep their work confidential, if they can; but the press may try to break that confidentiality, if it can, without fear of criminal prosecution if it succeeds. The government has no duty to provide publicity; it may avoid it, but it may not deny freedom of the press by resorting to using any special constraints of the criminal law as its weapon.

The main business of government is conducted within that middle ground in France, which has just as professional a civil service as Britain, and in the United States, where the government's attempt to encroach upon the middle ground by injunction was denied by the Supreme Court in the *Pentagon Papers* case. Neither of these countries practises government in a fishbowl. A combination of politics, self-interest, loyalty and responsibility can be effective enough without the criminal law in reserve. Nixon's tapes showed how indiscreet presidential talk can be, within the jurisdiction of a free and aggressive press, and we only found him out because he bugged himself.

But of course an arm's length relationship between the Cabinet

*From *New Society*, 24 June 1976.

and the press would provide a greater risk of disclosure than the Official Secrets Act does, however imperfectly the latter is enforced.

For there is always the possibility that some politician or civil servant will leak a decision he opposes if, but only if, he does not face jail or the sack; and that some paper will print what he leaks if, but only if, it will not be brought to court if it does. Those who favour the present criminal sanctions argue that the increased risk would be substantial enough to corrupt the general process of government.

If there is any genuine risk, they say, then the real decisions will be taken by a small cabal of ministers, who have more reason to trust one another, so that meetings of the Cabinet itself will be only for the rubber stamp. [. . .]

How much force is there in that popular argument for secrecy? We must make explicit a distinction the argument presupposes. This is the distinction between the *reasons* for a politician's decision, which are the considerations that actually move him or her to take that decision, and the *justifications* for his decision, which are the considerations he or she would present to the public if called upon to explain it. [. . .]

Of course, a politician's reasons and his justifications will never be identical. But it is desirable that there should normally be a considerable overlap, and deplorable when they have nothing in common at all.

The argument for compulsory secrecy of Cabinet discussions comes to this. It says that confidentiality must be guaranteed so that reasons that are not justifications can be given to Cabinet without fear that they will be given to the public as well. This argument begs the chief question at issue, which is the question whether that privilege is desirable in a democracy, and whether it is desirable at the level of Cabinet discussions and decision. [. . .]

Political decisions are reached, in Britain as in any other large democracy, through a series of discrete decisions taken by groups that are progressively more representative (because more positions and interests are represented in the group) and progressively more decisive (because they fix collective responsibility for progressively more powerful political units). Informal meetings in a minister's office are less representative and less decisive than departmental meetings, which are less representative, and vastly less decisive, than meetings of the Cabinet itself.

The ideal of open government, about which so much is said, is not the ideal of publicity spread over the whole process of political decision. *It is the different ideal that the gap between reasons and justifications should diminish as the process moves towards more decisive phases*. That ideal is not offended by a minister canvassing with his assistants reasons he would disown in public. It is shattered when decisions are taken in Cabinet, which is in normal circumstances as decisive an institution as Parliament itself, for reasons that have nothing in common with justifications provided when the Cabinet reports to the House.

The arm's length model of a free press works in a flexible way to enforce the ideal of open government. It offers little threat to the executive office where everyone knows how many and who are privy to what is said. But it forces those who manage the decision to take more care, as they broaden the groups that consider the decision, to argue on principles that are able to withstand publicity. The threat to secrecy provided by a free press works, in a practical matter, in exactly the right direction.

The partisans of secrecy miss that point. Their argument is weak because they fail to grasp the direct connection between the risk of publicity and the level at which the decision threatened by publicity is to be taken. Decisions become more decisive when they are taken by institutions that are more representative. When they are more representative the risk of a leak grows; when they are more decisive the threat of that leak improves rather than corrupts the process of decision. The Cabinet should be the first institution that loses the security blanket of the Official Secrets Act, not, as is often said, the last.

What shall we then say of the argument that if Cabinet meetings are not protected by the criminal law, then decisions will be taken by cabals, and presented to Cabinet for ratification only? If Cabinets really were rubber stamps, even on issues affecting the interests and concerns of those who had been excluded from the earlier decision of the cabal then the sense of collective responsibility that makes a Cabinet decision decisive would be lost. It is inconceivable that those whose voices are needed in the Cabinet for political reasons would accept that they were foreclosed by a decision in which they had taken no genuine part.

The critics say that government must be less efficient if the tenure-protected civil service cannot be brought into the political process, on a confidential basis, early on. That neglects the French experience. It also neglects the fact that there are pressures, internal to the civil service, that protect secrecy, and that these pressures could, as a practical matter, be reinforced under a less extravagant security system that did not label everything in sight 'confidential'. In any case the argument once again begs the question most in issue. Suppose the Official Secrets Act is amended so that a minister no longer feels so secure in circulating papers that display reasons for his decision that he does not take to be justifications as well.

Suppose that the laws and policies of the nation are different as a result. Do we have any reason whatsoever to think that they will be worse?

Secrecy and the US government*

DAVID CURZON

What is hidden by governmental secrecy? Secrecy hides the content of the decision-making process that consists of the premises of reality, the concepts of action, and the objectives and constraints that operate within this bounded deliberative process, and the character of the viewpoint that constrains debate. This answer leads to the real question: What problems might be hidden and exacerbated by keeping this content secret?

1. Secrecy can hide the fact that the premises of reality on which decisions are based can be wrong, or be such gross simplifications that they distort reality, or be deliberately biased in order to protect subordinates from the adverse judgements of a superior, or be based on prejudice and ideology. The advisers surrounding the President, as can be seen in the disclosures available, often formulate premises of reality that display remarkable ignorance. For example, in 1961, speaking as the top US expert on counter-insurgency, General Maxwell Taylor argued that 'the North Vietnamese will face severe logistical difficulties in trying to maintain strong forces in the field in South-east Asia'.[1] But 1961 was just seven years after the same forces in the same area defeated the French in a protracted war in which the logistical capacities of the Viet Minh were a significant element in their victory. These capacities were subsequently demonstrated again by the continuous flow of supplies down the Ho Chi Minh trail from North to South Vietnam under heavy US bombardment.

The general level of background knowledge operating in the deliberations on the Vietnam War is indicated by Daniel Ellsberg when he says that 'there has never been an official of Deputy Assistant Secretary rank or higher (including myself) who could have passed in office a mid-term freshman exam in modern Vietnamese history'.[2]

Secrecy not only permits such ignorance to continue unchallenged but creates the climate that makes it inevitable.

The problem of deliberate bias can be illustrated by McNamara's firsthand fact-finding missions to South Vietnam, which were the

*From 'The generic secrets of government decision-making', in Itzhak Galnoor (ed.), *Government secrecy in democracies* (Harper & Row, 1977) pp. 100–6.

source of important reports. L. Fletcher Prouty remarks that 'McNamara would be taken on an itinerary planned in Washington, he would see "close-in combat" designed in Washington, and he would receive field data and statistics prepared for him in Washington. All during his visit he would be in the custody of skilled briefers who knew what he should see, whom he should see, and whom he should not see'.[3]

The understanding of reality that is most significant in deliberations, however, may be grounded less in facts, even of these kinds, than in ideology, prejudice and idiosyncrasy. The reality premises contained in reports, briefings and memos have to enter minds in order to have any effect on actions. The limitations of these minds to receive and comprehend the strange and unknown, and the biases and opinions of formed and egotistical men, compete with the facts generated by embassies, intelligence agencies and expert analysis. What gets through? What images strike a response in the receiving mind of a Lyndon Johnson, a Richard Nixon, or a McGeorge Bundy? In 1964, for example, Lyndon Johnson told some reporters that he 'grew up with Mexicans. They'll come right into your yard and take it over if you let them. And the next day they'll be on your porch. . . . But if you say to 'em right at the start, "Hold on, just wait a minute," they'll know they're dealing with somebody who'll stand up. And after that you can get along fine.'[4] This may be regarded as mere prejudice, but it is more important for our purposes to see that it is a premise of reality and one that Lyndon Johnson presumably felt had been supported by his experiences. Few around him would have wished to contradict these convictions, and many pandered to them. But even if someone had tried to argue him out of his convictions, he is unlikely to have succeeded. These convictions form part of the world view that appeared in the confidential report on Vietnam that Johnson, as vice-president, submitted to President Kennedy in May 1961 after his trip to South-east Asia:

> The battle against Communism must be joined in South-east Asia with strength and determination to achieve success there – or the United States, inevitably, must surrender the Pacific and take our defences on our own shores.[5]

The premise of reality in this sentence, an exaggerated version of the domino theory in which the US must 'inevitably surrender the Pacific', surely played a significant role in determining the form of the continuation of Kennedy's policies on Vietnam. As Johnson says earlier in the same report, 'I took to South-east Asia some basic convictions about the problems faced there. . . .'[6]

The Nixon Watergate tapes offer us a direct glimpse of the ignorance operating at the highest levels of government. President Nixon and H. R. Haldeman, his Chief of Staff, are talking about a major international economic crisis.[7]

HALDEMAN: Did you get the report that the British floated the pound?

NIXON: No, I don't think so.

HALDEMAN: They did.

NIXON: That's devaluation?

HALDEMAN: Yeah, Flanagan's got a report on it here.

NIXON: I don't care about it. Nothing we can do about it.

HALDEMAN: You don't want a rundown?

NIXON: No, I don't.

HALDEMAN: He argues it shows the wisdom of our refusal to consider convertibility until we get a new monetary system.

NIXON: Good, I think he's right. It's too complicated for me to get into. (Unintelligible)

HALDEMAN: Burns expects a 5-day [sic] per cent devaluation against the dollar.

NIXON: Yeah. OK. Fine.

HALDEMAN: Burns is concerned about speculation about the lire.

NIXON: Well, I don't give a (expletive deleted) about the lire. (Unintelligible)

HALDEMAN: That's the substance of that.

Presumably the concurrence of the chief executive in many technical decisions is a matter of formality. But in those deliberations where the President must be an arbiter, the knowledge that he brings to bear may be minimal. Under these conditions, prejudice and ideology must provide the premises of reality and value that are needed in order to make a decision.

2. Secrecy can hide the fact that the objectives orienting a decision may represent the interests of a small group, or of one class, or of the personal interests of elected or appointed officials. For example, hearings before a sub-committee of the Senate Foreign Relations Committee disclose that high officials of ITT Corporation, which owned a subsidiary in Chile, had met in 1970 with officials of the CIA and the State Department and the White House in a 'prolonged and extensive pattern of consultation'. These consultations concerned plans contained in ITT memoranda suggesting an attempt by agencies of the US government to 'prevent the election of Salvador Allende Gossens, a Marxist, as president of Chile' by such actions as 'fomenting violence that might bring about a military takeover of the country'. President Nixon, according to ITT

memoranda before the committee, gave the US ambassador to Chile a 'green light' to 'do all possible short of military action to keep Allende from power'.[8]

Domestically also the protection or enhancement of the interests of a small group is often a dominant objective of policy, even when this conflicts unambiguously with the interests of the rest of the population. This was the case when the Nixon administration raised the support price of milk in exchange for contributions to the Committee to Re-elect the President from milk-producer groups. The fact that private interests influence both domestic and foreign policy is hardly a revelation, but the methods by which it is done and the extent to which it is done are secret, so that the public has little direct knowledge of what the real objectives of government policy are and how they are formed.

Secrecy can also hide the fact that there may be few legal or moral or electoral constraints operating in the deliberations. For example, the Pentagon Papers present no evidence that questions of international law or of morality were even formally discussed by those who approved general policies involving reprisal against civilian populations. Yet Telford Taylor, the chief counsel for the prosecution in the Nuremberg trials, in a discussion of the legal issues associated with the approval of these US policies in Vietnam concludes:

> [It] is clear that such reprisal attacks are a flagrant violation of the Geneva Convention on Civilian Protection, which prohibits 'collective penalties' and 'reprisals against protected persons', and equally in violation of the Rules of Land Warfare.[9]

In the case of electoral constraints, disclosures such as the Pentagon Papers provide excellent examples of how secrecy permits the electorate to be manipulated by selective information on government actions. During 1964, prior to the first US bombing of North Vietnam and during the presidential election campaign, the US was supporting raids by boat from South Vietnam for such activities as the 'destruction of section of Hanoi-Vinh railroad'.[10] These activities were kept secret from the US electorate and Congress. A major purpose of these activities appears to have been to provoke North Vietnam into actions that could be used as an excuse to obtain public and congressional support for bombing. A 'Plan of Action for South Vietnam', drafted in September 1964, listed five 'desiderata' for US actions, including 'they should be likely at some point to provoke a military DRV (Democratic Republic of [North] Vietnam) response' and 'the provoked response should provide good grounds for us to escalate if we wished'.[11]

3. Secrecy can hide the concepts of action that were considered and rejected. The use of tactical atomic weapons or the threat of mass murder, for example, might have been seriously considered and rejected narrowly or on grounds that show that such action could be used in the future. For example, the Pentagon Papers show that the threat of mass starvation was considered by senior US officials. McNaughton, in a memorandum of 8 January 1966, suggested that the destruction of locks and dams in North Vietnam might 'offer promise':

> It should be studied. Such destruction does not kill or drown people. By shallow flooding the rice it leads after time to widespread starvation (more than a million?) unless food is provided – which we could offer to do 'at the conference table'.[12]

In the opposite vein, secrecy can hide the fact that the concepts of action considered will be only a few of the actions that are conceivable under the circumstances. Those not considered or rejected may be superior to the action taken. But it is not possible for an outsider to make this judgement, since secrecy also hides the premises that underlie the adoption or rejection of a particular action. By doing so, secrecy can also hide the face that the actions taken may be 'irrational', even in the narrow sense defined above. For example, President Johnson's half-formulated doubts were apparently crystallized by Dean Acheson, a former US Secretary of State whom Johnson respected, who told him in a private meeting that 'the Joint Chiefs of Staff don't know what they are talking about'.[13] Acheson's conclusion was that the actions advocated by the Joint Chiefs of Staff were inconsistent with his perception of the reality in Vietnam.

4. Secrecy hides the fact that the deliberations are circumscribed by an ideology. This could only be illustrated by an extended case study, but the point itself is simple enough. There are two complementary ways of examining the debate and conflict in deliberations. The first is to recapitulate the conflicts of judgement of the debate. But, as Gabriel Kolko points out, that debate and conflict occur is often of less significance than that the debate is circumscribed, perhaps unconsciously, by the shared ideology of the participants.[14] An example of the effects of shared ideology is pointed out by the fact that no one in the US executive branch during the entire period covered by the Pentagon Papers ever presented the case of supporting the NLF. The ideology of the participants determined this absence, and any conflicts of judgement occurred within a perspective in which the NLF view of events in South Vietnam could not be presented. But this perspective

should not be taken for granted in an analysis. Any attempt to comprehend the US policy deliberations on the Vietnam War, in which premises of reality and objectives and concepts of action were heatedly debated, must begin with some characterization of, and explanation for, the limits within which this debate occurred. The second way of examining the conflicts of judgement in a policy debate, then, is to characterize the ideology shared by those who were disagreeing. This is usually implicit in the debate, and the participants themselves will usually not be aware of it; they may even deny having an ideology. Nonetheless, the word *ideology* is appropriate to designate this bounding of deliberation. In the case of US policy towards the Allende government in Chile, for example, if the ITT memoranda were representative of the deliberations, the implicit ideology can be most easily characterized as the protection of the common (or 'class') interests of the owners of US property in Chile and (if a domino theory was also one of the premises of reality) in the rest of Latin America.

5. Finally, secrecy can hide the fact that those exercising power may be persons inadequate to the moral and intellectual complexity of the problems that they face in the roles that give them so much power over others' lives. Individuals act differently in different situations, and the character and capacities of officials in the job of deliberation under pressure may be surprisingly different from their characters and capacities in more static circumstances, such as public meetings or private interviews and dinners.

The tapes of President Nixon and his aides discussing Watergate illustrate this point voluminously. Often newspaper stories provide glimpses of the psychological climate and quality of deliberations on momentous decisions. Some former aides to Henry Kissinger, for example, report that he told his staff on the afternoon of the 1970 US invasion of Cambodia, that 'our leader has flipped his lid. But you're all expected to rally round. If you can't, get out. We can't have any carping in the back room'.[15] This is hearsay, but it is terrifying hearsay, for it indicates that it may be possible that democracies, like totalitarian regimes, are modes of government that permit sufficient discretion to leaders for them to launch an invasion of another country for idiosyncratic, as distinct from ideological, reasons.

REFERENCES

1. *Pentagon papers* (New York, Bantam Books, 1971) p. 143. While this edition is a drastic abridgement, it is adequate as a source of illustration and is widely available.

2. Daniel Ellsberg, *Papers on the war* (New York, Simon & Schuster, 1972) p. 28.
3. L. Fletcher Prouty, *The secret team* (New York, Ballantine Books, 1974) p. 14.
4. Richard J. Barnet, *Roots of war* (Baltimore, Penguin Books, 1973) p. 87.
5. *Pentagon papers* (1971) p. 128: see Reference 1.
6. Ibid.
7. *New York Times,* 6 August 1974, p. 14.
8. *New York Times,* 22 March 1974, p. 1, and 23 March 1974, p. 1. As I was finishing this paper, corroboration of the US role in the overthrow of the Allende government was given in an article in the *New York Times,* 8 September 1974, p. 1, reporting on testimony to Congress by the head of the CIA.
9. Telford Taylor, *Nuremberg and Vietnam* (New York, Quadrangle Books, 1970) p. 145.
10. *Pentagon papers* (1971) p. 302.
11. Ibid., p. 356
12. Mike Gravel (ed.), *The Senator Gravel edition: the Pentagon papers* (Boston, Beacon Press, 1971) 4:43, cited in D. Ellsberg (1972) p. 295; see Reference 2.
13. Townsend Hoopes, *The limits of intervention* (New York, McKay, 1969) pp. 204–5.
14. Gabriel Kolko, *The roots of American foreign policy* (Boston, Beacon Press, 1969) p. 7.
15. *New York Post,* 13 June 1974, p. 33.

CHAPTER THREE

Parliament

Introduction

The role of parliament

London – When John Mackintosh, a noted Labour Member of Parliament, died the other day, his entire staff was dismissed on the spot. It consisted of one woman, a secretary.

This incident points up the antiquated and amateurish fashion in which the House of Commons works compared with the US Congress. It explains why the mother of Parliaments has become an almost helpless rubber stamp in many instances for government ministers and a growing bureaucracy.[1]

Parliament's role in a representative democracy is crucial. Yet political scientists tend to regard it ambivalently and at least one academic has dismissed it from his analysis of contemporary British government.[2] There is, however, a scholarly preoccupation with its decline. And whether or not there was ever a 'golden age' of British government in which Parliament was genuinely sovereign, its current failure to hold government properly to account leaves a serious gap in the political system. It is the *only* institution to which government is formally accountable.

In the first extract of this section Keith Middlemas argues that Bagehot's distinction between the real division of power and the dignified part of the constitution applies to Parliament. In his view it has lost both its positive power of initiating policy and its negative power of restraining government expenditure. So what functions are left to Parliament? Why does it find it so difficult to fulfil them in an effective way? And what are the consequences for government's management of information and therefore for policy-making?

Historically Question Time in the House of Commons is a device through which backbenchers can fulfil one of the most important of their remaining functions – scrutiny of government policy. Theoretically it is a mechanism by which Members can elicit information and thereby embarrass the government or make public certain aspects of policy. But how useful are MPs' questions? In the article below Martin Bailey and Charles Medawar reveal some of the restrictions and techniques of official evasion that the system has acquired. In 1978 a Labour MP, Jeff Rooker, forced the government to reveal its policy on questions. He asked each departmental minister to list all those topics on which it was *not* his practice to answer questions. Columns of *Hansard* were filled with the answers which ranged from 'Details of arms sales, operational matters, contract prices, costs of individual aircraft etc . . .' (Minister of Defence) to 'reasons for investigation or non-investigation of aircraft accidents . . .' and 'day-to-day matters of the English Tourist Board . . .' (Secretary of State for Trade). What the English Tourist Board might have to hide is never revealed.[3]

Concern that Parliamentary Questions have more of a ritual than a real value is not new. The feeling that Parliament needed a more powerful method of holding government to account can be traced back to the demand for Parliamentary reform, and in particular the call for a new Select Committee system, in the early 1960s. Richard Crossman, as Lord President of the Council and Leader of the House, was responsible for introducing a new set of Select Committees inquiring into a wider range of government policies than previously. It is somewhat ironical that it was in the same capacity that he wrote to the Chairmen of the new committees making it clear that ministers could not be questioned about certain areas of policy.[4] So perhaps it is not surprising that hopes that this reform might help redress the balance of power between Parliament and the executive have also been dashed. Leslie Chapman, a former regional director with the Ministry of Works, reveals below, in the extract from his book, how even the Parliamentary Accounts Committee, 'Parliament's watchdog on public expenditure', was weak and ineffective when it came to deal with clear cases of government waste. Yet, as he points out, if the tax payer has any hopes of his interests being protected, it is with this body that his hopes must rest.

Why are Select Committees so ineffectual? One argument is that MPs are insufficiently informed to pursue vigorous lines of questioning in their inquiries. Most MPs are dissatisfied with the staff facilities and the sources of information available to them. (For a more detailed account, two surveys of MPs' opinions are available.[5]) But past Select Committee inquiries indicate more intransigent problems. The Nationalized Industries Select Committee came into direct conflict with the government over its inquiry into the British Steel Corporation (1977–78).[6] The government refused to lay before the Committee certain papers relating to the Corporation's borrowing. Without this information, as the Report pointed out, the Committee was unable to fulfil its statutory duty of controlling the Corporation's borrowing. Committees have no power to insist on the submission of evidence of a verbal or written nature. During the Overseas Development Committee's inquiry into the renegotiation of the Lomé Convention the minister, Judith Hart, drew the Committee's attention to the fact there are certain categories of information that ministers cannot reveal.[7]

The weakness of the Select Committee system in Britain is often compared unfavourably with the power of the US Congressional Committees. But as Sir Angus Maude, a senior Conservative MP, points out in the extract from the Granada Television programme below, this criticism is based on a misunderstanding of the two constitutions. The House of Commons operates on the basis of the political party alignments within it. This means, Nevil Johnson has written, that the overarching activity is the competition between government and opposition with the result that Select Committees must always have a certain academic quality.[8] Another view, supported by parliamentarians as diverse as Michael Foot and Enoch Powell, is that Parliament best performs its functions on the floor of the house. The forum of debate should not, they think, move upstairs to the committee corridor.

In 1980, however, following the recommendations of the Select Committee on Procedure (see note 4, below) Norman St John Stevas, Leader of the House, introduced a new departmentally based Committee system designed '. . . to exercise effective control and stewardship over ministers and the expanding bureaucracy of the modern state.' Hugo Young, in the final essay in this book, describes it as a political achievement offering hope for more open government. But subtle forms of resistance to the new Committee system have not been slow to emerge. A directive leaked to Peter Hennessy of *The Times* listed instructions for civil servants appearing before Select Committees on how to cope with questions. They are directed not to disclose '. . . any information which the government wishes to be kept secret whether or not it is already classified information.'[9] And the new Committee system has already been beset by party division as the controversial report from the new Environment Committee on council house sales shows.[10]

The Lobby system

The symbolic importance of Parliament is confirmed in the Lobby system. It is the chief source of both formal and informal political news for correspondents. But does a system which is governed by rules more suited to a boys' boarding school, as Anthony King, a Professor of Politics points out in his discussion of the Lobby system, result in an informed view of political life? The extract from his discussion with a number of journalists reveals a division of opinion. The degree to which the Lobby can be manipulated by the government is made clear by David McKie, deputy editor of *The*

Guardian, in his account of the calculated leaking and briefing that takes place.

REFERENCES

1. Bernard D. Nossiter, London correspondent, *Washington Post*, 13 August 1978.
2. Peter Self, 'Are we worse governed', *New Society,* 19 May 1977, p. 334.
3. For a complete list of the questions that ministers refuse to answer see Brian Sedgemore, *The secret constitution: an analysis of the political establishment* (Hodder & Stoughton, 1980), Appendix 3.
4. *First report of the Select Committee on Procedure, session 1977–8,* HC 588, Vol. 1, Appendix D, p. 29.
5. A. Barker and M. Rush, *The Member of Parliament and his information* (Allen & Unwin, 1970); and Keith Ovenden, *The politics of steel* (Macmillan, 1969) ch. 11.
6. *First, second and fifth reports from the Select Committee on Nationalized Industries, session 1977–8: the British Steel Corporation,* HC26, 127, 238.
7. *Second report of the Committee on Overseas Development, sessions 1977–8: the renegotiation of the Lomé Convention,* HC 586, p. 36.
8. Nevil Johnson, 'Select Committees as tools of parliamentary reform: some further reflections', in S. A. Walkland and Michael Ryle (eds), *The Commons in the 70s* (Fontana, 1977).
9. Peter Hennessy, 'Whitehall men told what not to disclose', *The Times,* 27 May 1980.
10. For an examination of the issue of how useful it is for Committees to inquire into such areas of political sensitivity see Julia Langdon, 'Split provokes doubts in Select Committee system', *The Guardian* 20 July 1981.

The devaluation of
Parliament*

KEITH MIDDLEMAS

It was Bagehot who first observed the distinction between the real division of power and the dignified version of the constitution. Myths inevitably surround the formation of the National Government, the subsequent devaluation of the party system, the influence of industrial institutions, and the role of Parliament itself *vis-à-vis* the state apparatus in the 1930s and 40s, befogging textbooks, procedural manuals and contemporary debates about sovereignty inside Britain.[1] Yet in no complex modern society is it conceivable that present-day realities should instantaneously be reflected in continuous rehabilitation of traditional theory. In Britain especially it has been habitual to modernize the constitution by appeal to a remoter, purer and usually fictitious past, overlaid by recent abuses which may be remedied, rather than to advocate change – and this process is, inevitably, slow.[2]

To assess the change in party politics since 1911, and the balance between strategy for government and ideological preoccupation is virtually impossible on a statistical basis or, for lack of sound evidence about voters' opinions, from outside the system itself. The records inside – of party or institution – are necessarily biased and myopic and sometimes, where organization is concerned, extremely dull. But they do reveal a calculating face rarely displayed in public, a mundane, even cynical, preoccupation with what Burke called 'interest', more valuable than the selective offerings of election time. In the light of such evidence, between 1911 and 1945, it can be said that parties had become more homogeneous, the range and variety of views they presented diminishing, like the number of manifestos, in proportion to increasing central direction; inter-party warfare became a matter of stereotyped abuse rather than the rational discussion whose decline Edwardian parliamentarians had already become accustomed to deplore.

Great areas of national policy tended to become the prerogative of ministers and civil servants, acting within the curtilage of 'government', rather than of political leaders and MPs in the House of

*From *Politics in industrial society: the experience of the British system since 1911* (Deutsch, 1979) pp. 308–9.

Commons. Consequently, party strategy, organization, finance and propaganda were devised for electoral conflicts which provided, not administrations in the broad, nineteenth-century sense, but the personnel of Cabinets, the mandate for a set of policies, and the House of Commons majority which ensured tenure of the state apparatus so long as the Prime Minister determined. Well before 1940, Parliament as distinct from government had lost the power of initiating policy or legislation, except on the narrow front reserved for 'private members'; while even its negative power of restraint over government expenditure had been seriously curtailed by administrative changes contingent on the presentation of complex Estimates and the weakness of its Select Committees in the face of departmental secrecy.

This view is now commonly accepted,[3] in a decade increasingly disillusioned with Parliament after many years' devaluation of the language of political management.

REFERENCES

1. A survey conducted by the Hansard Society in the summer of 1977, for example, discovered that 49 per cent of the sample of secondary school leavers believed that the House of Commons made all the important decisions about the running of the country. See *The Times,* 17 August 1977.
2. See Paul Johnson, *The offshore islanders* (Weidenfeld & Nicolson, 1972).
3. As in Anthony Down's well-known hypothesis that electoral competition drives parties towards the ideological centre in an attempt to win the middle ground and thus elections.

How useful are MPs' questions?*

MARTIN BAILEY AND CHARLES MEDAWAR

Many MPs are seriously dissatisfied with the Parliamentary Question system which is supposed to be one of the main ways in which humble backbenchers can call government ministers to account.

In a survey of MPs by the *Sunday Times* and Social Audit (a pressure group campaigning for greater government accountability), one former Labour junior minister, Gwyneth Dunwoody, told us: 'Most ministers instinctively give answers which are inadequate and misleading.'

A Tory backbencher said: 'After a time you give up because it really does hurt to keep banging one's head against the Establishment's brick wall.' And two other MPs referred to Question Time as 'a game' and 'a farce'.

Others among the two hundred MPs we contacted were less damning. They acknowledged that the rules about tabling questions could be restrictive and the answers sometimes unhelpful but, as Sir Bernard Braine, Conservative MP for Essex, put it: 'The experienced MP knows how to get round the problems . . . The art consists of asking questions in such a way that ministers must answer.'

There is no doubt that PQs, as they are called, and their replies, can produce a wealth of information on some subjects as any reading of *Hansard* – in which they are published daily – shows.

MPs table about 35,000 Parliamentary Questions a year for ministers to answer. About 3000 receive oral answers in the Commons; the others receive written replies.

With oral questions an MP has the great advantage of being able to put a follow-up question (the so-called 'supplementary') to a minister after the initial reply has been given. Often a bland initial question masks an MP's real point, which he springs on the minister in the supplementary.

But our survey on MPs – plus an analysis of recent PQs – reveals that the system has acquired several restrictions and techniques of official evasion. One such is the vague and anodyne reply. Here are three others:

*From the *Sunday Times*, 30 March 1980.

1. *Taboo topics* Each government department simply refuses to answer PQs on a number of specified subjects, and there are now more than one hundred of these.

Many are described as 'security' matters and, though this must often be a legitimate explanation, it often arouses suspicion. For example, it has been established by precedent that the Home Secretary does not give detailed responses to questions on telephone tapping, so, despite the wealth of detail published in the press about this recently, William Whitelaw has provided no substantive information in reply to PQs.

Security apart, MPs in our survey told us they had been prevented from tabling questions on the day-to-day affairs of nationalized industries; issues involving commercial confidence; and the infringement of human rights in general, and in Indonesia and the USSR in particular. (MPs can, however, sometimes get round this type of restriction by raising the points in 'supplementary' questions to ministers' oral answers or by making them during the course of debates.)

The list of forbidden areas also includes such apparently innocuous subjects as farm-workers' wages, advice from the Welsh Office, government research contracts, the Sports Council and contracts for the Forestry Commission.

2. *Planted questions* Sometimes the administration gets MPs to put questions which will enable ministers to broadcast his department's achievements. In the past this has sometimes occurred on a massive scale: back in 1971 for instance, the *Sunday Times* revealed that the Department of the Environment had once prepared a 'bank' of friendly PQs to preclude critical ones in their minister's Question Time.

Such organized rigging of the system now seems unlikely but Table Office clerks say the practice of planting individual questions is still widespread.

When these 'planted' questions are answered orally they eat into the valuable minutes of Question Time, and ministers escape from probing PQs. It can also mean that MPs who later put down questions on the same topic may be simply referred to the original 'planted' answer.

A recent example of 'planting' occurred after two RAF jets crashed at Wisbech last September. On the suggestion of the Ministry of Defence, a PQ was tabled by Bill Walker, Conservative MP for the remote constituency of Perth – and this effectively pre-empted more critical questions from the local MP, Clement Freud.

3. *The disproportionate cost excuse* Ministers sometimes refuse to answer questions on the grounds that the information requested is not readily available, and can be obtainable only at 'disproportionate' cost.

Last year seven hundred PQs went unanswered for this reason. This represented only 2 per cent of all questions tabled, but the danger is that, since it is the minister and his staff who decide how much effort should be put into compiling a particular reply, critical questions may be the ones more often ruled too expensive.

A former Labour minister, Alex Lyon, told us that recently he asked the Home Office for the number of immigrants from the Indian sub-continent awaiting permits to settle in the UK.

Lyon had actually received a full answer to this question when he had tabled it in 1978. But when he asked for the same information last December the new Conservative minister of state, Tim Raison, refused a full response on the ground that it would 'involve disproportionate cost'.

The skilful MP will be able to circumvent many of the problems outlined above, but the 'cost' excuse will be harder to challenge.

The government now spends £1 million a year in answering the 35,000 PQs tabled every year. Sir Derek Rayner, the Prime Minister's newly appointed cost-cutter, has already received complaints from some Whitehall departments about this expense; funds could be saved, if further restrictions were made on the number of PQs.

But any attempt along these lines would provoke a storm of protest at Westminster. Despite all their criticisms, the vast majority of MPs in our survey told us that the right to table PQs was vital. As Labour MP David Clark put it, they remain 'the one essential weapon in the backbencher's armoury'.

The Public Accounts Committee: a case study*

LESLIE CHAPMAN

The superficiality and ineffectuality of the Public Accounts Committee's examinations is further illustrated by the handling of its questions about the Government Car Service, which [. . .] was abolished in Southern Region and maintained without reductions in the other regions. The remainder of the story is contained in the Comptroller and Auditor General's report[1] on the Appropriation Accounts (1974–5), Paras 145 to 150 (Appendix 4), and the sixth Report from the Committee of Public Accounts, Session 1975–6 (Appendixes 5 and 6). The Report paragraphs led, as they had done in the case of the maintenance expenditure, to the appearance of the PSA [Property Services Agency] before the PAC (10 May 1976).

The proceedings began with the chairman referring to the relevant paragraphs of the C and AG's report which made it clear that substantial savings were made by withdrawing the Government Car Service in the Southern Region from 1972 onwards. There was, said the chairman, a proved economy, and, that being the case, why was it that the PSA did not insist at that time on similar reductions, or at any rate planning similar action, in other regions? In reply Mr Cox made two points. He said first, that it was necessary for the PSA to satisfy themselves that the economies made in the Southern Region were genuine in the sense that there clearly was a saving for the PSA, and also to make sure that the additional expenses incurred by other departments did not exceed the saving to the PSA. Secondly, that the PSA had to be quite clear that the conditions in other regions were sufficiently similar to those in the Southern Region to justify similar steps being taken elsewhere. In answer to a further question Mr Cox said a report had been obtained from Southern Region 'last June' (that is, June 1975) as a result of which they (the PSA) became convinced that it was possible, and safely possible, to make the savings. In November 1975 all the regional directors were asked to make proposals for cutting down the numbers of cars. As a result, reductions from 172 cars to 87 were agreed for the car pools outside London. Asked if he did not think that the time between the Southern Region action and the proposed moves in the rest of the

*From *Your disobedient servant* (Penguin Books, 1979) pp. 89–95.

country (timed to be completed in 1978) was very long, Mr Cox said that he agreed. He explained the delay by saying that at the first inquiry the regional controllers (he meant, I think, regional directors) were not in favour of complete abolition. Secondly, there was a certain amount of administrative difficulty because the PSA had recently been set up and there was a good deal of reorganization going on. The supplies division of the Agency, which was responsible for the car service, was being turned over to a system of accountable management and it was not clear to people at that stage just how the financial arrangements would work. Mr Cox ended by saying that he did accept that it could and should have been possible to have followed up the Southern Region experiment more quickly than was the case.

But this time the chairman was not going to let up too quickly. If the withdrawal of the car service was made in the Southern Region in 1972, he said, it must have been done for a good reason. Someone must have been very clear that this was going to result in a substantial saving. (He might also have said, but unfortunately did not, that the C and AG's report had already covered this aspect very adequately in its references to the Southern Region action.) In these circumstances, said the chairman, and there is no way of telling whether he had his tongue in his cheek when he said it, it seemed to him particularly surprising that it took so long to deal with the other regions. Mr Cox replied, yes, it was true that the Southern Region action was taken as a result of a thorough management survey. He repeated that it was necessary to be certain that the costs were not being inflicted upon another department, and went on to say that unlike the Southern Region, which was fairly close to London, the remaining regions would always need a Government Car Service to look after ministers and senior civil servants visiting the regions in the course of their duties.

I shall come back to other parts of the evidence later on [. . .] but that covers what Mr Cox and the chairman had to say, and for the moment we will jump ahead to the findings of the PAC (Appendix 6). The relevant paragraph (number 69) reads:

Your Committee consider that the time between the abolition of the Southern Region car service in 1972 and the agreements to halve the car fleets in other Regions by 1978 was excessive. We think that the Department and Regional Directors should have realized from the outset that substantial economies were possible. The Agency informed us that most Regions need a car service for visiting ministers and senior officers. We accept this, but we look to the Agency to press ahead quickly with the reductions now decided upon and to make sure that no further opportunities are lost to make all justifiable economies.

In the next paragraph, dealing with the setting up of an inter-departmental committee to review the arrangements for the use and operation of transport services, the Committee says:

> We expect the inter-departmental study to be quickly concluded and all possible economies to be promptly implemented.

And in the final paragraph the PAC tries to make sure that wider lessons are learned. The paragraph reads:

> While the car service is not a major function of the Property Services Agency it involved sizeable expenditure and it has been shown that useful economies can be made. There may also be activities in other departments which may escape proper economy reviews because they are not central to the department's main functions and your Committee stress the need for all departments to seek out and effect economies over the whole range of their activities.

This was a very proper sentiment on which to close the proceedings. The ordinary reader can be forgiven for thinking that the taxpayer's interests had been served, that justice had been done and that there was a good chance that all would be well in the future.

But now, looking in more detail at the questions and answers (Appendix 5), it is possible to see how inadequately they covered the situation. It was claimed, first, that, at the beginning, other regional directors were not in favour of complete abolition. Of what significance is this defence? The choice was never between complete abolition on the one hand and total inactivity on the other. What was there to stop then the action now agreed to be possible, that is, an immediate 50 per cent reduction?

Next, take the explanation that it was necessary to be satisfied that the economies that had been made in the Southern Region were genuine in the sense that there would be savings to the PSA; and that any additional expense incurred by other departments would not have the effect of nullifying these economies. This was a sensible course of action. Indeed, it was more than sensible – it was an absolute prerequisite for any action at all, and it was never questioned at any time by anybody. The report of the Southern Region survey made it abundantly clear that if every car which had been supplied from the Government Car Service had to be replaced by hired car or taxi there would still have been a small but useful saving of between £5000 and £9000 a year at 1971 prices. This was the very least satisfactory result that could have been achieved in these improbable circumstances. The probable results – a much reduced use of *all* cars on official business – provided far greater savings.

All such inquiries had been made, and all doubts resolved before the Southern Region's action was taken. The discussions with the other departments also made it perfectly clear that the reductions did not in any sense affect the way those departments did their job, still less make it impossible for them to do it. It is, therefore, difficult to see the relevance of this defence. All the figures were available and all these doubts could have been similarly resolved in the other regions, as the C and AG's report makes obvious, in 1972.

As to Mr Cox's second point that the PSA had to be clear that the conditions in other regions were similar to those in London, he says they were now (1976) satisfied that this was so. But what stopped them from being so satisfied in 1972? The proposition that Reading is close to London and could, therefore, undertake a total abolition of its car service, where the other regions, being further removed, would always have to keep some cars for visiting ministers and senior officers is fair. But the Southern Region survey showed that the bulk of the use of the car service was not accounted for by these senior people but by junior staff, and that over 80 per cent of the total usage was by junior staff of just three departments. The Comptroller and Auditor General's report stated that his examination of requisitions and log sheets for regions outside London had shown a pattern of car usage in 1974–5 (which was when he carried out his survey) similar to that which had led to the abolition of the service in the Southern Region. It follows inevitably from this that had the other regions carried out this survey then they would have found that notwithstanding the need for cars in those regions for visiting VIPs, at least 80 per cent of the journeys could have been subjected to the kind of reduction made in the Southern Region. As a reason for delay, therefore, this answer too seems to be irrelevant.

Next, Mr Cox said that reports were obtained in June 1975 which resolved all their misgivings and doubts and uncertainties and made it possible for them to go ahead. What caused this action to be taken in June 1975, at least three years after it could have been taken? This, essentially, is a matter for speculation. It may be that after all the troubles and uncertainties of departmental reorganization this was the first opportunity that the PSA had had, and that in no time at all (five months, anyway) the report of June 1975 was followed by instructions to the other regions to make economies. That is one possibility. The alternative explanation is that by June 1975 it must have been apparent to the PSA that Exchequer and Audit Department was taking a close interest in the car service and that they, the

PSA, were, to say the least, going to be presented with some very awkward questions to answer.

Another reason for delay given was that the PSA had been recently set up and that there was a good deal of reorganization going on. I suppose it depends on what you mean by 'recently'. In fact, the PSA had been set up four years before, in 1971. While it was true that many changes in the structure of the department's headquarters were taking place (though not to any great purpose as far as the taxpayer was concerned), why could not changes in the car service be a part of that great reorganization? It involved very little work, no dislocation of other services, and it could be put through just about as painlessly as any kind of reduction could be. This had already been demonstrated in Southern Region and it is always easier to follow once such action has been shown to be practicable elsewhere.

Lastly, it was claimed that the accounting system was going to be altered and it was, therefore, not clear just how these financial arrangements would work. Now this is really very intriguing. What kind of accounting system was being envisaged, we wonder, which could cope with 172 cars but not with 87? Or rather, could cope with a reduction from 172 to 87 in 1978, but not in 1972? The government service has dreamed up some startling accounting arrangements over the years, but this one must have been one quite new to human experience.

The chairman, questioning the need even for the reduced fleets of 87 cars, said he could not believe that all those ministers travelled at the same time. The answer from Mr Cox was: 'Eighty-seven was the figure that we got down to, and that covered six regional offices in Scotland and Wales.'[2] There are no regional offices in Scotland or Wales. Each of those two countries has just one headquarters office, and I can only think that what Mr Cox meant was that this figure covered the fleets based outside London, other than those in Scotland and Wales (and Reading).[3] On that assumption, the reduced car service now provides something like fourteen or fifteen cars for each region on a full-time all-the-year round basis. It is well over three years since I left the department and much can change in that time, and in any case I never had the occasion to study the use of the car service in regions other than my own. Nevertheless, sitting here without any information or facts other than those published by the Comptroller and Auditor General I can say categorically that the car service proposed under this new reduced scheme is still wasteful and extravagant. My estimate of need would be between two and four cars per region.

There was a further question which was not asked, although a good many harassed taxpayers would no doubt have liked it to have been. Although the wasteful use of the car service was brought to an end in 1972 in Southern Region and perhaps will be, to a limited extent, by 1978 in the other regions, the waste did not suddenly start in 1972. It had been going on for years. Would it not have been relevant to ask for how many years, and why? And whatever the answer to that, relying for the moment only on Mr Cox's own statement that the Southern Region experiment should have been followed up more quickly than was the case, was it not appropriate to ask who exactly was responsible for the delay?

REFERENCES

1. For the record, the C and AG's report is wrong in one respect: paragraph 146 begins by saying that the examination of the car service was carried out by the department's Directorate of Management Services. It wasn't. The survey was carried out by a team of three, two of them my staff and one man borrowed from the Directorate of Management Services because they were short of work. All the subsequent work was done by Southern Region staff headed by the regional administrative officer, Norman Wright.
2. Para. 2384, Appendix V.
3. If Mr Cox's evidence should have read that the revised figure of eighty-seven cars related to the six regions *and* Scotland and Wales, the argument is substantially the same, except that this figure would then amount to about 11 cars per pool.

Select Committees:
A comparison with the
US Congress*

JOHN MACKINTOSH AND ANGUS MAUDE

Angus Maude I thought that at some stage in this argument we should hear about the Congressional Committees in the United States. And in case anybody should be impressed by this argument, let us get it quite clear at the outset, that it is wholly irrelevant and based on an entirely false understanding of the differences in the constitution of the United States and the United Kingdom. The fact of the matter is that in America, unlike Britain, the legislature and the executive are completely separated. Neither the President nor any member of his Cabinet is a member of either House of Congress, and the only way in which ministers can in fact be interrogated in depth is through the Senate and Congressional Committees. Members of the Senate, members of Congress, do not normally aspire to become ministers or members of the President's Cabinet. What they aspire to become is Chairman and Vice-Chairman of Senate or Congressional Committees. This is almost the ultimate ambition of a Congressman in the United States, to become Chairman of one of the important committees: Foreign Affairs, Finance, where the television cameras are always there and there is always a juicy scandal like Watergate to deal with. Yes indeed. (*Interruption*)

John Mackintosh Why does the Hon. Gentleman think it would be such a disaster if Members of Parliament were not all desperate to become ministers? It is one of the greatest weaknesses of the House of Commons that every back-bencher with ambition and ability wants either to become a minister or a shadow minister. Surely to become a permanent critic of the government is also an honourable and worthwhile objective?

Angus Maude It can be argued whether all Members of Parliament want to become ministers. It has been said that they either want to become ministers quickly or knights slowly. (*Laughter*) Either of

*From *The State of the Nation: Parliament* (Granada Television, 1973) pp. 156–7.

those is no doubt a harmless enough ambition. And it isn't the expert, as often as not, who really embarrasses the government. (*Hear, hear*) It isn't the expert always who improves Bills, discovers scandals. It is very often the rather thick uninvolved chap who perhaps has been half asleep through most of the minister's speech in a Standing Committee or on the Floor . . . (*Laughter*) And who suddenly wakes up and says 'What does that mean?' Or who wakes up and says 'Prove that!' Or 'Could I have the figures?' And very often it is almost by accident, as it were, by the ordinary common-sense bloke asking the ordinary commonsense question that the experts have never thought of, that we get improvements, the changes of policy and so forth, that really affect legislation. The Chamber is getting thin already with the number of Members that it has there. More Select Committees, more Legislative Committees, will make this infinitely worse. What we need is more informed debate in the House. And on the question of information, it isn't Select Committees that give you information, it is every Member's outside sources to which he can already get access. What a Member wants is not official information or officially inspired and provided information. It's the information which he has the nous and the commonsense and the acumen to go and find for himself.

The Westminster Lobby correspondents*

ANTHONY KING AND ANNE SLOMAN

The Lobby produces practically all the political news we all con-
sume, yet almost nothing is known by the general public about how
it actually works. And even among journalists there are profoundly
divergent views about whether the Lobby in its present form is a
good thing or not. Anthony Howard, the editor of the *New Statesman*, who for years has been the scourge of the Lobby:

Howard It's far too cosy. Politicians and journalists live in each
other's pockets under the system, and I often think probably they're
only talking to each other as well. No other country, I think, has
quite the same incestuous relationship as we have between parliamentarians and correspondents at Westminster. I've always said,
you know, that it's almost like Piccadilly before the Wolfenden
Report: there stand the Lobby correspondents waiting, soliciting,
for the politician to come out; they treat them as if they were their
clients and, you know, in some ways I think the fact has to be faced
that Lobby correspondents do become instruments for a politician's
gratification.

King Against this David Wood, the Lobby correspondent of *The
Times*:

Wood Generally speaking, I do not know of any group of journalists
who, on the whole – and I'm not saying we're never without sinners
by any means, any more than any other branch of the trade is – I
don't know of any branch of the trade where, at any rate, they aim
more consistently at a high standard than in the Westminster
Lobby.

King [. . .] What is the Lobby? How does it work? The name is easy
to explain. Members of the Lobby, unlike ordinary members of the
general public, can circulate freely in most parts of the Palace of
Westminster – most notably in the Members' Lobby itself.
   Much of the work of Lobby correspondents is like the work of
other journalists; but there are two special features of Lobby
journalism that the newspaper reader ought to be aware of. The first

*From *Westminster and beyond* (Macmillan, 1973) pp. 73–6, 79–81, 87.

is that Lobby journalists are under a strict obligation not to reveal the sources of their stories. There's a formal set of Lobby Rules which says that it's the Lobby correspondent's 'primary duty to protect his informants, and care must be taken not to reveal anything that could lead to their identification'. In other words if, say, a Tory MP tells a reporter that he and some friends of his are about to vote against the government, the reporter can publish the fact that a revolt is about to take place, but he mustn't identify the MP who told him.

The second thing about Lobby journalism is that members of the Lobby attend frequent briefings, given by ministers and other government and opposition spokesmen. These are not press conferences in the ordinary sense. Not only are the reporters present not supposed, in the usual way, to reveal their sources, but the fact that such briefings take place at all is supposed to be kept a secret. Indeed, a great deal of the Lobby's work used to be shrouded in an atmosphere of semi-secrecy, rather like the rites of a Masonic Lodge. One or two Lobby men weren't very happy when they discovered we were going to do this programme.

One set of regular Lobby briefings is given by the Prime Minister's press spokesman. Sir Harold Evans, who served at No. 10 for seven years under Harold Macmillan, describes what takes place.

Evans It happened customarily twice a day. There was a morning meeting, which was usually quite thinly attended because it was the evening papers and the agencies only. The spokesman always took those meetings. In the afternoon, one met at the House and that was a fuller meeting usually because the full Lobby would turn up for that. After one had talked to the Lobby at their two meetings during the day, one naturally expected to have follow-up questions from individuals, and one had to be available right through the evening and indeed often into the small hours if anything important was moving. At the weekends one also had to be ready to deal with individual inquiries. This was roughly the pattern of it. [. . .]

King The other main briefings are given on Thursday afternoons by the Leader of the House and, separately, by the Leader of the Opposition. [. . .] I asked Sir Harold Evans how these Thursday briefings differed from the ones Downing Street was responsible for.

Evans This was really a ministers' Lobby meeting and the Leader of the House, having gone through the business of the week, had an awful lot to talk about, usually, and on matters of depth and substance. And, since the Leader of the House is usually a top figure in government, obviously the Lobby were very keen to probe him.

King And similarly on the opposition side. Such briefings are important and they're worth describing because most people aren't aware they take place at all. [. . .] The trouble with most briefings, as David Wood says, is that, with so many people involved, they are almost mass meetings. He doesn't rely on them – at least not without further investigation – for information on what the government is doing. I asked him about what his main sources of information were. His answers were brief, but told one what one wanted to know. 'Do you have much private contact with ministers? Do you see individual Cabinet ministers alone, fairly often?'

Wood Yes.

King To talk to them about the work of their departments, the general political situation, and so on?

Wood Yes. I'm being cryptic . . .

King That's the way it looks from the journalist's side of the fence. How does it look from the politician's? I raised with William Deedes, the Conservative Member for Ashford and a former Minister in Charge of Government Information, the same point I raised with David Wood. How much contact is there in the normal way between Cabinet ministers and either the Lobby as a whole or individual members of the Lobby? William Deedes was less cryptic.

Deedes That depends a lot on the Cabinet minister. He can always invite, or ask himself to be invited – I think that's the way it has to go – by the Lobby, in order to give them information which he thinks is important to them. Apart from those formal, if private, occasions, how much he encounters individual members of the Lobby around the corridors and in the Lobby is very much up to him. He would probably know at least half of them, and they would take an interest in him. And it really depends on how forthcoming he is disposed to be towards them.

King And how often would a minister, say, have lunch or dinner with somebody in the Lobby, or several of them?

Deedes Open to any Lobby correspondent to invite any minister, any Member of Parliament, to lunch with him. And I think a good deal of very pleasant exchange goes on in this way. It is a very civilized way in which to discuss the work of a department and what ministers may be doing, thinking, contemplating. I think this is a very legitimate activity.

King [. . .] There is an aspect of the way the Lobby works that can lead to ill-feeling with backbenchers, as Gerald Kaufman explains:

Kaufman What backbenchers do resent, and it's a resentment I share, is that journalists should receive advance copies of parliamentary documents before they do, and should receive advance copies of parliamentary statements before they do. A backbencher finds it awfully difficult to put sensible and probing questions, say, to Sir Alec Douglas-Home when he's made a statement about the Pearce Report if he's neither seen a copy of the Pearce Report nor even seen a copy of Sir Alec's statement, whereas the journalists have both of these in advance and, therefore, when they meet ministers privately – as it's pretty certain they did with Sir Alec – they are able to ask much more probing questions. [. . .]

King Do the correspondents, the specialist correspondents, and the Lobby people need to work much more as a team in your view?

Kaufman I think that what they need is what American newspapers have, that is, a bureau. I think each newspaper needs a Westminster bureau with a political editor in charge and a large team with time and scope to deal with the extraordinary outflow of information and documents which comes from the government and the House of Commons.

King For John Whale, [of the *Sunday Times*] the major single difficulty about the Lobby is that the men in it have to be generalists.

Whale The difficulty that Lobby men have is that they're tied to a single source. This is true, of course, of a lot of specialist journalists – environment specialists, defence specialists – they need, crudely put, to keep the favour of the department that they write about if that department is to continue to supply them with information. But they have at least some expert knowledge to weigh against what they get from the department. Now Lobby men are just as much one-department journalists; they are in fact Downing Street correspondents. But they are not specialists; they have to cover the entire field of politics, the entire field of human life, they can't possibly know enough of the detail of legislation, of government planning, in order to check what is handed out to them from Downing Street.

The Lobby and other matters*

DAVID McKIE

Thursdays is always a pretty busy day in the House of Commons because you have the Prime Minister's questions and then they introduce the business of next week. [. . .] After that, if you are lucky, you may get to see the Leader of the Opposition who frequently has a briefing on Thursdays. That comes about half an hour after the other one, which means that all the points that have been picked up in the first one are then put to the Leader of the Opposition. One rule that proceeds from this is that stories that appear in the newspapers as leaks on a Friday morning tend to be more reliable than leaks on other days because they quite often come out of this sequence of meetings. So, 'Friday leaks are credible' is the first moral which I underline.

However, the best stories which come out of Lobby journalism don't actually come that way at all. Where they come from is the contacts you make – particularly with ministers, much less with civil servants and ordinary MPs – but you gradually get to know ministers and you find that they will tell you certain things which they don't on the whole tell you in formal briefings. You pick up rather more in the bars or in the corridors or on the phone, particularly on Sunday. Sunday is a good day for Lobby correspondents because if you ring up people at home they have actually got time to talk and they have got no one standing round (except their wives) who is going to let on that they have done so. Hence Monday leaks are not too bad – not always as good as Friday leaks – but not bad. [. . .]

It is these informal contacts which you make, because you are a Lobby correspondent, which are important. The basis of all conversations you have as a Lobby correspondent – and this is why they tell you things – is that they are unattributable. You don't say, 'Mr Denis Healey said last night that it is his secret ambition to put

*From an audiotape of a seminar organized by the Open University's Audio-Visual Research Group (1978). The original audiotape forms part of a collection of political material, put together by the Group with the collaboration of OU/BBC. This collection is housed in the Open University Library, Walton Hall, Milton Keynes MK7 6AA, and is available for use by outside researchers on application to the Media Librarian. See also Henry James p. 186, and W. E. H. Whyte p. 193.

Britain on the road to becoming an Eastern-European state'.
Nothing is ever as attributable as that. He tells you, but you disguise
it. All sorts of curious little phrases crop up every now and again
which disguise the fact that someone has talked. 'It was being said in
government circles,' is one: now I have never actually seen a
government circle; perhaps it is like a sort of fairy ring. I saw in the
paper this morning: 'Friends of Mr . . .' and I thought, 'I don't
remember that he has any friends.' What it means is, he is saying
this, but he doesn't want to be saddled with it.

These are the rules which apply initially to the parliamentary
Lobby, to the political correspondents, but the system has changed
very much over the last twenty years in that whereas the parliamentary Lobby used to be supreme and used to deal with all ministers on
all subjects, that has changed and you have now got, very necessarily, a lot of specialist Lobbies growing up. The reason for that is fairly
obvious. Subjects like defence, town planning and so on tend to get
very complicated. Not even the most diligent Lobby correspondent
can really keep them in his head. If the minister wants to have a
serious conversation with people about what is in his mind, he
doesn't want to address a lot of Lobby correspondents who knew
nothing about the subject until they came in the door. So now you
get a sort of labour correspondents' Lobby and a planning correspondents' Lobby and a defence Lobby and a social services' Lobby
and so on. They are not quite so organized as the Parliamentary
Lobby [. . .] but they work on the same basis that everything said is
unattributable and the informal contacts are rather more important
than the formal ones.

Of course, ministers quite often manipulate; they play off one of
these Lobbies against another. I remember when I was on the news
desk at *The Guardian,* and we had a great struggle with Peter
Walker, who was then at Environment, because he had a system: on
the whole when he had good news to give he gave it himself, and
when he had bad news to give his subordinate ministers gave it.
Now, on this occasion there was some ghastly thing which had to be
announced about housing and they set up a briefing with the
political correspondents, and it was quite obvious why: unless you
had great expertise in this field, you could not ask the devastating
questions which all the planning correspondents wanted to ask. We
spent a long time trying to arrange that our planning correspondent
or housing correspondent should go, saying that it was pointless
talking to the politicals, but they had the right to control it and they
had the political correspondents there, who all, of course, appeared
with little memos sent by their planning and housing correspondents
and stumblingly read all the questions out. Even so the minister did
well, because the supplementaries were not of the same standard.

So there are all these interlocking Lobbies, all operating on roughly the same rules. The first thing that will no doubt appeal to you in the whole of this analysis is the extreme ease with which any system of that kind can be unscrupulously manipulated and, indeed, *is* unscrupulously manipulated. [. . .]

There is also another danger besides straight manipulation. That is that because you get information in confidence all the time, and because Lobby correspondents, editors and deputy editors and others see politicians quite a lot, a sort of informal conspiracy grows up in which some stories are deliberately neglected. That doesn't happen very often, but it has happened in a very damaging way on certain occasions. The most spectacular in recent years was the Labour government's considerations of devaluation. A great deal of information which reporters acquired at that time was actually suppressed, because it was feared that if they wrote a story saying 'Government plans to devalue on Thursday fortnight' something dreadful would happen to the pound. And so it was felt that it was irresponsible to run these stories. Some were not actually written at all, others were written and kept out of the newspapers by editors. Of course, the devaluation took place. [. . .]

Another example of the way that governments behave is their tendency to put out bad news on Fridays. The reason they do that is because Saturday papers tend to have less space for news (particularly for political news) and the reading is more superficial. Shovel it out late on Friday night: papers are light-staffed, and there is just a chance that no one will notice, and, even if they do, that they won't make very great play of it.

CHAPTER FOUR

Whitehall

Introduction

A colleague of mine (was) on a Fabian Society working group on civil service reform. What, he asked, were the qualities which counted and were rewarded in an organization such as the British civil service; and he answered his own question with a judicious and impressive list. All these qualities, he suggested, were carefully and objectively assessed in Whitehall in deciding promotions and estimating potential. Then he added (and this is my point): 'One thing that you might think would count, but which in fact is given no attention whatever, is whether or not your advice has been any good.'[1]

The doctrine of ministerial responsibility ensures that there is no public assessment of the quality of civil servants' advice. Thus civil servants are protected from critical scrutiny. The only guarantee of responsible and efficient conduct is a belief in the principles of the anonymity and neutrality of civil servants. But Nevil Johnson, a Fellow of Nuffield College, Oxford, argues in the first extract in this section that these principles have resulted in negligible ministerial influence over their departments. Ministers do not meddle, in his view, in the internal affairs of the bureaucracy, which has now become the most powerful prop of a centralized state.

Government resistance to any suggestion of changing the relationship between ministers and their departments dominated its response to the English Committee proposals to improve the efficiency and accountability of the civil service.[2] Once again the service retreated behind the cloak of ministerial responsibility. But does the ethos of secrecy in the bureaucracy (a direct outcome of the Official Secrets Act) in conjunction with the anonymity of civil servants and their control over information mean that civil servants push policy in the direction they want? Henry James, a former Director General of the Central Office of Information, argues to the contrary. In the second extract he supports the traditional view that these characteristics result in a high quality of professional advice. But in the name of good decision making he declares, the process of advice and information assimilation should *not* be revealed to the public. The dilemma that secrecy can pose for the press officer, whose task, James declares, is to give objective statements of the truth, is revealed in a letter from a senior press officer to the Franks Committee.[3]

'Yes Minister', a lucid and witty BBC television series about the fictional adventures of an inexperienced minister in Whitehall presents a less flattering view of the role of the civil servant. The extract is taken from the episode entitled 'Open Government'. How near the truth is Jay and Lynn's portrayal? The extracts from the Crossman *Diaries* confirm the view that the successful press officer is one who can manipulate the media. But it is not in every case that the press officer puts his loyalty to his government first as Brian Sedgemore, a former civil servant, describes below in his account of the same press officer.

The dual role of the Foreign Office News Department in both managing information output for the media on a daily basis and in advising politicians on the communication of major policy issues is described next by W. E. H. Whyte, a former head of the department. He relates how briefings on what is going on in negotiations behind locked doors can be abused by the media with disastrous political consequences. Political pragmatism, therefore, is one principle which governs information management; pursuit of a policy goal is another. Joe Haines, a former press secretary to Harold Wilson, presents a rather different view to Whyte's of the workings of the Foreign Office News Department. In his extract on 'the Soames affair' he describes how the Foreign Office's power of information management enabled them to destroy Britain's hopes of negotiating entry to the EEC, despite instructions from the Prime Minister to the contrary.

Is there any justification for the anonymity and secrecy in governmental decision making advocated by the civil service ethos? Peter Kellner, a journalist, and Lord Crowther Hunt, a former minister, discuss five cases in the final extract, where, they argue, closed government has encouraged bad policy making and bad administration.

REFERENCES

1. P. D. Henderson, 'Two British errors: their probable size and some possible lessons', *Oxford Economic Papers,* Vol. 29, No. 2, July 1977, pp. 159–205.
2. *The civil service: Government observations on the eleventh report of the House of Commons Expenditure Committee, Session 1976–77* (HC 535) Cmnd 7117, March 1978.
3. *Report and evidence of the departmental committee on Section 2 of the Official Secrets Act 1911* (The Franks Report) (Cmnd 5104, HMSO, 1972) Vol. 2, p. 231.

The masters of the machine*

NEVIL JOHNSON

The modern state is inescapably a bureaucratic state, and the centralized state in Britain is no exception, though some of our mythology would have it otherwise. So it would be most appropriate to say something about the bureaucracy, or some parts of it, within the context of these reflections on the theme of political centralization. Moreover, there is a good practical reason for this. The bureaucracy in the service of the central government, though silent and withdrawn from the world of political argument in public, is one of the most powerful props of centralization. Indeed, it is more than that. It is the very model of that network of informal communication without which a centralization so arbitrary in its political will as that of Britain, would be rent apart by dispute. The corridors of Whitehall lead out to the interlocking worlds around it, and there are few in these worlds outside the central administration who are not susceptible to the style and manners of Great George Street, the home of Her Majesty's Treasury.

What follows refers chiefly to the civil service as we call it, the bureaucracy of the central government. There is in Britain no such thing as a single common public service – no *Beamtentum,* no *fonction publique.* [. . .] In fact there is now a remarkably heterogeneous and little-studied range of public services, some of which show little sign of a lively recognition of their public status and of the obligations stemming from that. However, there can be no doubt that it is the civil service which has been and still is politically the most significant and influential segment of the public bureaucracy, and this is why I shall be concerned chiefly with it. Nor do my remarks even refer to the whole of the civil service: janitors and typists, research scientists and tax collectors, such people do not figure in my argument. The group which is of political interest is small, no more than the three or four thousand people who constitute the group which advises ministers, supervises the execution of policy, controls the administrative machine, and hopefully finds time to look ahead. It is this group which, through its administrative skills, contributes most to holding the centralized state together.

A few years ago it would have been precisely definable as the administrative class of the home civil service, but after the changes consequent on the reception of the Fulton Report (1968)[1] these

---

*From 'The Leviathan at the centre', in *In search of the constitution* (Pergamon, 1977) pp. 93–96.

higher levels of administration have become vaguer and looser in outline. But the majority of the members of this controlling group are in fact still general administrators brought up under the old dispensation: so we do not need to worry too much about the effects so far of the winds of change.

It is commonly thought that England shares with a few other countries such as Prussia and France the distinction of having invented a loyal, neutral and apolitical civil service. This very idea is, however, highly misleading. The basic error in the comparison is that in such continental countries the bureaucracy was at its highest levels never really apolitical – its mission was to serve a particular view of the state and of its purposes. In virtue of this it shared in varying degrees in the authority of the state. In contrast the British bureaucracy, as it emerged in its modern professional form in the service of a parliamentary leadership which controlled the central government, was intended to be genuinely excluded from political authority. And it eventually became so excluded. In this respect the British civil service is almost unique: if the model is to be found anywhere else in the world, then it is perhaps only in India where it lives on as an echo of empire.

What I have just said would be taken by many as a compliment, a commendation of the British view of the proper understanding of the place of a civil service in the structure of government and politics. But my intention is not so complacent. It is often forgotten how relatively recent is the detached, politically neutral and anonymous higher official. True, the conception of the official as the detached and impartial adviser is certainly present in the ideas of the founding fathers of the British civil service, in Trevelyan, Northcote, Macaulay and others. Yet this idea assumed flesh more slowly than is often believed. For many reasons which I cannot go into, but amongst which the close social intercourse between higher officials and political personalities was certainly very important, the upper reaches of the civil service remained only imperfectly detached from politics and party until the end of the First World War. Until then there was an intimacy between the worlds of politics and of administration which even permitted politicians to exercise a small amount of patronage, not on behalf of family friends as earlier on, but by way of securing the support of men of ability whose services they needed. It was after 1920 that the civil service as it is now known rapidly took shape, largely under the influence of the Treasury whose official head also became head of the whole service, and for that reason was able to claim within the bureaucracy a centralizing influence with which there is nothing comparable elsewhere. In a social sense the spheres of politics and administration then drifted apart (though that rupture was not complete until after 1945), and the civil service cocooned itself within the ethos of the anonymous, impartial and politically indifferent servants of political masters. The service accepted its servitude to ministers, but for that bargain the politicians had to pay a price. This was that they accepted the ultimate irresponsibility of their servants and agreed not to meddle in the internal affairs of the bureaucracy. This is why ministers have today negligible influence *in* their departments as opposed to influence *over* what they do; it explains why the civil service has become a closed corporation, a contemporary equivalent to the medieval church whose members, moreover, enjoy 'benefit of clergy'.

The contemporary criticism of the bureaucracy which has been voiced most often is of the generalist, non-specialized, amateur character of those who make up its central and directing core. This has always struck me as a somewhat confused and muddle-headed criticism which misses the main point, besides overlooking the important fact that the logic of our governmental arrangements has required that ministers should be served by people who have certain qualities in common with them. And the traditional administrator with an education in the humanities was undoubtedly well adapted to understanding the political needs of ministers. But the crucial thing is that the administrative civil service (to use for a moment the old expression) has indeed its own expertise and special skill, and that is in the manipulation of the administrative system in the service of ministers: the civil servant is the master of the machine. If we then remember that the price paid for the neutrality and loyalty of officials was the withdrawal of the politicians from interference in the affairs of the machine, and if further we take into account the manner in which the powers of government have expanded, then we can understand without difficulty the pervasive influence which the civil service acquired. And, as I have already remarked, in a very real sense the civil service remained irresponsible. For success ministers take credit, for failure ministers (if any one at all) take blame. It is rare indeed for the civil servant to be identified with any act of commission or omission, or until recently even to be known to have any views of his own at all. But for this complete self-abnegation he gains complete security.

REFERENCE

1. *The civil service: report of the committee* (The Fulton Report) 4 vols (Cmnd 3638, June 1968).

The role of the Central Office of Information*

HENRY JAMES

It was in 1936, or thereabouts, that a government department first felt the need to have a press officer, a full time communicator addressing the public through the media on the policies of that particular department. But at the outbreak of war in 1939 the Central Office of Information was established to provide a means of communication to the general public and at that time, to perform a propagandist role both within and outside the country. A Minister of Information headed the department. After the war when the word 'propaganda' had become an even dirtier word than it was before, there was some discussion as to what the future role of the then Ministry of Information might be. In the post-war period it became more important that there should be a source of professional information flowing from government through the media. In 1946 Clement Attlee announced that the Ministry of Information as such would cease to exist, but that there was to be established a Central Office of Information which would provide a source of professional expertise for all government departments and ministers. It was implicit in this that there should not be a *Minister* of Information and that ministers and their departments should be entirely autonomous in their information policy (as they were or are autonomous subject to the overall policy of the government in their other policies). Since that time governments have scrupulously avoided establishing a position of a minister of information. [. . .]

The government itself has no policy of information. It is at the discretion of the individual minister. The Secretary of State for the Department of Health and Social Security, for example, will answer questions on his information policy. If a question arises as to the past effectiveness of how a policy was conveyed, it would be a question for the minister. How policy should be announced and to whom it should be addressed is the responsibility of the department, who alone can identify the audience to be addressed at any particular time. If we look to the day-to-day processes of information in a department, in addition to its responsive role, the information

*From an audiotape in a collection organized by the Open University's Audio-Visual Research Group with the collaboration of OU/BBC. See note, p. 178.

officer also has a role in explaining policy and its evolution in a political sense. The press office also has a positive briefing role; it has to explain the problems facing the department and the alternative methods of dealing with them. I have always argued that the essential role of a government information officer in a policy-making department is not so much to explain, at the time, the decisions of government and the consequence of these decisions but preferably before that to explain the problems that underlie them. The government has no prescriptive claim for space in newspapers or in any other medium. Successive governments are competitors for space as is any other source of news. So what is important is that the policy as it evolves, the problems facing departments, should be explained to specialist or non-specialist journalists before they happen. It is obviously much simpler and certainly much more lucid for the journalist who is faced with, say, a statement from the House of Commons on housing policy, to have had an additional or prior briefing. For any but the most informed journalist, it is clearly impossible for him to interpret the statement correctly without this. [. . .]

There is a responsibility on government, this is how successive governments have seen it, to explain their actions and their activities. Not necessarily for basic reasons of political achievement but simply in order that in a democracy the processes of government can be understood. We hear a great deal about open government and open government means to each person round the table something different. What I mean by open government is the fullest possible response at all times to the question that the journalist within whatever medium may put. There may be an element of speculation in the response because you have to anticipate events. I remember Roy Jenkins when he was Home Secretary in 1975 and delivering the Granada lecture, made this point about open government: he reserved himself the right to change his mind in private. I think that is a very fundamental and very significant phrase. If the processes of government, the processes of advice and information assimilation prior to decision, are open then the quality of the advice and the quality of the decision taking is going to suffer. He reserves the right to change his mind in private, to be affected by information now coming in without being criticized for having changed his mind from a fundamental vantage point already taken. He also believes that he has the right to take the advice he wants from where he wants. Roy Jenkins also made the important point that if, for any reason, the sources of information available to him became available to others, he would not want to use any sanction against the perpetrator of that leak or breach of confidence. As a career civil servant I feel very strongly about this: the process of decision taking has to be done in sensible privacy. The accumulation of information upon which decisions are based is part of a public process. But the invitation to submit evidence, the advice that the individual gives the minister, whether it be political or from a civil servant, I believe has to be confidential. Otherwise the quality of that advice is going to deteriorate. [. . .]

As civil servants we are apolitical. We don't have specific allegiances to either party. This does not mean we are political eunuchs, but it does mean that the quality of the advice we give will, hopefully be professional. We do not give political advice and we are not image-makers. This is another possible misconception of our role. [. . .]

The journalist knows that he will get from the government information services, at whatever level, not the voice of the minister; not the voice of the governing party, but the calculated combination of all these. You can always get political advice – in any government there are over a hundred ministers. There is no difficulty in getting political advice. But what the journalist and the media expect to get from the government information service are objective statements of the truth so far as it can be determined, dispassionately, objectively and practically.

Yes Minister*

ANTHONY JAY AND JONATHAN LYNN

[Jim Hacker has just been appointed as Minister for Administrative Affairs; Bernard is his Principal Private Secretary. Sir Humphrey Appleby is the Permanent Under-Secretary of State and Head of the Department of Administrative Affairs.]

The scene is the Athenaeum, at night. Sir Humphrey is having a quiet chat with Sir Arnold, Secretary to the Cabinet. Bernard comes in with a folder for Sir Humphrey, and is asked to join them. Clearly this is something of an honour for him.

Sir Humphrey (asks Bernard) Tell us what you make of our new minister.

Bernard Absolutely fine.

Sir Humphrey Yes, we'll have him house-trained in no time. He swallowed the whole diary in one gulp, and I gather he did his boxes like a lamb last Saturday and Sunday?

Bernard Yes, sir.

Sir Humphrey So long as we can head him off this open government nonsense.

Bernard But I thought we were calling the White Paper 'Open Government'.

Sir Humphrey Of course. Always dispose of the difficult bit in the title. Does less harm there than in the text.

Sir Arnold It's the law of inverse relevance: the less you intend to do about something, the more you have to keep talking about it.

Bernard But . . . what is wrong with open government, actually? I mean, why shouldn't the public know more about what goes on?

Sir Arnold Are you serious?

Bernard Yes. It's the minister's policy, after all.

Sir Arnold My dear boy, it's a contradiction in terms. You can be open – or you can have government.

Bernard But don't the citizens of a democracy have a right to know?

Sir Humphrey No. They have a right to be ignorant. Knowledge only means complicity and guilt. Ignorance has a certain dignity.

Bernard But if the minister wants open government . . .

Sir Humphrey (shocked) You don't just give people what they want, if it's not good for them. Do you give brandy to an alcoholic?

Bernard But . . . but . . . but . . .

*From 'Open government' in the BBC series 'Yes Minister'.

Sir Arnold If people don't know what you're doing, they don't know what you're doing wrong.

Bernard (insisting) But all the same, Sir Humphrey, I am his private secretary, so if that is what he wants . . .

Sir Humphrey (interrupting) My dear boy. You will not be serving your minister by helping him to make a fool of himself. Look at the ministers we've had. Every one would have been a laughing stock in three weeks but for the most rigid and impenetrable secrecy about what they were up to.

Bernard Then what do you propose to do about it?

(Slight pause)

Sir Humphrey Can you keep a secret?

Bernard Of course.

Sir Humphrey So can I. (Rises) Now, if you'll excuse me, I have to make a phone call. (Exits)

(Slightly awkward pause)

Bernard Well, I'd better be taking this to the minister.

(Rises to go)

A successful press officer*

RICHARD CROSSMAN

6 April 1966
Back in London I held the press conference which I had decided
should be my first action as the old Minister of Housing in the new
Labour government. We decided on this in the last week of the
election and Peter Brown had prepared for it very carefully indeed.
I started with the announcement that local authority mortgage
lending would be resumed. Then I turned to the February council-
housing figures and gave the press an explanation of the deplorable
facts and then some new information about our mortgage plan.
After this I went into the other room and did a piece for BBC
television on mortgages and a special northern piece announcing my
decision on Sheffield local government boundaries.

7 April 1966
A glance at the papers and I knew that Peter Brown had scored
another of his tremendous successes. He knows exactly when to call
a press conference, how to brief the press and how to make it a
success. We managed to get a front-page story in the *Mail* and the
Telegraph, under the headline HOME LOANS RESUMED, and a good
story in *The Times* and *The Guardian.* Only the *Daily Express* did a
major story on the headline CROSSMAN SHOCK – FALLING HOUSING
FIGURES. In terms of news value the *Express* was quite right. It was
legitimate for a Tory paper to say that the February figures were
deplorable. And they could all have led with the fact that the
Minister of Housing had suppressed the February figures during the
election and was still trying to cover the facts up. But, apart from the
Express, they didn't. They accepted from us what I call the establishment story: the official line put out by me and by Peter Brown
was printed practically intact on their front pages. When Steve saw
the press he was astonished. 'What is all this news?' he said to me.
He didn't know that a department can, with a good press officer,
make the news it wants. At least that press conference was a sign
that Peter and I haven't lost our cunning in this particular respect.

*From *The diaries of a Cabinet minister Vol 1* (Hamish Hamilton and Jonathan
Cape, 1975) p. 497.

Divided loyalties*

BRIAN SEDGEMORE

I was working as a civil servant in the Ministry of Housing and Local Government at the time when Crossman was minister there and for two years was private secretary to one of his junior ministers, Robert Mellish. Crossman deliberately created tension and friction with his civil servants. He would call huge meetings with the permanent secretary, deputy secretaries and all manner of senior people and then spend much of the time talking to some middle-aged architect – much to the embarrassment of everybody, including the architect. What Crossman wrote was a brilliant description of what was going on. If Crossman were alive today I suspect that the main change he would notice, to which I have already referred, is the replacement of departmental policies by inter-departmental civil service policies.

A private secretary in the civil service often has to make up his mind whether he is working for his minister or the department. Constitutional theory says that he is working for the minister but his promotion depends on the department. I took the decision that I was working for the minister and this got me into some trouble.

For instance there was one occasion when my minister, Bob Mellish, wanted to promote the idea in a speech of a national housing plan. I gave him a bit of help with the drafting and we put the appropriate passages into the official text of a boring speech which had been prepared by the department. The next thing I knew I received a call from the Chief Information Officer, Mr Peter Brown, a man who was good at his job, scrupulously fair and liked by everyone. He asked me if the passages in question had been cleared with the department. When I said 'No – the minister just wants to float the idea' he said that the speech should not be issued. I told him that I was sorry but that it was for the minister to say whether or not the speech should be issued and that he was definitely going to make the speech and wanted it sent out as a press release. After some argument Mr Brown agreed to issue a release of the speech. I deliberately refrained from trying to clear it with the department because I knew that if I tried it would have been stopped. The speech was quite a success. The *Financial Times* paid it the compliment of an editorial, Crossman asked Mellish about it and in due course a plan which made use of some of its ideas was published.

*From *The secret constitution: an analysis of the political establishment* (Hodder & Stoughton, 1980) pp. 30–1.

The FCO and the media*

W. E. H. WHYTE

The News Department in the Foreign Office is geared into the work of the rest of the Office. We are not regarded, myself and my colleagues, as being people to whom it shall be vouchsafed that 'little' which they are actually allowed to 'tell'. Instead, it is recognized that if we are going to be able to do our job properly we should be involved in the process, to put it slightly pompously, of policy formation; we should know what is actually going on; we should be in the position to advise on the public line that should be taken. We should be in a position, also, to have some judgement of our own as to how much we should, in any particular situation, be allowed to say and to explain. So we are not, or never should be, in the situation of merely being at the receiving end of a piece of information, a press release or piece of press blurb. i.e. 'Here you are, take it, give that to them and if they ask any more supplementary questions, you don't know the answers.' That is not the way in which any effective press work, in our view, can be done.

Secondly, let me explain rapidly how the day works. My day consists of getting into the Foreign Office slightly earlier than most people and, together with my colleagues, working through the night cables, the morning's newspapers, the agency tapes, the BBC monitoring reports and other bits and pieces; maybe a transcript of last night's television interview with, for example, Ian Smith, who was on 'Tonight', or maybe a videotape. Having worked through all of that, we assemble those topics which are of Foreign Office interest, or in which we have some sort of foreign policy interest on which we think we have a point to make, or on which we are going to get questions during the course of the day. Having assembled the agenda – a list of stories, points, or problems – I take part in the morning washing-up session with senior under-secretaries, all of whom are superior to me, and I have a chance to pick their brains or warn them what is coming up. The rest of my department is running around the Foreign Office, trying to assemble the material that we are going to be needing in the course of the day; trying to extract the background information; discovering whether this story or that is correct, incorrect; discovering what we are going to be able to say at the daily press conference and so on. By 11.45 every morning we have put all this together and we have our own washing-up session inside the News Department. Each of us has his own portfolio and

*From an audiotape in a collection organized by the Open University's Audio-Visual Research Group with the collaboration of OU/BBC. See p. 178.

dishes his particular bit of the dirt with everybody else so we all know what everybody else has produced and we agree amongst ourselves what line we are going to be taking. We then have a daily Press Conference at 12.30, which is frequently a modest affair – ten, fifteen minutes, probably not more than half an hour – at which the principal news agencies will be present: Reuters, and the Press Association on the home front: sometimes Agence France Presse, sometimes the Deutsche Press Agentur and then maybe an African News Agency (some of the African newspapers have been in a great deal recently) because of running Southern African stories. It gives us a chance to put on record any statements, announcements (a certain amount of routine gobbledegook, the announcements of the appointment of this or that new ambassador, and so on) for that day.

To give you a brief sample, our topic sheet for today – the things that were going to be troubling us or about which we were going to be questioned – ran like this:

RHODESIA
NAMIBIA
CSCE (CONFERENCE ON SECURITY AND
   CO-OPERATION IN EUROPE) BELGRADE
THE BEAGLE CHANNEL
PANAMA CANAL
THE HORN OF AFRICA, SOMALIA, ETHIOPIA
THE MIDDLE EAST

That is a fair indication of the things which, in the course of the day, we are concerned about, needing to know about and that we are putting together a line about which we have got straight (God willing) by the time we go to the press conference at 12.30.

The press conference is a small tip of the iceberg of what we are doing most of the time, which is background, non-attributable briefing. People come in all through the afternoon and sometimes into the evening; always down the telephone; frequently into and sometimes through the night and at weekends (the world doesn't stop turning). We have somebody on duty round the clock. For the most part and non-attributably, we give organized background briefings every afternoon to groups of correspondents, British and foreign, who organize themselves: Reuters, *Times, Daily Mail, Express, Guardian* all come in at about 3 o'clock–3.15 every afternoon. Another lot come afterwards. The BBC and ITN prefer to come on their own; so too does the *Financial Times*. The Americans come in once a week – or the French, the Germans, the Dutch and so on. It is roughly speaking the Lobby system applied to foreign policy, foreign issues. The basic defence of the non-attributability is that you can say a great deal more than you could if things were 'on the record', in quotation marks, liable to be thrown back at you.

In the course of all this there are, as far as I am concerned, a few basic principles. The first is that you have got to stick to the truth. It may not be the whole truth and it certainly won't *always* be the whole truth, but it really must if possible be nothing but the truth. Above all you must not give a chap a bum steer. If he comes to you and he has got a story or he has got the scent, even if you can't tell him all about it, you have on the whole to contrive to indicate that he is on to something which is either okay, or something absolutely not so. This is, I think, the basis on which your entire credibility hinges.

Secondly, when I first came to the News Department (and I was scared out of my wits) I had a kind of idea that you had an inner circle of highly trusted correspondents to whom you could tell everything, or very nearly everything – such as the Diplomatic Correspondent of the London *Times* – but I won't be invidious and pick them out. Then, I thought, you worked your way down through other, slightly more unreliable or potentially dangerous characters who were out to trip you up, catch you out or make use of something which wasn't really designed to be published at that moment – such as the *Daily Express*. Then, further out, you had really dangerous characters of whom you had to be very wary – such as *Der Spiegel* or the *Morning Star*. I very rapidly discovered that this is absolutely not so. Absolute nonsense. But with certain exceptions and certain nuances, what you can say to one person you can say to everybody. The faster our communications systems work and the smaller the world gets the more true this is. The difference between what you say to one man and what you say to another is mainly determined by how much he knows; how much he is interested; the space he has got; how many column inches he can command in his paper; or how much air-time he is going to be able to get for whatever he is putting together. This is the principal difference between say the *Financial Times* and *The Times* at one end and the *Express* and *Mirror* at the other. The purpose of the whole exercise is to explain as much as possible: lay it all out and try and get across what the facts are, what it is you are trying to achieve. The better informed somebody is when he starts, the more probable it is that he is going to be able to make use of what you can tell him.

In this process it is true that there are constraints. There are, firstly, foreign policy constraints. There is the fact that a lot of communication between governments takes place behind locked doors and if there are unilateral breaches of confidence, this can be exceedingly damaging to further communication, or damaging to whatever process of negotiation you may be engaged in.

We were in Malta the other day, as you may have noticed, talking
with the Patriotic Front. We were not very sanguine about how
these talks were going to go, thinking that we might well in fact have
a very quick punch-up and that would be that and we would all go
home and that would be breaking-point as far as serious talk with
them was concerned. It did not work out that way at all. We had two
and a half days of very interesting discussions at the end of which I
think we understood each other's positions very much better than
before. But whether we were basically near to a possible deal is
another matter.

Now they were very much on their best behaviour; they wanted to
show that they were statesmen, negotiating seriously about this very
difficult area, and they came up with a document. We said, 'Did you
have to give us a document, crystallizing your position? You are
going to get stuck with it and it is going to make everything more
rigid because it will instantly be published.' They said, 'Well, we do
want to give this document, but all right, no, we won't publish it.'
Well, that was absurd: within minutes the thing would have been on
Reuter's and every other wire. But it did not leak! They put the
clamps on their Roneo machines or whatever. To the astonishment
of all the journalists around all the usual sources dried up and, at
least until after we left Malta, nobody actually got sight of that
particular document. They were rather proud about it: they were
really showing that they could be responsible and all that. What
happens?

At the end of that day (day two of the talks) they go back to their
hotel in the late evening, they switch on their radio (they do what
they do everywhere else all round Africa and elsewhere, they listen
to the World Service of the BBC) and the lead item on that evening
in the BBC World Service is: 'Patriotic Front in Talks in Malta
Agrees to UN Force.' Now, they had agreed to no such thing and
they certainly had not told anybody from the press that they had
agreed to any such thing, so where did it come from? (It must be that
wretched British spokesman who was doing the briefing again!) The
following day started with a minor explosion from Joshua Nkomo
complaining about the way in which the BBC, that organ of the
British government (as the world knows) had been retailing (a)
what was meant to be a subject of closed negotiations in a manner
(b) which was, in any case, not accurate.

Well, I knew what was happening the previous evening, but only
when it was a bit late. The BBC correspondent on the spot for
External Services, Bush House, was briefed by me as to what was
going on in outline, mood and all that and in the end he asked me,
'Has anything actually shifted?' and I say, 'Yes, I think there has
been a little shift here and there. For example, whereas the Patriotic

Front were totally opposed to the whole idea of a United Nations force as part of a possible package in Rhodesia, they now are indicating that maybe in certain conditions, they would be willing to see some sort of a UN contingent performing some of the functions of referee during an interim administration, perhaps participating in the process of observing elections.' Back goes this ten minutes or whatever commentary piece which sets this point out among others in very careful measured terms with all the reservations. When it comes to the news editor at Bush House he looks down this and extracts a bald statement and puts it up front in his news at ten, or whatever: 'Patriotic Front in Malta Agrees to UN Force'. Patriotic Front in Malta goes through the roof, thereafter. Another example of the problems of explaining a little bit more to the press of what is going on behind locked doors than the people involved in the negotiations are willing to accept.

Perfidious foreigners*

JOE HAINES

When I joined Harold Wilson's Press Office in January 1969, his government had a record deficit in the opinion polls, had lost to the Scottish Nationalists a by-election at Hamilton where previously it had an 18,000 majority, had embarked on a fateful and fatal battle with the unions over 'In Place of Strife', was having its morale and energy sapped by constant talk of, and fitful attempts at, conspiracies to topple the leader, and had had its attempt to join the Common Market frustrated by General de Gaulle. It was like becoming a public relations officer for the army after the evacuation of Dunkirk.

Of all the government's misfortunes, the failure of the efforts to get negotiations going on entry into Europe – which from the narrow view of electoral popularity had had the least impact – rankled most of all in the official mind. The French President was seen as an old man harbouring the resentments of twenty-five years earlier, taking slow, deliberate and repeated revenge for the affronts dealt to him when he was a wartime irritant to Churchill and Roosevelt. If a spirit of revenge was within him, there was one, too, among some British officials, though with them the origins were of more recent date. Suddenly, in the first week of February 1969, the General gave them their chance, in an interview granted to the then British ambassador in Paris, Sir Christopher Soames.

That the General did not like the EEC, either as it had been created or as it had evolved, was well known, though perhaps the intensity of his dislike was not. In his meeting with Sir Christopher he had rehearsed, first, his familiar lecture about Britain being the principal satellite of the United States. British entry into the EEC as it stood then would change the whole character of the Market. Every country in the Community – except France, of course, which had managed to break away – was an American satellite and Britain's membership would only make matters worse.

The trouble was, he said, that Britain and France in their long history had never been friends, only allies when necessity compelled it, or rivals; there had never been a genuine partnership between them. De Gaulle was willing to try to change all that, to make a new start. He had little faith in the EEC, he went on, and would willingly

*From *The politics of power* (Jonathan Cape, 1977) pp. 74–81, 92–3.

contemplate its breaking up. To that end, he wanted Britain to launch an initiative designed to promote a new form of Free Trade Association in Europe, which would include agricultural free trade. If we agreed to do that then he would issue a statement supporting us.

He was willing, in effect, to be an accessory after the fact of the murder of the Community, but he had no wish to be caught with the gun in his hand.

The first British reaction was to ask why de Gaulle did not launch the initiative himself; if he did that, we would certainly then indicate our willingness to discuss the whole issue with him, though without prior commitment.

To do it de Gaulle's way meant that if the initiative succeeded Britain's reputation would be that of a country which, denied partnership in Europe, took retribution by destroying the most promising adventure in uniting Europe ever undertaken; if the initiative failed, as it almost certainly would have done, then Britain would have the odium, plus certain exclusion from the EEC for at least a generation.

The Prime Minister's reaction was precise on this point: 'We want to join the Common Market,' he said, 'not bury it.' But, on the whole, he refused to get excited about the development, taking the view that de Gaulle had said little to Soames that was different from what he had said when they had met at an earlier Summit. Few others shared that view, however; certainly not Dr Kiesinger, the Federal German Chancellor, with whom the Prime Minister had talks in Bonn on 11 February, six days after the de Gaulle–Soames discussion. Harold Wilson faced a dilemma in Bonn: if he told Dr Kiesinger about the proposals put forward by the General then he was breaking the confidential seal which de Gaulle had placed upon them; if, however, he did not disclose them, the British government would have been doubly suspect in German eyes, when news of the talks eventually leaked, for concealing them from the Federal Chancellor. Harold Wilson was pressed hard by the Foreign Office to 'tell all' to Kiesinger, but he refused, giving him only a sanitized outline of what the General had said.

In the event, it did not matter. When Harold Wilson returned home he discovered that the Foreign Office, against his clearly expressed wishes, had circulated an extensive, though far from complete, record of the Paris talks to our ambassadors to the other countries of the Community and to Washington, with instructions to disclose the contents to the governments to which they were accredited, with the additional information that the British government disagreed fundamentally with the General on almost every issue he raised. It was this behaviour which subsequently prompted Harold

Wilson to write in *The Labour Government 1964–1970: A Personal Record:*

> I was getting concerned . . . about the attitude which the Foreign Office, at least at official level, seemed to be taking against the French, and the joy that some purely procedural victories seemed to give them.[1]

On this occasion, the FCO were after a bigger prize than a 'purely procedural' victory. Having twice been thwarted by the General in our attempt to join the Common Market, they were determined to cast him in the role of the Community's Benedict Arnold. It was an opportunity to demonstrate our credentials for being a part of the new Europe and that it was the French who sought to betray it. That was the motive in informing France's partners of the way the General's mind was working. It had the incidental merit, too, of ensuring that the world outside Washington and the Community would soon hear of it. Then as now, to tell our European partners anything in confidence was equivalent to handing copies to Reuter's news agency, the Press Association, the Associated Press, United Press International and Agence France Presse. In my experience, only the National Executive Committee of the Labour Party can leak secret documents faster, more consistently and more accurately, and they are, of course, a much older institution. On this occasion, however, the secret *was* kept, incredibly, for about ten days, which only went to show how shaken the Community governments were by the news. Then *Figaro* and *France Soir* received a version of it – garbled, but with enough truth in it to blow the whole story open. The 'Soames affair' had begun, and from that moment the Foreign Office were active in exploiting it to what they conceived to be de Gaulle's disadvantage.

The News Department at the Foreign Office is unlike any other information office in Whitehall. Its staff are diplomats, many with considerable service abroad. They are specialists in their subjects, but with a solid general knowledge of British policy in any area of the globe. On completion of his spell of duty there, the Head of the News Department can expect appointment as an ambassador or High Commissioner. The department is integral to the policy-making function of the FCO, because publicity is not only at times essential to the success of the policy but it can determine the course that the policy will take. It would be inelegant to describe them as aggressive in their propaganda, but they are firm to the point of dogmatism, especially about NATO and Eastern Europe. They are suckled by a corps of highly-paid British diplomatic correspondents; in addition a substantial number of foreign correspondents stationed in London look to the Foreign and Commonwealth Office as a principal news source. But it is not only the News Department which has these contacts; the relationships between other FCO diplomats and journalists are close and extensive; if the FCO gives a luncheon or dinner for a visiting dignitary, or throws a cocktail party, journalists are represented. When the Foreign and Commonwealth Secretary sets off for a tour abroad, the newspapermen assigned to report the trip may well travel in his aircraft, paying the full commercial fare but enjoying the luxury of VIP travel. In so doing they inevitably jeopardize the independence they never stop talking about, but that is by the way.

When on Friday, 21 February 1969, the news about the Soames affair began to break, sketchy and inaccurate though it was, I was told by the News Department that they were proposing to leak to *Il Messagero* in Rome the version of the interview telegraphed to France's partners and to the US State Department. This ill-conceived manoeuvre was to be the means by which we exposed the perfidy of the French and displayed the innate decency and desire to be good Europeans of the British. It was true that General de Gaulle had placed an embargo of confidentiality upon his talk with the ambassador but, seeing that the story would be in an Italian newspaper, we were hardly likely to be blamed for breaking it. Had this clumsy exercise taken place – which was unthinkable – and had it succeeded – which was unlikely – the Italian government no doubt would have been condemned for leaking it, an eventuality which, if it did weigh heavily on the official mind, no one saw fit to mention. When I reported the plan to the Prime Minister he instantly vetoed it.

That evening, Harold Wilson was due to speak at a party rally in Felixstowe, some eighty-three miles from London but in the Friday rush-hour three hours or more away by road. It meant that once he left Downing Street he would be out of touch for several hours (communications between Prime Minister and Downing Street have since been improved).

Just before he left, at 4.20 p.m., he instructed me on the course the No. 10 Press Office was to follow: not to leak the story; not to deny the truth, but not to add to it. We were to 'keep our hands clean'. If the French decided to leak the story then we could not stop them, but Harold Wilson did not want Britain to be accused of being responsible.

There must have been a Black Santa operating that evening, for a wish was never so speedily unfulfilled. As the Prime Minister drove away I went to the general press office and found a message asking me to go to the Foreign and Commonwealth Office's press briefing at 4.30. I arrived in time to hear the official spokesman begin to read from a telegram in his hand. It was the same telegram which had been sent to The Hague, Bonn, Brussels, Luxembourg, Rome and Washington, and classified 'Secret'. The spokesman said:

General de Gaulle spoke to our Ambassador in Paris two weeks ago. He began by saying that it had been impossible to arrive at a European view because of the pro-American feelings of all the countries in Europe, and particularly ourselves, whereas France had succeeded in achieving a totally independent position. This was not so in the case of either Germany or Italy or the Nether-lands, and certainly not of the United Kingdom. The whole essence of a European entity must be an independent position in world terms and he was not yet convinced that it was possible for us to accept this.

Once there was a truly independent Europe, there would be no need for NATO with its American dominance and command structure. General de Gaulle went on to say that he had no part in the creation of the Common Market, neither did he have any particular faith in it. What was more, he was quite certain that if we and our friends joined it, it could no longer be the same. This would not necessarily be a bad thing. It might have been created differently and he by no means excluded that for the future.

But we seemed to have set our hearts on joining it, for better or for worse. He personally foresaw it changing and would like to see it change into a looser form of a free trade area with arrangements by each country to exchange agricultural produce. He would be quite prepared to discuss with us what should take the place of the Common Market as an enlarged European Economic Association. But he was also anxious first to have political discussions with us. His thought was that there should be a large European Economic Association but with a smaller Inner Council of a European Political Association consisting of France, Britain, Germany and Italy. But it was necessary first to see whether France and Britain saw things sufficiently in common, because this was the key to any such political association. General de Gaulle recalled a suggestion which M. Debré had made a few months earlier to our ambassador, that Britain and France should have talks together on political matters, saying that he had understood we were not interested in this. Our ambassador replied that we would wish to know what object the French had in view in these discussions. General de Gaulle replied that he would like to see talks between Britain and France on economic, monetary, political and defence matters to see whether we could resolve our differences. He would like to see a gesture by the

British government suggesting that such talks should take place, which he would then welcome.

That statement was given non-attributably to the reporters present, i.e. while they could use the substance of it, they could not quote directly from it, nor reveal its source. But sources nowadays are only secure on comparatively minor stories; in this case, the source was part of the story. By nightfall, every capital in Europe knew of it. By the following Monday, the French government had bitterly protested about the briefing, the British press was ferocious in its condemnation of the government and the Conservative opposition was jubilant at the Cabinet's embarrassment.

At one stroke, the senior diplomats behind the move had destroyed any hope of Britain negotiating to enter Europe while General de Gaulle was still in power (in fact, he resigned two months later, having recklessly committed the continuation of his presidency to the outcome of an unimportant referendum; but the FCO could not have anticipated that happening); reduced relations with France to the depths they plumbed when the first de Gaulle veto was applied in 1963; made the rest of the Community wary about Britain (Europe without France was inconceivable; Europe without Britain was not only possible, it was the current position); provoked an embarrassed ambassador to the edge of apoplexy and resignation; upset the fervently pro-European members of the Cabinet; given the opposition the time of their lives in the House of Commons; and enabled the British press to portray the government as being as inept abroad as they said it was at home. All in all, short of staging a military coup, it was quite an afternoon's work. As the Duke of Wellington said, 'The next greatest misfortune to losing a battle is to gain such a victory as this.'

I was not able to speak to the Prime Minister after the FCO briefing until much later in the evening. Predictably, he was angry, and well aware that he would have to bear the brunt of the Opposition's attack in the Commons as well as the criticism from overseas. The FCO, however finely they may have calculated would be the effect in foreign capitals, had totally failed to appreciate the disarray their action would cause at home; or if they had appreciated it, they chose to ignore it. In diplomacy, whatever the public, purist protestations of Prime Ministers and Presidents, the end is frequently held to justify the means, but at the conclusion of the Soames affair the government could not even enjoy that consolation. [. . .]

Defenders of the FCO can point out that temporary civil servants with a political background – which described me – are notoriously obsessional about the power of the civil service and hyper-

suspicious of its influence. Certainly many permanent civil servants
have told me that is the case. For my part, I was alarmed by the
complacency of senior civil servants when things went wrong, a
complacency born of the fact that while governments may come and
governments may go, the civil service will go on for ever, whatever
the nature of the regime. I saw them as insulated from the outside
world, the political world as well as the world of the working man,
by the stockade of neutrality and impartiality which they have
erected around themselves. Their resolution not to be involved
politically – though the fact that their top tier, in the main, went to
public schools where Conservatism is endemic, live in Conservative
constituencies which are part of or adjacent to the stockbroking
belt, and think conservatively, which makes them Conservative-
inclined voters – has led them to be politically ignorant, which is
neither the same thing nor a good thing. For the special reason that
diplomats might spend two-thirds of their adult life working abroad
– and when working in London are concerned only with overseas
affairs – they are, despite their skills, likely to be more ignorant than
most.

One example of this came in December 1975 when the FCO
drafted, for the Prime Minister's signature, a letter of con-
gratulation to Mr Malcolm Fraser, leader of the Liberal (i.e.
Conservative) party in Australia on his becoming Prime Minister; a
potty suggestion which came within hours of the elected (Labour)
Prime Minister, Gough Whitlam, being dismissed from office by the
unelected Governor-General, Sir John Kerr, using powers everyone thought had fallen into disuse.

The 'Soames affair', the leaking of the Prague telegram and
numerous other incidents convinced Harold Wilson when in opposition that changes in the structure of the FCO News Department
ought to be made if he returned to office. I proposed, and he agreed,
that we should place a professional information officer, not a
professional diplomat, at the head of the Department; not least for
the benefit of the press themselves. Some months before the general
election of February 1974, Harold Wilson suggested the solution to
Jim Callaghan and my nomination for the man to carry it out – Tom
McCaffrey, a Scot who was then Director of Information at the
Home Office, where he had worked with Jim Callaghan between
1967 and 1970 – and a former deputy press secretary at No. 10. At
one point in the Douglas-Home–Wilson correspondence over the
'Shakespeare' telegram, Sir Alec had regretted that a slip had been
made by a junior official (while still defending it). Under McCaffrey, who was politically sensitive, it seemed unlikely that such a
mistake, deliberate or inadvertent, would occur again. It was the
attitude which prevailed in the Department that counted.

Jim Callaghan was enthusiastic about appointing McCaffrey, and did so as soon as he became Secretary of State. By then I think, he had convinced himself it was his idea in the first place. With McCaffrey there, and with Tom McNally, head of the Labour Party's International Department, joining Callaghan as his special adviser, a new dimension was added to the advice given to the Secretary of State. But the service triumphed in the end. When Jim Callaghan became Prime Minister on 5 April 1976, he naturally took McCaffrey with him to Downing Street. The FCO machine had already insisted that a diplomat should be appointed to replace him, and the monopoly was restored. McNally, too, went to Downing Street and the new Secretary of State, Tony Crosland, was accompanied to the FCO by his special adviser at the Department of Environment, a young man whose principal expertise was in the field of housing and local government. Even though he later recruited a special adviser on Southern Africa, the clock had been put right back.

REFERENCE

1. Harold Wilson, *The Labour government 1964–1970: a personal record* (Penguin Books, 1974).

Civil servants and secrecy*

PETER KELLNER AND LORD CROWTHER-HUNT

On their appointment civil servants are required to 'sign the Official Secrets Act'. In practical terms, civil servants sign a declaration whose contents, taken at face value, prevent them from telling anyone else almost anything about their work:

> . . . I am aware that I should not divulge any information gained by me as a result of my appointment to any unauthorized person, either orally or in writing, without the previous official sanction in writing of the department appointing me, to which written application should be made and two copies of the proposed publication to be forwarded. I understand also that I am liable to be prosecuted if I publish without official sanction any information I may acquire in the course of my tenure of an official appointment (unless it has already officially been made public) or retain without official sanction any sketch, plan, model, article, note or official documents which are no longer needed for my official duties, and that these provisions apply not only during the period of my appointment but also after my appointment has ceased.
> . . .

[. . .] The unspoken heart of the argument for closed government is that private debate among civil servants and ministers produces more *rational* policies, freed from public pressure, which is assumed to be irrational. Wise men, cogitating quietly on the nation's problems, will produce 'right' answers, if they are shielded from the hubbub of the political marketplace. But once exposed to pressure groups and vested interests and newspapers that will get it all wrong, who knows what absurdities will result?

Various secondary arguments are deployed to make an essential contempt for democratic debate more palatable. In the course of one interview, a senior official of the civil service department involved in monitoring the response of government departments to Sir Douglas Allen's letter on background papers, deployed the following arguments:

*From *The civil servants: an inquiry into Britain's ruling class* (Macdonald, 1980) pp. 264, 275–81.

There are some people who want to get at the papers just to get at
the titillating stuff, who think politics is all about intrigue and that
sort of thing . . .
There would be an upsurge in sensational journalism. For
example, if all Public Health Inspectors' findings were made
public, a restaurant which was quite innocently doing something
wrong – and was happy to correct things once it was pointed out –
might quite unfairly be branded as a filthy restaurant . . .
If you sit Mr Begin and Mr Sadat down to negotiate, and
broadcast to the world everything they say, then do not expect
peace to come to the Middle East.[1]

As in many bad arguments there is a good argument struggling to
get out. The good argument is that – quite apart from military
secrets – certain kinds of government information are properly kept
confidential. In a mixed economy any government will have access
to commercial confidences; in a society where money markets are
allowed to function with some freedom, some aspects of monetary
policy cannot easily be anticipated in public. That argument,
however, is about specifics, not about the generality of closed
government. The fact that examples lie readily to hand where most
reasonable people would concede the government's right to secrecy
does not invalidate the *principle* of open government – just as the
laws of libel and contempt should not invalidate the *principle* of free
speech: nearly all rules have their exceptions.
The central argument of both civil servants and ministers, however, does not concern the sensible exceptions. It concerns the
character of policy-making, of government administration, and of
democratic debate. The essence of Callaghan's minute, and of the
ideas that circulate in the Cabinet Office and the CSD, is that closed
government is better government. The odd thing is that they
provide little if any evidence for this hypothesis. On the contrary, a
number of instances of closed government that have come to light
suggest it can actually encourage bad policy-making and bad administration.
Five recent examples of questionable decision-making behind
closed doors are:

1. *Concorde* In the 1960s, when the important decisions were being
taken, there was no effective opportunity to challenge publicly the
government's false optimism about its prospects. And because
there were no adequate outside checks, the internal system of
checks and balances – with the Treasury supposed to act as a
questioning foil to departmental enthusiasm – was allowed to fail
unnoticed. Professor David Henderson, chief economist at the

Ministry of Aviation from 1965 to 1967, recently said: 'Even now we don't know whose opinions counted at what stage, what figures were accepted on what evidence at what stage, what outside checks were made. How can one justify that? How can we pretend to be trying to learn lessons from experience?' Henderson was asked whether outside, independent checks were ever made on the economics of Concorde: 'Not that I'm aware of . . . It offends the British administrator's sense of what is orderly. (The Treasury) can question the departments, it can disbelieve them, but it has no independent checks.'[2]

2. *Oil sanctions* When Thomas Bingham QC inquired in 1977 and 1978 into the breaking of oil sanctions against Rhodesia he found that a secret decision was taken in 1968, involving the Commonwealth Secretary, George (now Lord) Thomson, civil servants, and oil companies, to allow the oil companies to help arrange for oil to reach Rhodesia. The crux of the decision was a 'swap' arrangement, whereby the French oil company Total sent oil into Rhodesia on behalf of the British companies Shell and BP. The details were negotiated between the oil companies and Alan Gregory, an Assistant Secretary at the Ministry of Power. The arrangement allowed ministers to say that no *British* oil was reaching Rhodesia, although Parliament was never told what decisions had been reached. Following the report of the Bingham inquiry, evidence emerged that not even the full Cabinet was ever told of the swap arrangement: and the Prime Minister of the day, Harold Wilson, has denied knowing of its essential details. According to Wilson, the minute of the relevant meeting with the oil companies was indeed sent to No. 10. But:

> It was not circulated to the Cabinet either by the Foreign Office or by No. 10. . . . There is no record of my seeing it. . . . It would have been inconceivable for my Cabinet colleagues, myself, the Attorney-General or the officials to have connived at any action brought to our notice constituting a body blow to our sanctions policy.[3]

3. *Child benefits* In May 1976 the Labour Cabinet decided to defer a scheme to end family tax allowances and replace them with cash child benefits. Since tax allowances went to the father, while child benefit payments would be received by the mother, the move was designed specifically to help women. Barbara Castle, as Secretary for Social Services, enthusiastically piloted the legislation through Parliament. In April 1976, however, Callaghan became Prime Minister and replaced her with David Ennals. A few weeks later,

caught between Treasury caution and pay policy fears (if the take-home pay of husbands suddenly fell with the switch to payment to wives), the Cabinet deferred the scheme. A month later *New Society* published the Cabinet minutes of the crucial meeting: these showed that a decisive argument was the reported opposition of the TUC to the child benefit scheme. In fact the TUC had been told the day before by Denis Healey that the problem was *Cabinet* reluctance: this was the main reason why the TUC went cool on the scheme. In other words, Healey deceived both the TUC and the Cabinet about the other's true beliefs, and so persuaded both to acquiesce in a change of policy. Only the leak of the Cabinet minutes, and the subsequent checking by the *Sunday Times* of TUC records, revealed how Treasury officials, through Healey, overturned both Labour and TUC policy.[4] In the event the full child benefit scheme was delayed two years: had it not been for the *New Society* leak, the delay might arguably have been longer.

4. *Education planning* In 1975 the Education Arts and Home Office Sub-Committee of the Commons Expenditure Committee asked to see certain internal planning papers drawn up within the Department of Education and Science. In accordance with their rules for responding to Select Committees the Department's officials refused. These documents were supplied, however, to the international Organization for Economic Cooperation and Development. The OECD then published a highly critical study of the DES's planning, based on the papers that MP's had not been allowed to see. The OECD condemned the DES's planning approach as merely 'identifying existing trends' and then seeking to cater for them as best it could in the future – whereas the OECD argued that educational planning should be more positive, and consider the objectives of educational policy. The OECD concluded that in the DES 'there is no attempt at a new identification and formulation of educational goals in a world where the traditional canons of knowledge, values, attitudes and skills are continually questioned'.[5]

The OECD also criticized the DES for its lack of openness. This, it said, had two serious consequences:

One is that in certain cases policy is less likely to be understood and therefore less likely to be whole-heartedly accepted when the processes that lead up to it are guarded as arcane secrets. The second is that goals and priorities, once established, may go on being taken for granted and hence escape the regular scrutiny which may be necessary for an appropriate re-alignment of policy.[6]

5. *Tax relief and public schools* Labour's October 1974 election manifesto promised to 'withdraw tax relief and charitable status from public schools'. The promise was not implemented, and Sir William Pile, permanent secretary at the Department of Education until 1976, played a part in the process. In October 1975 he briefed Fred Mulley, the Education Secretary, on 'technical problems to which at present nobody knows the answers'. Pile's minute, dated 9 October, is a gem for connoisseurs of civil service delaying tactics:

> First, the term 'public schools' has no definable meaning. . . . There are substantial problems of definition involved in discriminating between one kind of school and another. Secondly, there is at the root of the matter the problem that charitable status is not enjoyed by the schools as such but by the institutions which provide them. . . . Thirdly, any progress in relation to the withdrawal of tax reliefs is critically dependent upon finding ways of redefining charities or discriminating between charities. . . . Treasury ministers are satisfied that it is not practicable to discriminate between policies and covenants intended to finance school fees and other policies and covenants. Last, an independent school provided by a charity enjoys a 50 per cent relief from rates on the school site. . . . The withdrawal would involve legislation and the question of discriminating between one kind of school and another would of course have to be faced.

Pile concluded that immediate responsibility for action 'lies primarily not with you but with the Home Secretary, the Chancellor of the Exchequer and the Secretary of State for the Environment. . . . I cannot think of anything that we ourselves can usefully do in the interim'.

One possible course Mulley might have taken was not suggested: enlist the help of tax and education experts outside government who were sympathetic to its policies. It would have been remarkable if widening the debate would not have prompted any suggestion as to how Pile's 'technical problems' might be overcome. Yet Mulley's officials were pressing the very opposite tactic. When Joan Lestor, a junior minister in the department, was preparing to speak at a Cambridge Union debate, an Assistant Secretary, M. W. Hodges, prepared the following advice:

> In the light of the government's legal advice, it would appear inadvisable for Miss Lestor to suggest any date by which *charitable status*, as such, might be expected to be withdrawn from the public schools. It would be advisable to speak rather in terms of the *fiscal benefits* associated with charitable status – a fine distinc-

tion, perhaps, to the ears of a lay audience, and indeed one which may be lost on them; if so, so much the better.

Those examples are, in detail, very different: but there is one important factor. In each case the decisions that were taken reflected not so much wise, rational men arriving at considered judgements, as ordinary frail mortals using closed government to hide their inadequacies. As Lord Armstrong – again candid in retirement – described Whitehall's obsession with secrecy: 'It obviously is comfortable, convenient, and one has to say it allows mistakes to be covered up.' Asked whether it also allowed incompetence to be covered up, Armstrong replied, 'Of course it does.'[7]

REFERENCES

1. Interview with author.
2. 'Newsweek', BBC TV, 9 November 1978.
3. *Hansard,* 7 November 1978, cols 743, 748.
4. *Sunday Times,* 20 June 1976.
5. Quoted in *Eleventh report from the Expenditure Committee* (HC 535, HMSO, 1977) Vol. 3, p. 111.
6. Ibid.
7. 'Newsweek'; see Reference 2.

PART THREE

Confrontations

This part consists of four case studies: Nuclear Power Policy; The Concorde Project; The Reporting of Northern Ireland; and The Publication of the Crossman *Diaries*. In all these cases the latent conflict between state power and the demands for freedom of information have become manifest. There have been several such confrontations in recent years, from Oilgate[1] to the 1978 ABC trial.[2] More recently, a battle took place in the high court between the British Steel Corporation and Granada Television. Granada published, in a television programme, confidential memoranda concerned with the conduct, by the state corporation, of a vital industrial negotiation. But, claims Ronald Dworkin, rather than arguing in favour of the important principle that the law should not prevent the press from publishing truthful information of public importance, unless for the gravest of reasons, Granada conceded that it had acted unlawfully.[3] The press, claims Dworkin, failed 'to identify and protect the nerve of the ideal of a free press in a free society'.

The rationale for choosing the case of nuclear power is that it has such massive social and political implications yet it is probably more bound by secrecy than any other area of policy. The Concorde project was not only colossally wasteful but it is a salutary example of how decision-taking behind closed doors leads to disastrous policy-making. The problems of media coverage of Northern Ireland are continuing ones which have tested, to the point of breaking, the principles of independence and impartiality on which our broadcasting institutions are based. Finally, we have included an analysis of the conflict that arose over the publication of the Crossman *Diaries* because it both symbolizes and reaffirms all the traditional values and myths of the constitution which sustain a closed and élitist system of government.

REFERENCES

1. Martin Bailey, *Oilgate: the sanctions scandal* (Coronet 1979).
2. David Leigh, *The frontiers of secrecy* (Junction Books, 1980) pp. 230–43.
3. Ronald Dworkin, 'The press is still fighting the wrong freedom battle', *Sunday Times*, 10 August 1980.

CHAPTER ONE

Nuclear power policy

Introduction

A seminar on 'How to live with the news media in difficult times' has found an appropriate speaker for one of its main sessions. The topics include 'The best time to release bad news and how to minimize press comment and criticism', and the man dealing with them is Mr Harold Boltek, the company secretary of British Nuclear Fuels.[1]

Britain's nuclear power programme has not been a success. It has been expensive, and not very productive. 'For thirty years scarce resources have been devoted to a technology whose economic and social value has consistently proved less than claimed by its advocates . . . There is no consensus over reactor type . . . The nuclear plant industry is ill-structured and uncompetitive in world markets.'[2] And yet over this period around 90 per cent of all government research and development in energy has been invested in nuclear power. 'Our return for this heroic expense of effort and finance is a modest 11 per cent of our electricity supply – representing a miserable 3 per cent of all forms of energy consumed in the country.'[3] Every year, the performance of the world's big nuclear power stations is tabulated, and the stations are ranked in order of performance and reliability. The best of the British stations came 105th on the list; two others were ranked at 107 and 113. Three Mile Island came last at 115.[4] Bowden compares present government policy to a land-based Polaris system: 'It is indefensible, but unstoppable.'

Nuclear power is a huge and complex issue. Decisions made in the field of nuclear energy policy affect every man, woman and child in this country. So why have successive governments (to transpose Gowing's words) treated nuclear technology as 'something wholly apart from normal procedures, whether democratic, constitutional, diplomatic or economic?'[5] And why did nuclear power only become a subject for political debate in the seventies, when Britain had been involved in programmes of nuclear research since the Second World War?

Margaret Gowing describes how the wartime secrecy over the atomic bomb distorted constitutional government in Britain. The War Cabinet never discussed the subject; Mr Attlee, the Deputy Prime Minister, knew nothing about it. The new Labour government took office, 'unprepared and uninformed', ten days before the atomic bomb fell on Hiroshima. Subsequently, the Labour Cabinet as a whole was excluded from discussing Britain's bomb. These decisions were taken by a small, inner group of senior ministers. The minimum of information was given to Parliament and to the press. Gowing contends that post-war secrecy soured Britain's external relations, particularly with her former allies. Secrecy also had profound effects internally, on the industrial development of nuclear technology. The British government refused publication of any reports about atomic energy, even those concerning non-technical, non-secret material: the Americans classified information only about production processes and military uses. Consequently when private industry clamoured to enter the nuclear field in the fifties, it was quite ignorant of the size and complexity of the problems it would be facing. The result, claims Gowing, was painful disillusion. Secrecy postponed the integration of atomic energy into programmes for defence, foreign relations, scientific research and energy for many years.

Roger Williams, in a recent major study of British decision-making in the nuclear field,[6] describes how, in the post-war years, Britain's work on nuclear energy was divided into three parts: research; weapons research; and production. In 1954 these three were grouped together under the Atomic Energy Authority (AEA). This body, because of the security aspects of the atomic energy project and because of its huge financial demands, had considerably more autonomy than the other public corporations. The AEA worked in conjunction with the Central Electricity Generating Board (CEGB), 'the effective voice of the electricity supply industry', training its personnel in the techniques of nuclear power and advising the electricity authorities on the nuclear side of new power stations. In 1971, British Nuclear Fuels Limited (BNFL), a new public body, was set up to take over responsibility for the fuel side of the AEA. BNFL shared a chairman with the AEA, and had similar limits on its accountability to Parliament. Apart from the public bodies there were the consortia, groups of companies who carried out the construction of nuclear power stations under the instructions of the AEA.

Williams's main conclusion about British nuclear decisions is that Britain has settled for handling too many twentieth-century problems with nineteenth-century political and administrative attitudes and machinery. This, he claims, is one of the major reasons for her continuing decline. Britain's nuclear decisions, alleges Williams, have been insular and inflexible, and have shown considerable naïvety about the political ramifications and momentum of technology. Above all, they were formulated in a system which lacked the public accountability to recognize and remedy weaknesses as and when these became apparent. The closed policy sub-system, argues Williams, 'was inadequate and confused to an extent which made sound policy almost by definition unattainable.'

The key factor in explaining the limited politicization of nuclear energy in Britain, claims Williams, is the socio-political culture: a culture which encourages consensus, and trust in public authorities. Be that as it may, the 'nuclear community' of decision-makers (once described by Tony Benn as a highly-organized scientific, industrial and technical lobby) ensured that nuclear policy was safely labelled as a purely technical, non party-political issue. Opponents or critics of nuclear energy were frequently dismissed as emotional, irrational, even élitist: twentieth-century Luddites.

In 1976, Michael Flood and Robin Grove-White published their book *Nuclear prospects: a comment on the individual, the state and nuclear power*.[7] This marked a turning-point in the nuclear debate. Nuclear policy was not only a technical matter, they argued; any new technology has social and political side effects, which affect us all – this was particularly true of nuclear power. Before Britain committed herself irreversibly to this technology, these social and political questions must be acknowledged and made the subject of public debate. In their extract in this section, Flood and Grove-White discuss the possible political and civil liberties implications of the security measures which might be thought desirable in an energy economy dominated by plutonium. They describe the passage of the Atomic Energy Authority (Special Constables) Act 1976, by which the then Secretary of State for Energy, Tony Benn, set up a private, permanently armed force which, contrary to both common law and constitutional practice, is virtually insulated from Parliamentary control.

Nuclear prospects provoked a response from JUSTICE, the British section of the International Commission of Jurists. They found these arguments disturbing, and expressed their concern (in evidence to the Windscale Inquiry) that Britain's nuclear power programme could have profound implications both for the rule of law and for the fundamental liberties of the citizen. Government statements on surveillance, for example, had apparently created a new crime in English law: subversion against the state. JUSTICE was fearful that any society which tended to respond to dissent with increasing violence ran the risk of turning into what they termed a 'security state'.[8]

In our second extract, Roger Williams makes a plea for greater accountability in the machinery of nuclear decision-making. Policy-making to date has been concentrated in a closed system of interested parties, for neither individual ministers nor Parliament are adequately equipped to assess the value or significance of what the AEA are doing. Even with billions of public money at stake, British government, in relation to nuclear development, has mostly amounted to no more than 'ratification, indifference or bewilderment'.

Abbreviations

AEA	Atomic Energy Authority
AGR	Advanced gas-cooled reactor
BNFL	British Nuclear Fuels Limited
CEGB	Central Electricity Generating Board
NII	Nuclear Installations Inspectorate
SGHWR	Steam-generating heavy water reactor

REFERENCES

1. Item from *The Guardian* Diary, 21 April 1981.
2. William B. Walker, Review of *The nuclear power decisions, International Affairs*, Vol. 57, No. 2, Spring 1981.
3. Robin Cook, *No nukes!* Fabian Tract 475 (The Fabian Society, 1981) p. 10.
4. Vivian Bowden, 'Reliability drops – but the price goes up', *The Guardian*, 9 July 1981.
5. Margaret Gowing, *Reflections on atomic energy history* (Cambridge University Press, 1978) pp. 23, 14, 12, 20.
6. Roger Williams, *The nuclear power decisions: British policies 1953–78* (Croom Helm, 1980).
7. Michael Flood and Robin Grove-White, *Nuclear prospects: a comment on the individual, the state and nuclear power* (FOE, CPRE, NCCL, 1976).
8. JUSTICE, *Plutonium and liberty* (JUSTICE, 1978) pp. 5, 9, 17–18.

The political impact of nuclear security*

MICHAEL FLOOD AND ROBIN GROVE-WHITE

The most important objectives of increased security measures in an energy economy dominated by plutonium would be the prevention of nuclear terror and social dislocation. The risks of possible failure to guard against nuclear malevolence might provide a practically unlimited justification for any measures thought desirable. The obvious, and serious, civil liberties' implications of the methods should not disguise this fact.

However, such measures could have 'spillover' effects on the polity generally. In the paragraphs that follow, we argue that free political debate of the full range of issues raised [in a] nuclear programme might well be prejudiced by the security measures adopted. The implications of this for parliamentary democracy itself could be serious.

We consider just three aspects.

1. *News media* Anxiety by the security services to prevent terrorist incidents could have ramifications for news media discussion of day-to-day nuclear power matters. The present strict executive embargo on information relating to existing small-scale and (presumably) infrequent movements of plutonium may well be extended to cover the larger commitments of the projected FBR programme. We may speculate that information about plutonium practices and movements might become subject to a D Notice[1] – a step which could be justified, in our view, by present criteria.[2]

News media editors would then have two reasons for being cautious about publishing stories relating to important aspects of the nuclear power programme – the existence of a D Notice and increased possibilities for falling foul of the Official Secrets Act [. . .]. They would be concerned, understandably, to avoid infringing either sanction. This concern would express itself probably in consultations with D Notice Committee or government officials whenever uncertainties arose.

But such consultations might also tend to make editors suscepti-

*From *Nuclear prospects: a comment on the individual, the state and nuclear power* (FOE, CPRE, NCCL, 1976) pp. 18–23.

ble to executive opportunism – in this case, pressure to quash politically embarrassing stories relating to the nuclear power programme where no genuine security implications existed.

Such incidents have occurred in the past. For example, a former minister is reported to have commented sweepingly in 1963 on frequent abuses by ministers of D Notice procedure.[3] There is also at least one graphic example of governmental abuse of authority to deter publication on a matter relating to the nuclear power programme.[4]

The greater the need to sustain the momentum of the nuclear programme – for reasons of national economic policy as much as for reasons of energy security – the more awkward for government might be public or parliamentary hesitations about the programme on grounds of safety or economics (for example). Executive temptation to influence the flow of information on more 'sensitive' nuclear matters, even where bona fide security interests were not at stake, might thus be considerable. Such influence might be made easier than at present by the genuine security considerations that would apply to certain aspects of the fuel cycle.

Such manipulation of D Notice or Official Secrets Act procedures could contribute to serious ignorance in Parliament and public alike of the routine ups and downs of the nuclear power programme.

2.*Pressure groups* Suspicion breeds suspicion. If bodies outside government think their phones are being tapped and their activities regularly monitored, they inevitably take measures to avoid such surveillance. This in turn leads to increased interest by the authorities, who may be led to measures still less favourable to personal privacy. As the nuclear programme grows this cycle of response and counter-response might exacerbate the climate of suspicion and increase tension. It would be subtly corrosive of freedom of speech.[5]

3. *Armed force and the constitution* The passage of the Atomic Energy Authority (Special Constables) Act 1976 has given the AEA a permanently armed Constabulary whose duties include the guarding of plutonium and its related installations. So far this force is small.[6] But almost certainly a national commitment to the fast breeder reactor would require the development of a very large force indeed[7] to provide armed support.[8] It is a major step in several ways.

In the paragraphs that follow we suggest that during the passage of the Act in the first half of 1976, Parliament accepted security measures which are seriously at odds with parliamentary control of nuclear power. But in the circumstances, we argue, Parliament may have had little choice. For the brutal message of the Atomic Energy

Authority (Special Constables) Act seems to be that plutonium security is not simply more important than democratic controls. It may actually be *incompatible* with those controls.

The Special Constables Act confers extensive powers on the AEA's Special Constabulary to carry arms, to engage in hot pursuit of actual or attempted thieves of special nuclear materials and to arrest on suspicion. Few would doubt the necessity for such powers for guarding plutonium and similar materials.

However, it is notable that despite the urging of a significant body of opinion, the government did not assign these functions to either the regular police or the Army.[9] Building on the existing private constabulary of the AEA, the government preferred instead to create a private permanently armed force.

In these circumstances, a central feature of the Act is, *prima facie*, disturbing. Despite the Special Constabulary's broad powers and the almost total public ignorance of its structure and code of conduct,[10] the line of its accountability to Parliament is extremely thin.

The Constabulary is employed by, and hence responsible to, the AEA. The AEA, being a nationalized industry board, are formally responsible to the Secretary of State for Energy. And the Secretary of State is in turn responsible to Parliament. It is important to understand the *nature* of the Secretary of State's relation to the AEA. He has only limited powers over the Authority's administration[11] and, as a matter of public policy, he is not answerable to Parliament for their day-to-day activities.[12] The line of accountability from Constabulary to Parliament is thus attenuated and, despite assurances given by ministers during the passage of the Bill, it is probable that many of the questions MPs will most want to ask about the Constabulary's actions and attitudes will in future be regarded by the Table Office as lying outside the sphere of the Secretary of State's responsibility.[13]

Throughout the passage of the Bill, ministers sought to reassure doubters that this chain of accountability was 'proper' and 'regular',[14] even in the exceptional circumstances to which the Bill was addressed. Indeed it was even claimed by Lord Shepherd, Leader of the House of Lords, that the Bill provided 'about as watertight a position for parliament, and for the public, as one is likely to be able to legislate for'.[15]

Not all MPs agreed with this assessment. Recognizing that the Bill implied the almost complete insulation of a private armed force from public or parliamentary view, Alan Beith MP argued it 'could be regarded as a very dangerous threat to civil liberties'.[16] In the House of Lords, Lords Avebury and Mansfield contended that the Bill provided for quite inadequate parliamentary controls over 'a

situation wholly new in our history',[17] involving 'a quite new departure in our constitutional thought on carrying arms'.[18]

Ministers made just one small gesture in response to these
libertarian urgings. In a letter to Beith, the Secretary of State
undertook to be 'ready to answer in the House in relation to any
incident in which weapons were fired by the AEAC other than for
training purposes'.[19] Beith regarded this 'extremely limited'[20] assurance as unsatisfactory. It had no statutory force and was in any event
highly restricted. Nevertheless, it was all that the government
offered, other than repeated assertions of the existence of adequate
'accountability'.

The enacted Bill is therefore deeply disturbing on civil liberties
grounds, in and of itself. It creates a private armed force, which may
grow steadily as the nuclear power programme grows. It is a force
with extensive powers of pursuit and arrest, yet its manner of
operation is, and will continue to be, completely unfamiliar to the
public at large. It is unlikely that MPs will even be permitted to ask
Questions in Parliament about its conduct.

Why has this situation come about?

Throughout the debates in Lords and Commons, a paradox was
evident. Ministers were fully seized of the range of issues at stake.
To Tony Benn, the possibility of plutonium theft presented 'an
exceptional risk and danger'.[21] At the same time he acknowledged
that the Bill's extension of the right to bear arms, in order to meet
the threat, ran 'against the grain for anyone with our tradition'.[22]
Repeatedly throughout the Bill's passage, the urgency of the need
for armed protection was both stressed and regretted.

Yet the government's response to these acknowledged difficulties
was perplexing. Despite the fact that the Secretary of State's right of
intervention in the Authority's running of the Constabulary could
be exercised only in the most exceptional circumstances,[23] ministers
appeared wilfully to exaggerate the extent of the Secretary of State's
authority. There seemed to be considerable anxiety amongst ministers at all stages of the Bill's passage to emphasize the 'control'[24] the
Secretary of State would exercise over the Constabulary. But the
fact of the matter was, as Alan Beith pointed out, 'The Bill gives a
great deal of power and responsibility to the Authority, but very
little to the Secretary of State. The Authority is not answerable to
the House. The Secretary of State is – and that is the crucial issue.
. . . In this legislation, the Secretary of State does not have enough
powers.'[25]

Why then did the Secretary of State choose to leave his powers so
limited? It would have been consistent with Tony Benn's view of the
seriousness of the situation if he had decided to bring the Special
Constabulary within his own authentic control, on a day-to-day

basis, rather than leaving it as a mere 'technical service of a nationalized industry'.[26] Ministers, particularly interventionist ministers like Tony Benn, are not usually so reluctant to innovate on important matters – and the issues at stake would have assured Benn the support of civil libertarians like Beith and Lords Avebury and Mansfield, had he chosen to do so. The Secretary of State's decision not to take such powers demands an explanation.

A profoundly disturbing possibility may be suggested – that greater ministerial powers over the Constabulary would actually *inhibit* the effective guarding of special nuclear materials and installations.

If it is accepted – as it may well be – that flexibility and furtiveness are central to the Special Constabulary's effectiveness in its vital tasks, it becomes hard to challenge the argument that public knowledge of its activites – through direct parliamentary accountability or public availability of its Standing Orders – could prejudice this effectiveness.

It seems reasonable therefore to suggest that the government may have been advised by the security services *not* to give powers to a minister, precisely in order to avoid the possibility of answerability for the Constabulary's actions.

As Alan Beith realized, the only way the Secretary of State could be more than nominally responsible to Parliament would be if the Act made him first responsible for its actions. By avoiding direct responsibility, the Secretary of State's own formal ignorance of the Constabulary's day-to-day behaviour became constitutionally established.

If this reading of the Special Constables Act's passage is correct, civil nuclear power has already presented Britain with a frightening dilemma. Effective security of nuclear materials demands parliamentary (and hence public) ignorance. But public ignorance on matters of this importance is totally incompatible with an appraisal of the full implications of a growing nuclear commitment.

It is a difficulty which will grow steadily as the nuclear industry's need for armed protection grows. Democratic control of armed force and the interests of security will be increasingly at odds. The passage of the Atomic Energy Authority (Special Constables) Act 1976 suggests that, faced with the pressures of a fast breeder programme, parliamentarians may increasingly opt for security at the expense of long established prerogatives.

REFERENCES

1. A D Notice is a formal letter of *request* circulated confidentially to editors of newspapers, radio and TV news drawing attention to named items of news

regarded by the defence authorities as secrets of importance, publication of which would be contrary to the national interest. Such Notices are issued by a committee composed partly of government officials and partly of representatives of various press and radio organizations – the Services, Press and Broadcasting Committee (more familiarly, the D Notice Committee). See Radcliffe Report (Cmnd 168, HMSO, April 1962) paras 122–153 for a full account. [See also pp. 79–92 of the present volume.]

2. The subjects covered by D Notices relate principally to 'naval, military and air matters the publication of which would be prejudicial to the national interest'. But 'rigid interpretation of the wording of this formula (is not insisted upon), so long as a clear case of national prejudice of a "military" nature can be made out' (Radcliffe Report, para. 13). We suggest that information about plutonium practices could certainly give rise to national prejudice of a 'military' nature.

3. 'In May 1963. Lord Balfour of Inchyre (former Parliamentary Under-Secretary for Air) said he did not believe that there was a minister in the government who could put his hand on his heart and say that he did not know of instances where D Notices and the public relations system have been used to cloak individual or departmental failure.' David Williams, *Not in the public interest* (Hutchinson, 1965) p. 86.

4. In the early 1950s, the *Daily Express* was warned off a story with no security implications, relating to gross negligence during construction work at Windscale, by an explicit threat of prosecution under the Official Secrets Acts. A later admission by the senior Ministry of Defence official responsible made it clear that the threat had been an empty one. It had been made to shield the government from the embarrassment that would have followed from revelations of incompetence. (Oral evidence of Chapman Pincher, 14 December 1971 – Franks Report (Cmnd 5104, HMSO, 1972) vol. 4, pp. 237–8.)

5. The observations in this paragraph have been based on conversations with individuals engaged in a wide range of pressure group activity. They apply with particular force to groups active in areas (for example, defence) where security considerations are important.

6. 'Approximately 400'; see HC Debs (23 February 1976) Col. 18.

7. The AEA's 400 constables are required principally to guard the four most important AEA/BNFL installations handling special nuclear materials (Harwell, Winfrith, Dounreay and Windscale) and their associated transports. Ministers have refused, on security grounds, to disclose the more precise deployment of the force (see HC Debs (23 February 1976) Col. 18), so it is not possible to make a watertight estimate of the likely numbers of future armed men the nuclear industry might require. For discussion purposes, we make the modest assumption that the permanent guarding of a single sensitive installation and its transport calls for an average of fifty constables (not unreasonable perhaps when issues such as shift work, leave, administration, and planning staff are included). In view of present US practice and the numbers of attacks on foreign nuclear installations we assume that *all* UK nuclear installations may come to need armed guards – a possibility that was raised during the passage of the Special Constables Act (e.g. HC Debs (26 February 1976) Col. 709). In our reference year, this would mean guards would be required for fifty FBRs, fifty LWRs and associated fuel cycle facilities and transports. A modest guess at the scale of a future constabulary thus yields a minimum figure of 5000 armed men. We should emphasize we have no authority for this figure. It may be compared with the 17,000 uniformed officers of London's Metropolitan Police (who are, of course, unarmed).

8. The present Special Constabulary has no remit to guard the CEGB's property. So it is reasonable to assume that a CEGB force with broadly similar powers

would be thought necessary should the CEGB come to operate its own FBRs and guard its own special nuclear materials.

9. Before and during the Bill's passage, the Police Federation and a number of MPs and peers pressed the view that the creation of a separate AEA armed police force should be avoided if at all possible. Similarly, several MPs and peers urged that the guarding of nuclear installations and transports should be placed, unequivocally, in the hands of the Army.

10. A state of affairs that will certainly continue – as the Special Constabulary's Standing Orders will not be published (HL Debs (27 May 1976) Col. 416) and minimal information is likely to be made public about the organization or composition of the constabulary (see HC Debs (23 February 1976) Col. 18). By comparison, a crucial ingredient in public confidence in the ordinary police is the general knowledge that exists of police behaviour and controls. Police day-to-day conduct is openly regulated by both common law and administrative prescription (e.g. Home Office circulars). And general public familiarity with police force structure, ranking etc, has also acted to foster public understanding of their role. With the AEA's Special Constabulary, such devices will not exist.

11. While the Secretary of State may give the Authority 'such directions as he may think fit' (Atomic Energy Authority Act 1954 S 3[2]), and such directions may be 'general or particular in character' (S 3[3]), he has the duty not to intervene in detail in the conduct by the Authority of their affairs unless in his opinion 'overriding national interests so require' (S 3[3]).

12. Erskine May, *Parliamentary practice* (Butterworth, 18th ed., 1971) p. 326, for the detailed application of public policy in this area.

13. 'To be in order, a Question must relate to a matter within the government's responsibility or which could be so made by administrative or legislative action. . . . Some Questions are out of order because refusals to answer, by successive administrations, have been so consistent that such subjects cannot be *raised* by way of Questions.' For example 'Questions that relate to details of arrangements for national security; . . . and to matters of detail within the *day-to-day responsibilities of nationalized boards.*' (*Report from the Select Committee on Parliamentary Questions 1971–72,* paras 5–6). The emphases are ours. In a letter to Lord Avebury, dated 7 June 1976, Lord Shepherd, Leader of the House of Lords, sought to give a reassurance that parliamentary oversight of the AEA's Special Constabulary would be genuine. 'I am satisfied,' he wrote, 'that no provisions in either House would preclude the Secretary of State from answering any questions *raised* in either House.' (Our emphasis again.) This begs precisely the point at issue.

14. Tony Benn, HC Debs. (26 February 1976) Col. 704.

15. HL Debs. (27 May 1976) Col. 423.

16. HC Debs. (4 May 1976) Col. 1232.

17. The Earl of Mansfield, HL Debs (27 May 1976) Col. 411.

18. The Earl of Mansfield, HL Debs (18 May 1976) Col. 1274.

19. HC Debs (5 May 1976) Col. 1230.

20. HC Debs (5 May 1976) Col. 1231.

21. HC Debs (26 February 1976) Col. 702.

22. HC Debs (26 February 1976) Col. 708.

23. See Reference 11.

24. For example – 'As for control by Parliament . . . control will be exercised by (the Secretary of State)': Alex Eadie (Under-Secretary of State for Energy), HC Debs *Standing Committee B* (27 April 1976) Col. 9.

25. HC Debs (4 May 1976) Col. 1238.

26. Eldon Griffiths MP – HC Debs (4 May 1976) Col. 1233. Griffiths and the official opposition supported the government in its formal detachment from the Constabulary's procedures and practice.

Tradition versus technology*

ROGER WILLIAMS

In the atomic energy field in Britain one feels that secrecy having begun as a necessity continued as a convenience and eventually became an obsession. In my view, only since 1975 and in respect of Windscale has British civil nuclear power approached real accountability. Judged by the criterion of openness – itself the first requirement in public accountability – each of the main political reactor decisions – 1955, 1957, 1960, 1965, 1974 and 1978 – was an improvement on the one before, with the last two markedly more open than the other four, though even then far from fully open. But always one must remember that the reactor choice questions – 1955 (Magnox), 1965 (AGR), 1974 (SGHWR) and 1978 (AGR) – were squarely based on much earlier, and exclusively internal, AEA decisions. And always too one must remember the obscurity with which the CEGB conduct their affairs.

To ask for enhanced public accountability is to be directed first, and often last, to Parliament. What in this respect can Parliament claim to have achieved?

Incredible though it may seem, the first full parliamentary investigation involving the AEA was conducted by the Estimates Committee in 1958–9, when the Industrial Group of the Authority was examined.[1] The Estimates Committee proved an 'affable watchdog'[2] and the ensuing report mostly commended the AEA, but it has been suggested[3] that the great pains taken by the Authority to assist the Committee and the complexity of the subject matter together ensured the Authority a favourable report. The AEA, by this time committed to the AGR, were also then considering the reactor concept which later became the SGHWR, but the Committee felt incompetent to judge whether resources could in fact be spared to develop this extra system, though they did think the AEA should encourage more and earlier consortia participation in research and development.

The AEA has fallen outside the province of the Nationalized Industries Committee and this Committee in 1962[4] dealt with the Authority only peripherally in looking at nuclear energy. In spite of

*From *The nuclear power decisions – British policies 1953–1978* (Croom Helm, 1980) pp. 324–31.

this, it has been said that the Committee 'exhibited considerable ability'[5] in tackling the technical issues at stake, and [. . .] they certainly revealed real areas of difference between the AEA and the CEGB, concluding that 'the evidence which has been recited suggests defects in the existing structure and organization which may mean that money is not being spent to the best advantage'.

The Public Accounts Committee, using the reports prepared for them by the Comptroller and Auditor-General [. . .] have frequently investigated the AEA's accounts. Confining themselves to the financial side of nuclear energy, and so ordinarily avoiding the technical arguments for particular policies, the Committee have in this field, as in others, usually offered valuable and searching criticism. Their analyses have, of course, been retrospective, and also there have been some important time gaps in their work. It is of particular interest that until the early sixties they found the AEA's accounts to be at best mostly unintelligible, and strongly, and ultimately successfully, urged their reform.[6]

The new Science Committee, having in 1967 chosen nuclear energy for their first study, also in that inquiry found themselves confronting the matter of public accountability. They were told[7] then by the Minister of Technology that 'there has been every reason for relying on the advice of the Authority as the chosen instrument, in all questions of atomic research and development . . . the AEA contains within itself the machinery for giving advice to the government'. It was not thought 'necessary, right or proper, or possible' for Mintech to duplicate the advisory machinery of the AEA, though individual projects were evaluated in Mintech 'to the best of our ability'. The AEA were much closer to Mintech than were other public corporations to their ministries and although Mintech was developing a techno-economic analysis unit, the technical side of nuclear proposals currently could not be assessed other than by the AEA: 'when the Authority decides what particular reactors it wishes to build for research purposes, than I would be glad to leave it to them because at this stage one would not even have the facts upon which an economic assessment could be made. Their decision . . . would be one based entirely upon a scientific assessment . . . and here I do not think it would be open to me to have a sensible alternative view unless the expenditure . . . was so great as really to be beyond the capacity of the country to pay for it.'

Sir Friston How, Secretary of the Atomic Energy Office, had told the Estimates Committee[8] essentially the same thing in 1959: it was inevitable that the Authority should have a fair margin of freedom because 'in this curious sphere' only the people available to them had sufficient knowledge to know what was worthwhile; there had naturally, therefore, been no attempt to create a parallel bureaucracy in Whitehall. Or as a minister put it in 1960,[9] he was 'advised by the best experts available' and was bound to take their advice since it was rather higher than his own knowledge of the subject.

The Science Committee's opinion of all this in 1967[10] was that 'neither the Minister of Power nor the Minister of Technology appeared to have any very effective technical check on the activities of the AEA and the consequent allocation of public funds for the Authority's purposes'. The Committee were 'not satisfied that, between them, the two ministers are adequately equipped to assess the value and significance of what the Authority are doing'. Thus it could even be argued that the entire gas-cooled reactor technology line might not have been the best one to follow. The Committee therefore recommended 'a technical assessment unit capable of advising the government on the merits and prospects of particular projects proposed to be undertaken by the Authority'. The minister's reply[11] was that he 'foresaw very real difficulties in establishing such a unit', and that the Authority were 'the repository of nearly all the national expertise in the nuclear field'. He did, however, intend to set up an Atomic Energy Board to advise him and he hoped this would meet the Committee's objective. The Committee persisted on that occasion that such a board was not the sort of independent agency they had in mind, but in their subsequent studies they took their own opinions of policy more seriously and never properly returned to the accountability theme. The Committee's investigations [. . .] were of considerable value, but as should also be clear, they were far from adequate in getting full accountability. Judged against that objective there were too many subjects which the Committee did not address, their inquiries were for the most part insufficiently thorough, and they mostly failed to see themselves as primarily an instrument of inquiry. It might have helped had they been able to draw on some permanent techno-economic expertise located, say, in the Comptroller and Auditor-General's office, if such an arrangement could have been made.

The work of these various committees apart, one can pass quickly over Parliament's other devices for securing public accountability. In the nuclear field, debates, especially in the Lords, though infrequent, were often interesting and even informative; statements and answers to Parliamentary Questions were as usual under close ministerial control.

Now the quest for more accountability is never a popular one to make. Lord Rothschild found that in the early seventies with his report on civil science, and he also encountered on that occasion a reluctance or refusal even to acknowledge what accountability might mean. Certainly an annual report, answerability to ministers who are themselves never culpable to the point of resignation, and occasional appearances before parliamentary committees do not add up to the real thing. Yet common sense alone suggests that there is likely to be a strong, though obviously not infallible, correlation between the extent to which proposals are analysed and criticized in advance of a commitment and their soundness in practice afterwards. Even then nuclear decisions, in common with others in technology, emphasize the contrast between the horizon of decision-makers, measured at best in years, and the timescale of the technology, measured in decades.

Unhappily, it is basic to human nature to shy away from full and public accountability, and in Britain there are the Official Secrets Acts, the thirty-year rule, a multiplicity of lesser devices and the whole political culture to reinforce this trait. It is all grotesquely inadequate when millions, even billions, of public money are at stake, but it is going to be very hard indeed to change. By comparison, Britain's other nuclear problems, technological, organizational, and industrial have really all been derivative. Many would have arisen no matter what the policy system, but their form, severity and chronic character all were greatly affected by the particular closed system in which they arose.

It may be necessary to say here that one is not suggesting that government should not 'govern', that it should abdicate from responsibility. One is saying rather that in respect of Britain's nuclear development, government mostly amounted to ratification, indifference or bewilderment. One might have thought that, faced with matters which they could not really be expected to understand, decision-makers would have sought safety in opening out policy arguments so that outsiders might identify weaknesses insiders were either not qualified to assess or which they were prevented from even acknowledging because of institutional affiliations. Instead, on grounds of commercial security or constitutional propriety, the arguments were repeatedly closed up and decisions made on an inadequate basis of true knowledge.

In any mature polity the wise use of power must involve the sharing of information and the uncertainities and costs of technology have only underlined this. But in Britain, at least until the mid-seventies, healthy debate was not to be. Instead the AEA inherited on their creation a tradition of high priority and deep secrecy. The organization was from the first a powerhouse of ideas and enjoyed wide outside support, amongst the public and media and within Westminster and Whitehall. The civil service backgrounds of the AEA's first two chairmen perfectly bridged the internal demands and the external supports. The net result was that the level of nuclear spending was set independently rather than by evaluation against alternatives, and this having been the way things

began, this was how they continued. The Authority's later position
that 'massive government financial support is essential to the satisfactory launching of a development programme for nuclear power'[12]
was obviously correct but, remembering that in the post-war period
Britain has found it increasingly difficult to hold a position in the
second rank of states, less costly routes to nuclear power than a
large development programme would certainly have had attrac-
tions.

The civil nuclear enterprise appealed on many different grounds,
as exciting science, as challenging engineering distinct from
weapons work, as a more or less urgent social need, and last, but by
no means least, as a symbol of national vigour. Commitment once
entered into on these kinds of consideration, technological momentum took care of the rest and the Authority grew from 17,000 in 1954
to a peak of 41,000 in 1961. In the end, a good case can be made out
that not only was British energy research and development strategy
thrown out of balance, but British technology much more generally
as well.[13]

On the other hand, in Britain there never was created, and
understandably there never spontaneously developed, a capacity to
criticize the development of nuclear power, cogently, constructive-
ly and with full techno-economic rigour. Policy was much the worse
for this lack and it was this gap which in part the nuclear opposition
of 1974–8 and also the Royal Commission attempted, albeit very
imperfectly, to fill. But where might a critical capacity have established itself? Possibly it might have arisen within government itself
had not the AEA and CEGB been regarded from that perspective
as both in a sense themselves part of government and simultaneously a mutually monitoring binary system. Possibly it might have
developed within Parliament had not all the committees which
investigated nuclear power, with the partial exception of the Public
Accounts Committee, both lacked professional assistance and
valued their own opinions above their ability to ferret out information. Possibly the party system might have served had politicians
known how to relate the various issues, technical, economic, industrial and ethical, to party ideologies, or at least to party lines.
Possibly the university world could have helped had it been officially
thought worthwhile encouraging there on a continuing and disci-
plined basis a faculty for public policy analysis.

What is particularly remarkable in this connection is how differently nuclear safety and nuclear economics were handled in
Britain. Sponsorship had been separated from regulation by 1960
and although the AEA gave substantial assistance until at least
1962, a deliberate effort was thereafter made by the Nuclear
Installations Inspectorate (NII) to establish an independent regula-

tory capacity. No doubt there were weaknesses in the NII's approach, and the Inspectorate did not become fully separate from the nuclear sponsoring department until the creation of the Health and Safety Executive in 1975. Nevertheless, it was thought possible to create an organization with an informed view of safety, and distinct from the AEA. The creation of the National Radiological Protection Board in 1970 was another step in the same direction, and even within the AEA the Safety and Reliability Directorate enjoyed a far-reaching independence. Yet similar moves as regards nuclear economics were repeatedly refused and a policy monopoly tolerated, and even defended, as being inevitable. The point is sharply brought out by considering, as one of many similar examples, some words by N. L. Franklin,[14] chairman of the Nuclear Power Company but formerly of the AEA and BNFL, made in 1977 in respect of the public acceptability of nuclear power. Franklin was of course concerned with the safety aspect and here he felt that the public could be educated in the generality of the subject, to the point where they could realize there was a problem. But beyond that, evaluation of risk, especially at low levels, he saw as depending centrally on skills and specializations which could not be acquired by the public at large through education. Such evaluation was a matter rather for experts, and this arrangement could be publicly acceptable 'provided the public can be reassured in clearly visible ways that the organizational and institutional arrangements are such as to promote checking of one group of experts by others who are as well qualified and suitably independent'. It is, as should now be very clear, exactly such an independent check which has been totally missing in regard to nuclear power economics. Yet protests such as those of Lord Robens apart, nuclear power clearly has been publicly acceptable in Britain in the economic sense. It is perfectly understandable why the safety rather than the economic aspects of nuclear power should eventually have come to be a major matter of public concern, but one can still regret the possible overemphasis on this as compared with the virtual indifference on the part of the public to the economic questions. At the same time, nuclear power as well as government having lost most of its mystique in the seventies, one can suggest that the long-term failure to deal fairly with the public as regards nuclear economics substantially worsened suspicions when these eventually arose about nuclear safety.

Certainly, so long as it is considered enough to rely on the amateurs which ministers and MPs – and in this type of case officials too – must be, on journalistic investigation which however good is necessarily intermittent, and on academics and private individuals, then so long will policy continue to be essentially unaccountable, and because unaccountable, inadequate more often than it need be.

[. . .] It is certainly easy to overlook the enormous technical achievements of the last quarter century. But it remains the author's conviction that Britain can have a much more successful industrial future than she has had an immediate past, especially where nuclear power is concerned. It is also vital that public decisions should aim at social effectiveness as well as commercial efficiency. The structure in which decisions are taken and implemented is thus for two quite separate reasons absolutely fundamental. With due respect to such bodies as the Waverley, Powell and Vinter Committees, and the Nuclear Power Advisory Board, if a small fraction of the detailed effort which went into designing British nuclear reactors had gone into designing an adequate policy system and getting the responsibilities right, the benefits must surely have been enormous. But then, the design of reactors is obviously a highly specialized matter, whereas it has been traditional to regard the design of a policy system as a matter of reflex common sense and experience. Unfortunately, tradition and technology seem to make poor bedfellows, which has been so much the worse for Britain where tradition has enjoyed such a special place.

REFERENCES

1. HC 3 16-1 (1958–9).
2. *Nuclear Power*, September 1959, p. 81.
3. Nevil Johnson, *Parliament and administration: the estimates committee 1945–65* (Allen & Unwin, 1966) p. 60.
4. HC 236 I-III (1962–3).
5. David Coombes, *The Member of Parliament and the administration: the case of the select committee on the nationalized industries* (Allen & Unwin, 1966) p. 111.
6. HC 252 (1960–61), report, paras 105–9.
7. HC 381-XVII (1966–7), p. 188, para. 3 and Q. 970–84.
8. HC 3 16-1 (1958–9), Q. 19.
9. HCD 625 c. 952.
10. HC 381-XVII (1966–7), report, para. 154.
11. HC 40 (1968–9).
12. E. P. McTighe, 'The development of the UK nuclear power industry', *Atom*, December 1970, pp. 242–53 (53).
13. See, for example, Mary Goldring, 'The atomic incubus', *New Society*, 28 October 1965.
14. N. L. Franklin, 'Nuclear power in Western society', *Journal of the British Nuclear Energy Society*, Vol. 16, October 1977, pp. 303–14.

CHAPTER TWO

The Concorde project

Introduction

A potentially significant hardening of Conservative hearts against Concorde was revealed yesterday when the influential Tory MP, Mr John Biffen, denounced the plane as a 'flying overdraft' and said that no more should be built. Mr Biffen . . . told a meeting of Watford industrialists: 'The simple, inescapable truth is that the British taxpayer lost money when Concorde was developed; is also losing out when the plane is being built and – even more hurtful – whenever it is flown. The powerful technological and business lobby that has sustained Concorde over the years must be told they have had their day. [. . .] Mr Biffen [. . .] said that the Concorde affair showed the difficulties of controlling high-technology investments once they have become 'a substantial vested interest feeding upon public procurement and taxpayer finance'.[1]

Concorde is a major public expenditure project. And it has been a tragic waste of scarce national resources. Conceived in the late fifties, in the wake of a series of abandoned projects and in the aftermath of the disastrous Comet crashes, it was hoped at the time that a 'prestige project' would restore Britain's position as a leading aeronautical power. Collaboration with France, once established, became a convenient excuse for continuing, against all the odds. The words 'Anglo-French relations' were frequently used to stifle rational criticism. Andrew Wilson, former aviation correspondent of *The Observer*, has described the strangely uncritical attitude of the media towards Concorde.[2] In the sixties, the BBC dropped appearances by Mary Goldring of *The Economist* after complaints by the aircraft industry. 'Panorama' producers admitted that it was nearly impossible to get approval for an objective programme. When, eventually, one was made, 'the night before transmission someone entered the cutting room and removed two minutes of material which contradicted the pro-Concorde testimony of the Aerospace Minister, Gerald Kaufman'.

Economically, environmentally and socially, Concorde has been a disaster. No planes have been sold. The world's airlines found Concorde totally uneconomic. (During the sixties, projected sales had been estimated variously at between 160 and 500 aircraft.[3]) Based on estimates since acknowledged to have been invented,[4] Concorde, according to the latest House of Commons Select Committee Report[5] has so far cost British taxpayers around £900m. The estimated cost for 1980–81 alone adds another £34.6m. (Earlier Select Committee Reports[5] had their figures censored out before publication, ostensibly for reasons of 'commercial security'.) The 1981 Committee also reveals that while the 1962 Anglo-French Agreement provided for equal sharing of costs, Britain has in fact paid considerably more than France. It was further predicted that in the period up to 1983 this disparity would increase, with the UK figure rising to 58.6 per cent.

Many countries found the plane environmentally unacceptable. Concorde is considerably noisier than the jumbo jet; it has had to be granted special exemption from the Heathrow airport noise limits.[6] The British government took a 'colonial' attitude to their projected routes. These were largely based on the assumption that Third World countries would put up with supersonic booms that were unacceptable in Europe and America. India, and several African countries, spoilt this scenario by refusing overflying rights.[7]

And in the long term the British aircraft industry has not benefited from the concentration of government funds into this one high-technology project. Potentially important and successful developments, such as the wide-bodied jet and the vertical take-off jet fighter, have been held up and starved of the necessary investment.

The Industry and Trade Committee, reporting in April 1981, 'we-e left with the uneasy feeling that the inherent difficulty of the multiplicity of contracts, the number of interested parties and the participation of two sovereign states had meant that the project had acquired a life of its own and was out of control'. They recommended that the government should take all possible steps to abandon the project – by 1985 at the latest. On 14 July 1981, it was announced that the Thatcher government (in which Mr John Biffen was Secretary of State for Trade) had rejected the Committee's recommendations. Once again, Concorde had been reprieved.

In the extract in this section from a detailed examination of the project, Annabelle May describes how short-term political objectives have constantly frustrated attempts to cancel Concorde. Since this account was written, in 1978–9, Barbara Castle has published her *Diaries*.[8] These throw more light on the cancellation manoeuvres within the 1974–9 Labour government. According to Castle, it was Benn and Foot who, because of TUC pressure, argued that the project should continue, after a committee of ministers had recommended cancellation.

REFERENCES

1. *The Guardian* 27 September 1977.
2. Andrew Wilson, 'The Concorde tragi-comedy', *New Statesman*, 7 May 1976.
3. Andrew Wilson, *The Concorde fiasco* (Penguin Books, 1973).
4. Annabelle May, 'Concorde – bird of harmony or political albatross: an examination in the context of British foreign policy', *International Organization*, Vol. 33, No. 4, Autumn 1979, p. 492.
5. *Second report from the Industry and Trade Committee, 1980–81, 'Concorde'* (HC 265, April 1981).
6. Jeremy Bugler, 'The Concorde Scandal', *New Statesman,* 30 January 1976.
7. Annabelle May (1979) pp. 507–8; see reference 4.
8. Barbara Castle, *The Castle diaries 1974–76* (Weidenfeld & Nicolson, 1980) p. 106.

Concorde: the politics of technology*

ANNABELLE MAY

Concorde was an entirely political aeroplane. The plan was to show the French that we were good Europeans.[1]

Sir George Edwards, the Chairman of BAC, gave his view of the problems in a lecture delivered in 1972. The essence of the difficulty, he concluded, was that high technology is long-term, whereas matters of politics are short-term. 'Long-term stability is essential if the nation is to obtain value for money from advanced technology. . . . These international programmes in Europe try men's very souls, but . . . collaboration puts an iron rod through what would otherwise be a jelly programme . . . they are very difficult to get started but they are almost impossible to stop.'[2]

The British government's objectives in entering into the Concorde Agreement appeared, with hindsight, to be obvious. It was frequently referred to in the press as 'the price of entry into Europe'. Roger Williams, in his study *European Technology*, discusses what may be referred to in simple terms as the 'aims and objectives' of collaboration. But the situation, as he acknowledges, is a complex one. 'Governments,' he writes, 'typically view collaboration more as a means than as an end, and the effective end to which it is then a means is not always one which can be openly admitted. Within the European Community the nominal end is long-term integration, variously construed. . . . But both within the Community and without, governments invariably have other, and more national, tactical and strategic ends in mind than the overt one, so that cooperation or collaboration comes to be regarded as, for instance, a means of keeping the Americans out, of strengthening the national capability, or of preventing an unfavourable collaborative development between other European nations. The integrative potential of technology must as a result be assessed against the fact that the technological field is, or can be, particularly suitable for the furtherance of other and more general foreign policy objectives.'[3]

*From 'Concorde – bird of harmony or political albatross: an examination in the context of British foreign policy', *International Organization*, Vol. 3, No. 4, 1979, pp. 500–5.

Williams's analysis stresses the interdependence between domestic and foreign policy. And Nau has claimed that in no other country, even France, 'was the national character of technological and industrial developments during this period more evident than in Britain'.[4] But was the economic folly of the Concorde project due to 'the impact of the attitudes, commitments, and politics of Britain's top political leaders', rather than, as it is more frequently argued, 'the subversion of government policy by powerful agencies and groups, either in the bureaucracy or in the private sector'?[5]

It was perhaps unfortunate that the decision to collaborate with France should have been taken at a time when, according to a former British Ambassador in Paris, there was to be every possible source of strain on Anglo-French relations over a period of years, for a variety of reasons.[6] Patrick Gordon Walker wrote in April 1964, before he became Labour's Foreign Secretary, that Labour's defence and foreign policy were based upon the realities of the world. 'There are only two superpowers,' he declared, 'that can afford the full panoply of nuclear weapons . . . there are in addition great powers, that can play an important part in the world. Because of her resources, her place in the world, her Commonwealth connections, Britain can hope to be the most significant of these great powers.' With regard to Europe, the 'fundamental political question at issue,' according to Gordon Walker, was whether Britain could enter the EEC without severing her independent relations with the United States and the Commonwealth. The whole aim of a Labour government, he concluded, would be 'to heighten and enhance Britain's influence in the world'.[7]

But the new Labour government, coming into office in October 1964, led by Harold Wilson, soon found that it had inherited a balance of payments deficit of £800m. Richard Crossman later recorded in his diary that Concorde had been almost the first subject put to the new Cabinet at its first meeting. 'We were told that something dramatic must be done and Concorde should be scrapped because of the economic crisis.'[8] In a White Paper (known subsequently as the 'Brown Paper', as it was prepared by George Brown) the incoming administration declared its intention to cut out 'expenditure on items of low economic priority, such as "prestige projects". The government,' the paper went on, 'have already communicated to the French government their wish to re-examine urgently the Concorde Project.'[9] The statement caused a furore. Accusations and denials of American pressure flew back and forth. According to George Brown, a consistent opponent of the project, an investigation was set up within the Ministry of Aviation. As a result, the ministry was, as one senior official described it, split down the middle. But, he went on to explain, as Concorde was their major project, the civil servants believed that Roy Jenkins, the new Minister of Aviation, would not destroy their morale by immediately opposing it.[10] According to George Brown, the investigation concluded that Concorde was a financial disaster; that there would be no markets for it; and that there was no hope of any spin-off. And the Cabinet, though divided into the 'brutal economizers' versus the 'more internationally minded' – these are Crossman's phrases – initially agreed, by a small majority, that it should be cancelled. It was only at this stage that they realized that they were dealing with an international treaty, rather than with a trade agreement.[11] At the time, the Foreign Secretary, Patrick Gordon Walker, as Lord Gore-Booth has pointed out, was largely absent, seeking election to Parliament. 'There could thus be no firm top level ministerial direction of day-to-day foreign policy.'[12]

There has been much discussion, both then and since, on the absence of a break clause in the agreement. But this discussion would appear to be, as one former Ministry of Aviation official put it, yet another 'red herring'.[13] Tony Benn now claims that there was a secret clause, a clause which provided that considerable compensation must be paid by either side in the case of unilateral withdrawal.[14] His statement is confirmed by, among others, Morien Morgan. Speaking of the situation in 1964, Morgan said: 'It wasn't cancelled largely because we'd – the Ministry – with full authority of the government, got a non-cancel clause in.'[15] Eventually, Patrick Gordon Walker, in conjunction with the Attorney-General and the Lord Chancellor, persuaded the Cabinet to consult the legal advisers to the Foreign Office. They all stressed the dire consequences of cancellation. Not only would we be liable to pay huge damages, but we would lose our credibility as Europeans. It was then agreed that Jenkins should go to Paris and present a choice of options to the French government. In the House of Commons a Bristol MP was quick to point out the irony of the situation: here was our best European being sent off to wriggle out of the Concorde project, after Britain had already broken both the EFTA and the GATT agreements.[16] Jenkins met with a cold reception. The French refused to compromise. With hindsight, some of the British ministers and officials involved now think that if the government had held firm, the French, under pressure from their own Finance Ministry, might have accepted the situation. But this can only be speculation. The final decision would have rested with de Gaulle.

Concorde was to reach Cabinet level again in 1967–8, following devaluation and a succession of defence cuts. But this time, due to pressures of the domestic situation, it was overtly acknowledged to be an issue of national prestige. Crossman recorded in January 1968, after a divided Cabinet meeting on public expenditure costs:

'After I left I gather that Concorde was discussed, and it was decided we could not abandon it. Economically, of course, the saving would be enormously worthwhile, but I don't think this Labour government can in the same package cut the F-111, withdraw from East of Suez, and scrap the Concorde without demoralizing people absolutely.'[17]

When the Tories came back in 1970, led by Edward Heath, the assumptions behind the project were once more called into question. Initially, Heath refused to commit himself. He declared in a television interview that it was the government's intention to look closely at the whole field of government expenditure. Concorde's fate, he assured his questioner, would be decided entirely on economic grounds. Tests were being carried out to determine the 'economic return' of the aircraft, and when they were completed the Chancellor would announce the results to Parliament.[18] The disputed treaty clause was no longer the overt reason for continuing with the project. On 11 December 1972 Tony Benn was to make this clear in the House of Commons. 'In September 1968,' he declared, 'we . . . outlined the procedures which in effect, would free each government to consider what action they should take either by agreeing to continue or by deciding not to do so. Since 1969 the government, in effect, have had freedom of action restored to them for this purpose.'[19] But in 1970 the EEC negotiations were once more at a sensitive stage. John Davies, the minister later obliged to recant the initial 'lame duck' policy, became responsible for Concorde, first as Minister of Technology and subsequently as Secretary of State for Trade and Industry. He acknowledged the complexity of the issue: 'If you are running a business, there is nothing more dangerous, and in the end more calamitous, than to go on with something simply because you have spent a lot of money on it.' If he had been chairman of a company, responsible to shareholders, Davies said, he would have cancelled Concorde. 'But I wasn't, and nor was the government. . . . They had answerability to a treaty arrangement with another country. They had very big problems with regard to the maintenance of employment, and very big problems with regard to the development of high-level technology, so-called.'[20] It has been suggested that Heath's eventual decision to turn the problem over to the Central Policy Review Staff (the CPRS, or 'think-tank') was an attempt to 'de-politicize' it, in the sense of removing it from the arena of discussion within the government itself at a time when the European situation was a difficult one. As Heath himself explained in a lengthy interview in 1972, part of his strategy in setting up the CPRS was that he wanted it to deal with transdepartmental problems, '. . . because in Cabinet so often I have seen a problem come up with which two departments are concerned. They didn't settle it themselves, so it came to Cabinet. They each put in papers. Then there was always an argument about which facts and figures were right, and you sent them away to get all that sorted out. Then there was an argument about the consequences and so on. So what I've tried with the CPRS is to get all this sorted out before it comes to the Cabinet.'[21]

Lord Rothschild, Director General of the CPRS, questioned in December 1972 on BBC television, described the study done on Concorde as 'comparatively short-term'. His remarks were challenged by Professor Robert Nield, a Cambridge economist who had worked in the Cabinet office during the 1950s and later became Economic Adviser to the Treasury in the 1960s, under the Wilson government. While acknowledging the need for a unit in Whitehall which did not have to concern itself with day-to-day problems but which could respond to crises and pressures, Nield declared that Concorde was precisely the kind of issue that somebody in Lord Rothschild's position should refuse to touch. This was, Nield went on, because 'it is the sort of old maid in the pack . . . any new chap that comes into the system will be handed it, and will produce a report just like the last one. And on it goes. . . . Everybody knows it's a white elephant, but they can't kill it'.[22] The CPRS Report on the implications of Concorde is a classified document. But, says the *Sunday Times* team, the first sentence reads: 'Concorde is a commercial disaster . . .' Yet, apparently, it went on to claim that the international consequences of cancellation would be too great.[23]

According to Andrew Wilson,[24] there was yet another attempt at cancellation when the Labour government was re-elected in 1974. A strong lobby of 'economizers', led by Roy Jenkins and Denis Healey, was convinced that Britain should finally cut its losses. Tony Benn's decision, in March 1974, to disclose the development costs to Parliament for the first time, gave their case additional support. But once again it was the Foreign Secretary, James Callaghan, who was worried about the repercussions in Europe. The Prime Minister, Harold Wilson, flew to Paris for a summit meeting with the new President of France, Valéry Giscard d'Estaing. After much hard bargaining, agreement was reached. The Concorde production line was to be limited to the construction of sixteen planes. This final compromise recognized the fact that Concorde could never be an economic proposition.

REFERENCES

1. Sir Richard Way, Permanent Secretary, Minister of Aviation, 1963–6, in an interview.

2. Quoted in Roger Williams, *European technology: the politics of collaboration* (Croom Helm, 1973) p. 130.

3. Roger Williams (1973) pp. 162–3; see Reference 2.

4. H. R. Nau, 'Collective responses to R and D problems in western Europe: 1955–8, 1968–73', *International Organization,* Vol. 29, No. 3, Summer 1975, p. 635.

5. Stephen Blank, 'Britain: the politics of foreign economic policy, the domestic economy, and the problem of pluralistic stagnation', *International Organization,* Vol. 31, No. 4, Autumn 1977, p. 714.

6. Interview with author.

7. Patrick Gordon Walker, 'The Labour Party's defence and foreign policy', *Foreign Affairs,* Vol. 42, No. 3, April 1964, pp. 393–8.

8. Richard Crossman, *Diaries of a Cabinet minister* (Hamish Hamilton & Jonathan Cape, 1975) Vol. 1, p. 57.

9. *The economic situation* (HMSO, 26 October 1964).

10. Interview with author.

11. Interview with author.

12. Sir Paul Gore-Booth, *With great truth and respect* (Constable, 1974) p. 327.

13. Interview with author.

14. Interview with author.

15. OU Archive (see p. 178). See also Harold Wilson, *The Labour government 1964–70: a personal record* (Penguin Books, 1974) p. 527.

16. 701 HC Debs 423–4.

17. Richard Crossman (1976) Vol. 2, p. 638; see Reference 8.

18. 'This Week', Thames Television (24 September, 1970).

19. 848 HC Debs 115–6.

20. OU Archive (see p. 178).

21. Interview with Edward Heath by Charles Wintour and Robert Carvel, 'My style of government', *Evening Standard,* 1 June 1972.

22. 'Friday Talk-In', BBC Television (8 December 1972).

23. J. Barry, P. Gillman, R. Eglin, 'The Concord Conspiracy,' *The Sunday Times,* 8 February 1976.

24. Interview with author.

CHAPTER THREE

Northern Ireland and the media

Introduction

In recent years, the social and political conflict in Northern Ireland has illustrated the power of the state to circumscribe the broadcast media's coverage of events, issues and points of view there. This has been handled not through overt censorship, but rather through *mediated* intervention, in which spokesmen in the sphere of politics have defined the permissable limits, and these conceptual orientations have been picked up and reproduced within the media.[1]

Conflicting definitions of the principles of independence and impartiality have resulted in confrontation between the state, the broadcasting institutions and the programme makers. The media must function as a fourth estate in the context of Northern Ireland, as distinct from the executive, the legislature and the judiciary, a former BBC Controller of Northern Ireland has declared.[2] This does not entail, however, the adoption of special criteria. Rather, he continues, it depends on deploying the best professional skills and 'scrupulously fair dealing'.

Richard Francis's view that Northern Ireland is 'an everyday problem'[3] would appear to accept the dominant government definition of the situation. Northern Ireland, we are told, is not in a state of emergency or of war. This is not a view shared by many reporters of the current scene. Yet in face of criticism that the IRA are winning the propaganda war, Francis was reassuring.

> The assumption appears to be widespread that the appearance of an apologist for a terrorist organization is necessarily going to win public sympathy. Every piece of research that the BBC has done on these occasions, and there have only been five in the last ten years, has shown that as a result of the broadcast, sample audiences have come out of it being much more strongly antagonistic towards the terrorists and much more sympathetic towards the security forces.[4]

The problem of achieving independence and impartiality in Northern Ireland coverage takes an even more specific form as Philip Elliott, a sociologist, outlines in the first extract in this section. Secrecy, he argues, has been brought fully into play; journalists are dependent on official sources and if they are considered hostile they may be cut off from the regular flow of information altogether. In the second extract Peter Taylor, a television journalist and former reporter on the 'This Week' programme, describes how the Independent Broadcasting Authority responded to government pressure by censoring or calling for fundamental changes in 'This Week' programmes on Northern Ireland.[5]

Annan commended the BBC for dropping its mistaken policy towards Northern Ireland in the 1960s of trying to build a consensus.[6] The deliberate decision to ignore controversial issues, such as the civil rights marches, was fundamental to the management of news.[7] But the abandonment of this policy has not been matched by the abandonment of the official consensus which, Peter Taylor argues, makes informed discussion of the problem impossible. It is only this year, with the portrayal of Irish history on our television screens for the first time (in BBC2's 'Ireland: A Television history' and Thames Television's 'The Troubles'), that the view that Northern Ireland's problems are primarily religious is challenged.

Northern Ireland, more than anything else, has exposed the weaknesses in the structure of British broadcasting. It has revealed the power of government to exert influence and pressure on the transmission and content of programmes. And government has ultimately had an ally in the broadcasting authorities themselves whose definition of impartiality has usually accorded with the state's definition of the situation. In 1971, Lord Hill, Chairman of the BBC, wrote to the Home Secretary:

> As between the government and the opposition, as between two communities in Northern Ireland, the BBC has a duty to be impartial no less than in the rest of the United Kingdom. But, as between the British army and the gunmen, the BBC is not and cannot be impartial.[8]

Northern Ireland postscript

The importance of many measures taken in Northern Ireland lies in their subsequent application to the mainland. Robert Fisk, writing in *The Times*,[9] described the aftermath of the Ulster Worker's Council (UWC) strike in 1974. During this strike, Protestant workers cut off all the public services, leaving the authorities virtually powerless. Even army technicians did not have the skill to operate the sophisticated Belfast power station. As a direct consequence of this incident, a whole network of standby generators was secretly installed in Northern Ireland in 1975, plus standby generators at post office telephone exchanges. Civil servants at Stormont Castle discussed the powers which might be used to restrict news broadcasts by the local BBC in the case of a 'loyalist' *coup d'état.*

Fears that the same thing could happen in Britain, if extreme circumstances brought about 'militant industrial unrest', have since led to telephone exchanges on the mainland being similarly equipped. There is also a document in existence in Whitehall, claims Fisk, which suggests 'the kind of measures that might be taken in a national emergency to curb the ability of the BBC radio and television to broadcast statements by the leaders of a politically inspired strike'.[10]

REFERENCES

1. Philip Schlesinger, *Putting 'reality' together: BBC News* (Constable, 1978) p. 206.
2. Richard Francis, 'The BBC in Northern Ireland', *The Listener,* 3 March 1977.
3. Extract from evidence in *Third report from the Defence Committee 1979–80, the D Notice system* (HC 773, 1980), p. 48.
4. Richard Francis, writing in *The Listener,* 9 July 1981, p. 46.
5. For a detailed chronology of TV programmes dealing with Northern Ireland that have been banned, censored or delayed see Paul Madden, 'Banned, censored and delayed' in *The British Media and Ireland* (Information on Ireland 1980).
6. See *Report of the Committee on the future of broadcasting* (The Annan Report) Cmnd 6753, HMSO, 1977) pp. 269–71.
7. For a more detailed account, see Thames Television, *The Troubles* (Thames & MacDonald Futura, 1981).
8. Philip Schlesinger (1978), p. 212; see Reference 1.
9. *The Times,* 6 November 1975.
10. See also Richard Crossman, *Diaries of a Cabinet minister* (Hamish Hamilton & Jonathan Cape, 1977) Vol. 3, pp. 636–7, for a revealing account of the Labour Cabinet's discussion about jamming radio stations in Ulster.

The British approach to information management*

PHILIP ELLIOTT

There is more to information management than making information available. If the carrots of hospitality and handouts do not
work, there is no shortage of possible sticks. In Northern Ireland the
army has not been above strong arm tactics, freezing out or haras-
sing journalists whom it considered hostile to its cause. _The Guar-
dian_ correspondents, Simon Winchester and Simon Hoggart, both
record army attempts to bring them into line by cutting them off
from the regular flow of information.[1] In the case of _The Times_
correspondent, Robert Fisk, the process went further with threats
of legal action.[2] In other recent cases against Mark Hosenball and
Duncan Campbell the threats have been translated into action,
though it is impossible to be absolutely certain that it was their
activities related to Northern Ireland which prompted the action.
The third and most effective technique of information management, secrecy, has been brought fully into play.

Not all the blame for the secrecy which pervades British society
can be laid at the door of those who refuse to make information
available. Newspapers themselves hide much away by sticking to a
black-and-white view of the world in which heroes and heroines
contest with villains. Some grey does creep into the up-market
Sundays. They have more time for reflection and credit their
readers with the ability to cope with some of the complexities of life.
Soon after the death of Magella O'Hare, for example, readers of the
Sunday Times were told that there was something not quite right
about the army version that she died in the line of fire between a
soldier and a gunman. Months later there was another reference to
the incident as a case of black propaganda such as the army no
longer engaged in. Whether this was black propaganda in the
relatively familiar sense of putting out a misleading account or in the
much more sinister sense of an attempt to manufacture an atrocity
to follow the death of the Maguire children, the incident which led
to the foundation of the peace movement, has yet to be revealed.
Suffice it to say that it is unlikely that any but avid news consumers,

*From 'All the world's a stage' in James Curran (ed.), _The British press: a
manifesto_ (Macmillan, 1978) pp. 153–5.

compulsive readers of the small print or people with access to the
Irish papers know that a soldier has since been charged with Magella
O'Hare's murder.

It is safe to assume that this is known to many British journalists,
whether from published or unpublished sources. It provides an
example of another feature of journalism which, if not peculiar to
the British case, is found there in exaggerated form. For all the
public protestations about being the reader's representative, the
eyes and ears of the British public, journalists appear to get much
more satisfaction from being 'in the know' themselves, from hob-
nobbing with the great and famous, than from passing their information on to those on whose behalf they are supposed to collect
it. To criticize this tendency is not simply to denigrate another man's
pleasures. There is clear evidence, as for example in the operation
of the Lobby system, that 'in-group journalism' actively obstructs
the right to know. Indeed, one wonders whether British journalists
would be prepared to recognize that the public, as opposed to
themselves as a specially privileged group, enjoy such a right. The
phrase is one which speaks not only to the greater openness of
American government, but also the greater democracy of American
society. In the United States particular groups set less store by their
privileged access to information as a sign of their position in the
national pecking order. If, as in Britain, information has such a
value, then it is natural that there should be a tendency to husband
and hoard it, rather than scatter it abroad. The extension of the
analogy is that seeds kept in barns grow few crops. In-group
journalism is impotent journalism, so far as the democratic process
is concerned.

Journalists' jealousy of their status is not the only reason why the
public's right to know in Britain amounts to little more than a public
right to be patronised. There are plenty of other groups jealously
keeping guard over the little bits of information they have at their
disposal. Some, such as the professions and the local authorities,
have the backing of occupational sanctions; others such as the
courts, the government and the civil service have been able to make
use of the full resources of the law. Members of Parliament are in
the peculiar position of having their own quasi-legal procedure to
fall back on in the form of contempt of the House. Such sanctions
are symbolic of the British approach to information management
which can be summed up in two all-pervasive principles: when in
doubt say nothing; and an appeal to the press (or the public) is a
confession of weakness. Against this background it is hardly surprising that British journalists are inclined to play their cards very close
to their chests. Such sources as there are have to be protected even
at the cost of allowing them to contradict, in public, statements

which were apparently made in private – the situation which arose in the recent Lobby débâcle over Sir Peter Ramsbottom and Peter Jay. The practice becomes a good deal more questionable, however, when the source produces stories, not statements. The margarine industry's recent creation, 'the killer cow', may be acceptable as just another addition to the stock of public entertainments. Even so, it took time and close attention to realize that behind the headline was another campaign to wean the housewife off butter and on to margarine. Army stories designed to make a political point and show the need for a tougher security policy in Ulster, such as appeared towards the end of Merlyn Rees' time as Secretary of State, need much closer evaluation. In such cases the story is not the leaks but the leaking. As things stand, the British press is all too likely to be grateful it has a story to print. Because the supply is so limited, there is little hope that stories will be scrutinized rather than used; but because it is limited, information which does come out is particularly likely to need scrutinizing to reveal the source's motives and interests.

An information policy founded on secrecy implies there is something to hide. In all probability there is, but the stock in trade of the national press is simply to put on a fit of pique when confronted by some small cog in the system, a headmaster or a hospital administrator who dares say nothing but knows little anyway. It is a pity more journalists do not follow Claud Cockburn's advice: 'never believe anything until it has been officially denied'.[3] As it is, much of the reporter's job is simply to act as a recorder of what the official sources are willing to tell him. Even the McGregor Commission was struck by the 'heavy reliance on official sources and spokesmen' (10.71) it found in the press.[4] Several British correspondents in Ulster have recorded their surprise at finding they have been fooled by the official sources in the province. None have put it more engagingly than Andrew Stephen, who wrote in *The Observer* 'the sad experience for most British journalists once they start working in Northern Ireland is that the word of the authorities cannot automatically be relied upon'.[5]

REFERENCES

1. S. Winchester, *In Holy Terror*, (Faber & Faber 1974); S. Hoggart, 'The Army P.R. Men of Northern Ireland', *New Society*, 11 October 1973, pp. 79–80.
2. See Fisk's story in *The Times*, 8 February 1975.
3. Claud Cockburn, *I Claud*, (Penguin 1967).
4. *The Royal Commission on the Press* (the McGregor Commission), Final Report, Cmnd. 6810, HMSO 1977.
5. Andrew Stephen, (1976), 'A Reporter's Life in Belfast', *Observer*, 29 February 1976.

Reporting Northern Ireland*

PETER TAYLOR

Nowhere, in the British context, has the relationship between state, broadcasting institutions and programme makers been more sensitive and uneasy than in matters concerning Northern Ireland. Conflict arises whenever broadcast journalism challenges the prevalent ideology embodied in government policy and reflected in the broadcasting institutions it has established. In principle, the broadcasting authorities should stand between the media and the state as benevolent umpires, charged with the task of defending each against the excesses of the other, guardians of the public interest, upholders of a broadcasting service alleged to be the finest in the world. In practice, where Northern Ireland is concerned, they have become committed to a perspective of the conflict which identifies the public interest increasingly with the government interest. To question the government's ideology is to court trouble. The deeper the crisis and the more controversial the methods used to meet it, the greater the strain on the institutions of broadcasting forced to choose between the journalist's insistence on the public's right to know everything and the government's preference for it not to know too much.

The Irish question hangs over British politics like an angry and stubborn cloud that refuses to go away, despite the insistence of successive generations of British politicians that the cloud is just passing. The cloud has been there for four hundred years. The words of British politicians from Robert Earl of Essex, servant of Elizabeth the First, to Roy Mason, servant of Elizabeth the Second, echo down the centuries voicing frustration with and issuing warnings to the Irish that have changed little over four centuries. The shadow of the current ten-year cloud under which we stand is no longer and darker than its predecessors. Northern Ireland is different, not because there is no consensus but because the nature of the consensus that exists makes any informed discussion of the problem difficult, if not increasingly impossible.

The official consensus runs something like this: Northern Ireland is a state in conflict because Catholics and Protestants refuse to live

*From *Index,* Vol. 7, No. 6, November/December 1978, pp. 3–10.

together despite the efforts of successive British governments to encourage them to do so: we (the British), at considerable cost to the Exchequer and our soldiers, have done all that is humanly possible to find a political solution within the existing structures of the Northern Irish state: now the two communities must come up with a political solution they are prepared to work and accept themselves: the terrorists, in particular the Provisional IRA, are gangsters and thugs: they are the cause, not the symptom of the problem.

This is, of course, a British mainland perspective. Others see it differently. When Jack Lynch, the Irish Prime Minister, suggested that Britain should withdraw from the North and encourage the reunification of the country, Westminster – and much of Fleet Street – was outraged at his impertinence in suggesting such a solution to a 'British domestic problem'.

To challenge these cosy assumptions about the conflict – deliberately fostered by those in high places either because they are convenient or because they believe them – is to run the risk of being branded at best a terrorist dupe, at worst a terrorist sympathiser. Journalists and politicians rash enough to dissent have felt the lash of tongues from both sides of the House of Commons and been called 'unreliable'. Yet some of us working there as journalists have come to believe that the conflict is political and not religious: that its origins lie in the conquest of Ireland by England and the subsequent establishment of a Protestant colony in Ulster to keep the province secure for the Crown; that the immediate conflict stems from the partition of the country fifty years ago, an artificial division designed to be only temporary, engineered by the British to guarantee Protestant supremacy in the remaining six counties of Ulster; that the Provisional IRA may lay claim to the mantle of the 'terrorists' who drove the British out of the twenty-six counties in 1919–20 in a campaign every bit as bloody and unpleasant as the IRA's current offensive to drive the British from the remaining six counties; and lastly (and currently most sensitive of all) that not all the RUC's policemen are wonderful.

The second battle of Culloden

Why has the issue come to a head over the past twelve months? The last great battle was fought by the BBC in late 1971 over 'A Question of Ulster', which the Corporation succeeded in transmitting despite enormous pressure from the Unionist government at Stormont and the Tory government at Westminster. The marathon programme was notable more for the fact of its transmission than its content. It was hailed as a victory for the Corporation's independence, but as Philip Schlesinger[1] has pointed out, it was a success story amidst general defeat, for had the BBC not resisted the political pressures, it would have undermined its own legitimacy and public confidence in the institution. In the years that followed, Northern Ireland was gradually relegated to the second halves of the news bulletins and the inside columns of the newspapers. Ulster ceased to be a story. When the media did return to the subject, coverage continued to be guided by the numbing principles outlined by Philip Elliott in his UNESCO report,[2] that the story should be simple, involving 'both lack of explanation and historical perspective'; of human interest, involving 'a concentration on the particular detail of incidents and the personal characteristics of those involved which results in a continual procession of unique, inexplicable events'; and lastly, a reflection of the official version of events to consolidate the 'production of a common image'.

But there were occasional squalls in spite of the media's generally low profile. In 1976 the IBA banned a 'This Week' investigation into IRA fund raising in America before a foot of film had been shot, not because the subject matter was particularly contentious but because the 'timing' was felt to be wrong. The film was transmitted a week later, but it was a warning shot.

Meanwhile, Merlyn Rees, Secretary of State for Northern Ireland until the summer of 1976, negotiated the ending of internment and a cease-fire, his patience and persistence winning the respect of the public – even some Provos with whom he was brave enough to negotiate – and the goodwill of journalists. We felt that he was trying. His successor, however, Roy Mason, was a man hewn from rougher rock. His acquaintance with Ireland had begun as Minister of Defence (a position unlikely to encourage perspectives when the army was faced with its closest and most pressing security problem since the war). For him the problem was one of security and the present, not politics and the past: results were what he wanted, not history lessons or the niceties of media philosophy as expressed by the BBC's then Controller of Northern Ireland Dick Francis:

> The experience in Northern Ireland where communities and governments are in conflict, but not in a state of emergency or a state of war, suggests a greater need than ever for the media to function as the fourth estate, distinct from the executive, the legislature and the judiciary. But if the functions are to remain separate, it must be left to the media themselves to take the decisions, within the limits of responsibility, as to what to publish, when and how.[3]

Under Mason, journalists were more than ever courted as allies in the war, not recorders of it. After only a few months in office, the new Secretary of State is reported to have made his position brutally clear to Sir Michael Swann, Chairman of the BBC, at a private dinner at Belfast's Culloden Hotel, where he accused the BBC of showing disloyalty, supporting the rebels and purveying enemy propaganda. He is also said to have remarked that if the Northern Ireland Office had been in control of BBC policy, the IRA would have been defeated. Sir Michael later referred to this encounter as 'the second battle of Culloden'. Mr Mason shares the textbook view expressed by the Army's senior counter-insurgency expert, Brigadier Frank Kitson:

> The countering of the enemy's propaganda and putting across of the government's point of view, can be achieved either by direct action, as for example the provision of leaflets, or the setting up of an official wireless or television network, or *by trying to inform and influence the existing news media* (my emphasis).[4]

But Kitson adds a warning: 'The real difficulty lies in the political price which a democratic country pays in order to influence the ways in which its people think.'

The BBC was first in the firing line. Despite pressure from the RUC and the government, in March 1977 the BBC's 'Tonight' programme transmitted Keith Kyle's interview with Bernard O'Connor, an Enniskillen schoolmaster who alleged ill-treatment by the RUC's plainclothes interrogators at Castlereagh detention centre. If Northern Ireland is the most sensitive issue in British broadcasting, interrogation techniques are its most sensitive spot. Although under severe attack from Roy Mason and his unnatural but strongest ally in the House of Commons, the Conservative spokesman on Northern Ireland, Airey Neave, who accused the BBC of assisting terrorist recruitment and undermining the police, the BBC stood firm. In a letter to *The Times*, the Chairman, Sir Michael Swann (no doubt with Culloden in mind) wrote:

> The BBC has a responsibility to make available to the whole UK audience as truthful a picture as it can of the state of affairs in Northern Ireland.[5]

Whilst the BBC was having its showdown with Roy Mason, at the beginning of 1977, ITV's 'This Week' was having the odd desultory clash with the IBA and the Northern Ireland Office: the IBA did not like a Provisional Sinn Fein spokesman calling for 'one last push' to get the British out, delivered at the end of a film about the fifth anniversary of Bloody Sunday. The sound was subsequently taken

down and the 'offensive' sentiments lost in crowd noises and
commentary.

Intolerable restrictions
Because the structures of ITV are vaguer and less rigid than the
BBC's hierarchical pyramid, where decisions are constantly referred
upwards, its programme makers have traditionally been more
protected against political interference from above. Until recent
years and the growing political imperatives that the Northern Irish
conflict has placed upon it, the IBA was cautious in wielding its
power over news and current affairs. But the Authority, now more
powerful and confident with every decision it takes, increasingly
tends to arrogate to itself the functions of judge, jury and execution-
er. If the programme companies, powerful and influential bodies in
their own right, disagree with the Authority's decision, there is no
redress. Television journalism is increasingly hampered by restrictions that Fleet Street does not have and would never tolerate. The
Sunday Times may decide to publish and be damned – Thames
Television cannot. It is the IBA that takes that decision for it. The
Authority has always had an impressive panoply of weapons to hand
in the form of wide-ranging statutes which give it the power to stop
programmes that offend 'good taste and decency', are likely to
'incite to crime and disorder' or are 'offensive to public feeling'. But
most awesome of all is Section 4 I (f) of the 1973 Broadcasting Act,
which makes it incumbent on the Authority to see that 'due
impartiality is preserved in matters of political controversy or
matters relating to current public policy' (my emphasis).

As always, the interpretation and use of these statutes is a
personal matter that depends on the predilections of the person at
the top. In recent years the tone and style of the Authority has been
set by its Chairman, Lady Plowden, who is believed not to favour or
encourage investigative television reporting. Add to this a general
public antipathy towards Northern Ireland and it is not surprising
that the Authority tends to err on the side of caution when faced
with controversy. Nor is the Authority, despite its protestations,
immune from political pressure. In the end, when the interests of
state and the interests of journalism conflict, the odds are that the
former will triumph, particularly when the latter may be challenging
the ideology which the Authority itself, by its structure, is bound to
reflect. There is no statute in the Broadcasting Act that says that the
interests of the state must be paramount. There is no need for one.
Nor are the pressures from government on the Authority – or from
the Authority on its contracting companies – overt: there are no
official memoranda saying 'Thou shalt not . . .', rather letters
'regretting that . . .' and suggesting 'wouldn't it be better if . . .'.

When it comes to Northern Ireland the pressure is constant. It consists of not just the standard letters of protest from government and opposition to the IBA and the offending contracting company, but personal meetings between the Chairman of the Authority and the Secretary of State and Chief Constable of the RUC. These discussions are confidential, but their results gradually filter down through the broadcasting structures suggesting that more 'responsible' coverage would be welcome (there is little talk of censorship. Government and broadcasting authorities are usually far too adept and experienced to fall into that trap); that 'This Week' might 'lay off' Northern Ireland for a while, or that 'another reporter' might cover it. And the pressures on the contracting companies are also formidable: in a couple of years' time the IBA has the power to renew or withdraw their lucrative licences; the second channel, much desired and lobbied for by ITV, is a gift for government to grant or withhold. ITV is in the end beholden to both institutions; it takes courage to challenge them. Small wonder then that controversial coverage of Northern Ireland is tolerated rather than encouraged.

Propaganda exercise
The problems that 'This Week' has faced in the past year illustrate the difficulties confronting journalists attempting to report Northern Ireland as fully and freely as they would a conflict less close to home. The trouble started with 'In Friendship and Forgiveness' (August 1977), an alternative diary of the Queen's visit to Northern Ireland, her last engagement in Jubilee year. The world's press flocked to Belfast as never before even at the height of the 'war' in 1972, admittedly more as prospective vultures at the feast, awaiting the Provisionals' much-vaunted promise to 'make it a visit to remember', than as recorders of Her Majesty's progress through carefully chosen parts of her troublesome province. ITV's cameras covered the events live. ITN's senior newscaster declared from the Belfast rooftops that he could almost feel 'the peace in the air'. For Roy Mason the royal visit represented a proconsular triumph which the world was there to record. The Provisionals' threats proved empty: they were humiliated, if not defeated. Television brilliantly orchestrated the royal progress as it had throughout Jubilee year, but nowhere had its orchestration carried such political overtones which, however lost they might have been on its audience, were certainly not overlooked by the government officials who encouraged it. As a propaganda exercise its success was complete: it presented a picture of a province almost pacified, with grateful and loyal subjects from both sections of the community taking the Queen and her message to their hearts.

The reality was different. More than anything, the royal visit highlighted the political divisions of the province: to Protestants it represented a victory for their tradition which they felt had been under attack for so long, whilst for many Catholics Her Majesty came as the head of a state they refused to recognize. Such was the context in which 'This Week' placed its report, filming events that went largely unnoticed and unreported by the army of visiting pressman – the funerals of a young IRA volunteer shot dead by the army whilst allegedly throwing a petrol bomb and a young soldier shot dead by the Provisionals in retaliation; a Provisional IRA road block in Ballymurphy; a Republican rally in the Falls Road; the Apprentice Boys parade in Derry and an earlier sectarian sing-song; Loyalist street celebrations in the Shankhill; and a four-hour riot – which *was* widely reported. This potent mixture was intercut with scenes of the royal progress and interviews with proponents of the two conflicting traditions, John Hume and John Taylor, who placed the visit in its current and historical perspective.

The programme, scheduled for transmission a week after the visit, was banned by the IBA. (All 'This Week' programmes on Ireland have to be submitted for the Authority's approval prior to transmission, which is rarely the case with other sensitive issues that 'This Week' covers.) The IBA took exception to a section at the beginning of the film in which Andreas O'Callaghan, a Sinn Feinner from Dublin, stirred the crowd at the Falls Road rally with these words:

> While there is a British army of occupation on our streets, any Irishman who has it within his means, meaning any Irishman who can get his hands on a gun or weapon, he has the duty not to keep that gun in cold storage or even less to use that gun against the people who are fighting the British Army, let them get out and fight the British Army themselves . . . As long as there's one British soldier in any part of Ireland, there will always be people who will struggle, there will always be people who will resist.

These words could have been reported by any newspaper journalist but not, apparently, on television. Seeking refuge in Statute 4 (1) of the 1973 Broadcasting Act, the IBA deemed it likely that these words might constitute 'an incitement to crime' or 'lead to disorder'. Thames were advised to seek legal advice. Thames' counsel concluded:

> In the context of the programme and having regard to the careful way in which it is presented, I think it is unlikely that the excerpt could have any such effect. Having expressed my own opinion, I

do recognize that in a matter of judgement of this sort, it might be legitimately felt that the film with O'Callaghan's voice reproduced could have such an effect.

Significantly he added:

All things are *possible*, but the section requires the Authority to consider what is *likely*.

He also pointed out that Section 4 (1)b of the Act requires a news feature to be 'presented with due accuracy and impartiality'.

Accordingly, to play safe and to get the programme on the air, we decided to drop O'Callaghan's words and replace them with my neutered paraphrase in reported speech:

Andreas O'Callaghan went on to urge Irishmen to carry on the fight against British soldiers in Northern Ireland using whatever weapons they could lay their hands on. It was an open call to arms.

Counsel felt that we were now in the clear. The IBA decided that we were not. Two minutes before transmission a phone call came from the Authority ordering Thames not to show the programme. A previous film I had made on 'Drinking and Driving' was put out in its place.

But the O'Callaghan speech was not the only section of the programme that worried the IBA. They were anxious about the Provisional IRA road block in Ballymurphy, which they suspected we had set up. We had not. My commentary made the position clear:

Whilst the Queen was being welcomed at Hillsborough, the Provisional IRA mounted a road block in the Ballymurphy estate a few miles away. We were told earlier in the day that a snub to the Queen was planned. This was it – more propaganda than military exercise. Perhaps for our benefit, perhaps as a morale booster for their supporters. The checkpoint lasted five minutes. But it happened – within half a mile of any army post round the corner, out of sight.

Nevertheless the Authority remained worried that we might be in breach of the Northern Ireland Emergency Provisions (Amendment) Act 1975 by 'aiding and abetting the offence of wearing a mask or hood in a public place'. Thames' counsel implied that this was nonsense.

Finally, the IBA expressed concern over my final lines of commentary delivered over film of the soldier's funeral in his Yorkshire mining village:

> The events of that week drew to a close not on the streets of Belfast, but in the lanes of a Yorkshire mining village. There the army buried Private Lewis Harrison, the two-hundred-and-seventieth British soldier to die in Northern Ireland. For his family, the funeral was a bitter end to the Queen's Jubilee visit. It marked for them as only such grief can, the historical truth that lies behind the bewildering complexities of Ulster. Private Harrison died not because the Queen visited Ulster, but because the power she represents remains in that part of Ireland.

It was the last sentence that caused the agony. The IBA argued that it presented an 'incomplete' picture of the problem, there being no mention of religion, of Catholics and Protestants and the army keeping them from each other. I argued that to amend the sentence as the Authority requested was a distortion of the essence of my report. After much discussion, my words were allowed to stand.

Dictating 'the issues'

'In Friendship and Forgiveness' was finally transmitted two weeks after the visit, trickling out over the ITV network in slots that ranged from Friday teatime and Sunday lunchtime to nearly midnight on Ulster Television. By then the visit was history, the impact and topicality of the film lost. Significantly, the film finally shown was not materially different from the version banned two minutes before transmission. Was there collusion with government to prevent a mass audience seeing a different version of 'reality' presented at peak time, whilst memories of the event were still fresh? What damage would this perspective have done to the cosmetic presentation so carefully served up by the media? One can only guess. One Northern Ireland Office official I spoke to afterwards said he thought the film 'stank'.

We had not planned 'In Friendship and Forgiveness' in advance. We had gone to Belfast to prepare a programme that examined conditions in the prisons and the issues of Special Category Status. When we saw the unreported impact of the royal visit, we changed tack. We then returned to complete the prisons film we had started, 'Life Behind the Wire'. The programme, which included film secretly shot by the UDA inside the compounds of the Maze prison, showing prisoners parading openly in paramilitary uniform unchallenged by prison officers, highlighted the conflict between the government's insistence that the prisoners were common criminals lacking political motivation, and the inmates' view of themselves as political prisoners. Again, the programme was designed to examine the political nature of the conflict in Northern Ireland. The politicians did not like it. During the research period, the Northern Ireland Office suggested I make a profile of Roy Mason's first year in office. The prisons, they repeated, were not an issue. They prefer to dictate the 'issues' themselves. Airey Neave called for 'the most immediate action to stop the flow of Irish terrorist propaganda through the British news media'. He protested to the IBA about the 'myth that the terrorists in Northern Ireland are heroic and honourable soldiers'. Interestingly, Unionist politicians attacked not 'This Week', but the government for tolerating such a situation in a British gaol. For their own political reasons, they welcomed our taking the lid off Long Kesh, which Harry West, their leader, referred to as a 'terrorist Sandhurst'. The government preferred the lid to be kept on. No one questioned the accuracy of the picture we presented.

We submitted the film to the IBA. They had no objections, although one of their officials remarked that the political perspective of the film disturbed him. The real outcry came over two weeks after the programme had been transmitted, when the Provisional IRA shot dead Desmond Irvine, the Secretary of the Northern Ireland Prison Officers' Association, whose remarkable interview was the backbone of the film. Prison Officer Irvine agreed to the interview after long discussions with his colleagues, and decided to do it openly, fully aware of the risks he was taking. The Northern Ireland Office did not wish him to be interviewed. Political critics of the programme, and of 'This Week's' previous coverage did not hesitate to lay responsibility for his death at our door, despite the public declaration by the Association that they did not blame the programme for PO Irvine's death. Nor was Desmond Irvine displeased with the film or his own contribution to it. A few days before his death, he wrote to me saying:

I found the programme to be an accurate description of life at the Maze. Congratulations have poured in from many sources, including many messages from Great Britain. Your superb handling of a very delicate topic and the manner in which it was presented resulted in praise from staff and prisoners. Thank you for all your help.

His death, however unconnected it may have been with the programme, placed another weapon in the hands of 'This Week' critics and those who wished to curb or prevent coverage of sensitive corners of Northern Ireland policy and practice. Moral pressure

could now be applied even more forcefully not only to the programme makers, but to those to whom they were answerable.
'Putting lives at risk' and 'responsible reporting' took on a new
dimension.

These arguments were widely used to try and stop 'This Week'
from making and transmitting its next film, 'Inhuman and Degrading Treatment', an investigation into allegations of ill-treatment by
the RUC at Castlereagh interrogation centre. It proved to be the
most delicate issue that 'This Week' has tackled in Northern
Ireland, highly sensitive because it questioned the interrogation
techniques that were the cornerstone of the government's security
policy. The undoubted successes that Roy Mason claimed in putting
the 'terrorists behind bars' were in 80 per cent of cases the direct
result of statements elicited – in theory voluntarily – in police
custody, on which a suspect could be convicted in the absence of
further evidence. For several months in 1977 there had been
growing disquiet, initially amongst Catholics, eventually amongst
Protestants too, concerning the manner in which these statements
were being obtained. The allegations of ill-treatment were persistently dismissed by government and RUC as terrorist propaganda,
the last cries of defeated and discredited organizations. During our
numerous visits to Belfast the allegations grew stronger and more
widespread. We had off-the-record discussions with senior figures
in the legal field, who expressed growing anxiety at the way in which
they believed some confessions were being obtained. They felt that
our investigating the issue, within the context of the crisis and the
special legal framework designed to cope with it, would be neither
irresponsible nor untimely.

'Lay off Northern Ireland'
We examined ten cases of alleged ill-treatment in the programme.
Each case had strong corroborative medical evidence. We asked the
RUC for a background briefing and assistance, acutely aware of the
dangers of being taken for a ride by the paramilitary organizations
whose causes were undoubtedly helped by the propaganda generated by the issue. After lengthy discussions, the RUC refused all
cooperation. There were to be no facilities nor, more significantly,
any interview with the Chief Constable. The Northern Ireland
Office, washing their hands of the problem by saying it was 'one for
the RUC', were quick to remind me of the death of Desmond
Irvine.

We pressed ahead. Six days before transmission, we sent a
detailed telex to the RUC – without whom the IBA thought the
programme incomplete – listing the cases and medical evidence and
outlining a script of the programme. Three days later, word came

back that there was still to be no interview. No doubt the various hot lines buzzed. The day before transmission, the Chief Constable offered not an interview but an RUC editorial statement to camera. This compromise was unwelcome to the programme makers, but in the end we were forced to accept it. No statement – no programme. The institutions had triumphed again. A few hours before the programme was due to go out, the chief constable put his men on 'red alert', publicly declaring that his policemen were being put at risk by a television programme. Nothing happened. The Chief Constable, who invited Lady Plowden to lunch at his Belfast Headquarters, complained to the IBA that the programme was 'seriously lacking in balance'. (Whose fault was that?) The Northern Ireland Office issued an unprecedented personal attack on the reporter who had 'produced three programmes in quick succession which have concentrated on presenting the blackest possible picture of events in Northern Ireland', pointing out that 'after the last programme a prison officer was murdered'. Roy Mason accused the programme of being 'riddled with unsubstantiated conclusions' and being 'irresponsible and insensitive'. (Privately, senior legal figures welcomed the programme. They believed it to be accurate and welcome.) Letters of 'stern and strict' complaint were dispatched to the IBA and Thames Television, accusing 'This Week' of 'consistently knocking the security forces in Northern Ireland'. A showdown was in the air. It came eight months later – a period in which 'This Week's' producer David Elstein was told to 'lay off Northern Ireland' – in the form of the Amnesty Report.

Amnesty International had sent a mission to Belfast to examine the allegations of ill-treatment a week after 'This Week's' Castlereagh investigation. The government and RUC announced their intention to give the delegates every assistance, whilst refusing to discuss individual cases. Amnesty was given the facilities 'This Week' was denied. Few could argue that their report would be unbalanced or one-sided. In the event, the Amnesty Report was a devastating document. 'Maltreatment,' it concluded, 'has taken place with sufficient frequency to warrant a public inquiry to investigate it.'[6]

The Report was widely leaked ten days before publication. National newspapers reported its contents and the BBC's 'Tonight' programme quoted extensively from it. In the light of the leaks, 'This Week' planned a programme to discuss the Report through interviews with the usual Northern Ireland cross-section of people – mainly politicians – each of whom had read a copy of the report with which we had provided them. Over half the interviewees were well known for their staunch support of the RUC. The IBA banned the programme. There was no appeal. The decision was clear-cut. By chance, the eleven members who constituted the Authority had met that morning and reached a decision, it was argued, which it was impossible to countermand. On what legal grounds the decision was made was not, and still has not been, made clear. The Authority declared that it would be premature to discuss a report 'until it is public, thereby giving those involved and the general public a chance to study it in detail'. As Enoch Powell commented when told on his arrival at the studio that the programme had been banned: 'If we did not talk about what was premature, we would not talk about very much!'

There was no invocation of sections of the Broadcasting Act, as in the case of 'In Friendship and Forgiveness'; no discussion of amendments or compromises that might make it more acceptable as in 'Inhuman and Degrading Treatment'. The fact that the government had issued a ten-page reply to an unpublished report a matter of hours before the planned transmission of the programme, cut no ice with the Authority. The ban was an act of political censorship pure and simple: the pressures which had mounted over the past year at last had the desired effect. The IBA proved unable, perhaps unwilling, to resist them.

REFERENCES

1. Philip Schlesinger, *Putting 'reality' together: BBC News* (Constable, 1978) ch. 8.
2. Philip Elliott, 'Ethnicity and the media', Essay on Reporting Northern Ireland (UNESCO, 1978).
3. Richard Francis, in a lecture at the Royal Institute of International Affairs, February 1977.
4. Frank Kitson, *Bunch of five* (Faber, 1977) ch. 23.
5. *The Times*, 22 March 1977.
6. Amnesty Report (Amnesty International, 1978) p. 68.

CHAPTER FOUR

The publication of the Crossman *Diaries*

Introduction

The battle over publication of the Crossman *Diaries,* the *Sunday Times* and the publishers on one side, the Secretary to the Cabinet and the Attorney-General on the other, challenged the traditional British ethos of government secrecy. It had been Crossman's deliberate intention to do so; in writing the *Diaries,* he had set out to challenge oligarchical political power. And while the case ended in an apparent victory for the advocates of disclosure, the Attorney-General, declining to appeal, declared himself satisfied that a major issue of principle had been decided in his favour. Cabinet confidentiality had, for the first time, been established on a legal footing.

Keith Middlemas, the academic who advised the *Sunday Times* on the presentation of their case in the Crossman *Diaries* case, discusses the historical background to the judgement and concludes that the habit of secrecy is an analogue of Britain's political and social values.

Cabinet secrecy and the Crossman *Diaries**

KEITH MIDDLEMAS

The Lord Chief Justice's judgement and the decision of the Attorney-General not to appeal in the case of the Crossman *Diaries* do not mark the end of the running battle between governments and ministers or ex-ministers over the revelation of Cabinet proceedings. In the narrow interpretation given to the issues raised during the trial, several difficult questions were ignored; and the implications of what was decided suggest that Times Newspapers and the publishers may have won a victory, but that the Attorney-General has at least not lost his campaign. It is certainly ironical that Richard Crossman, by his headlong and deliberately reckless assault on the conventions surrounding Cabinet secrecy, should have helped to reinforce them by a wide and far-reaching interpretation of the law.

Historians and political scientists have a natural interest in the progressive unravelling of the procedures of central government, and while the former may be happy to have the time restrictions periodically reduced – as in 1967 the fifty-year ban on public access to Cabinet and departmental papers was cut to thirty years – students of politics find it harder to state when the line between necessary secrecy and open government should be drawn. The Crossman case, however, raised questions not only of when, but of what should be revealed; and, contrary to expectations in Whitehall, the result will probably be of greater importance than the report of Lord Radcliffe's Committee of Privy Councillors. In the light of the decision, and of the Lord Chief Justice's judgement that it is for the courts to decide where the public interest lies, it no longer signifies so greatly what guidelines are given to ministers on appointment: the testing area has shifted away from the Cabinet Office. [. . .]

The post-war period

For the post-war period, Cabinet Office procedural documents are not available, but on the evidence of ministerial statements, correspondence, and memoirs, it seems that the conventions of 1934 were

*From *Political Quarterly,* Vol. 47, 1976, pp. 39, 45–51.

not greatly changed. Authority for approval of publication was still vested in the PM and was delegated for convenience to the Cabinet Secretary; the only legal sanction in cases of evasion was the Official Secrets Act, since the argument of public interest could only be applied where manuscripts had already been submitted for approval; the category of war memoirs was for the second time partially exempted; a clear distinction was made between the right to publish of civil servants and of ministers; and a certain right of equity still obtained for ministers to set the record straight in regard to their own acts and careers. Churchill's war memoirs contained many exemptions from the rules, but they had been, as he acknowledged, allowed by the authorities: others, such as Lord Birkenhead's life of Lord Cherwell, slipped through the net. Generally, the rules were given strong support by politicians, notably by Attlee, in a public correspondence with Aneurin Bevan in 1952 following the latter's resignation.[1] But Bevan's criticism that collective responsibility could not last beyond the life of one government, won a degree of sympathy from historians, if not from constitutional lawyers.

Civil servants such as Hankey and Tom Jones suffered severely from these inhibitions (Jones's *Whitehall Diary*, ending in 1931, was not permitted until 1969). They were only seriously challenged in the early 1960s by Hugh Dalton, whose third volume of memoirs *High Tide and After* with its detailed instances of Cabinet discussions, ministers' private conversations, and talks with civil servants, was probably closest in style and content to Richard Crossman's diaries. Surprisingly, its frankness was not challenged by the Cabinet Office either at the time, or when Dalton's diaries reappeared in the 1973 biographies of Morrison and Bevan; nor were the lesser indiscretions of Attlee himself (*A Prime Minister Remembers*), Reginald Bevins, Anthony Nutting, or Walter Monckton.

A new trend emerged in the later 1960s, which may have caused the officials some worry. Ministers and senior officials began to give verbally the substance of Cabinet secrets, while avoiding open responsibility. Books such as Peter Jenkins' *The Battle of Downing Street* (1970) and especially *Denis Healey and the Policies of Power*, contained information which could only have been provided from the very top. None of them, however, provided a sufficient cause for action until Crossman deliberately provoked it.

Convention had by this time modified the original formal element to the point that the Cabinet Secretary, with reference to the PM, exercised complete control; and that control had effectively brought Cabinet ministers into line with civil servants. Ministerial discussions and confidential exchanges with civil servants, however, were still ranked in a lower category of secrecy; and some form of licensed evasion was tacitly recognized by both Cabinet Office and ministers – a grey area where a claim to rebut public attacks could be made.

This compromise was what Crossman challenged, on grounds of hypocrisy as much as public benefit. It had inherent weaknesses, quite apart from the root assumption that ministers would behave according to the gentlemanly code, and exercise tact and discretion. While it might cope in a reasonably civilized way with politicians' propensity to leak, and at the same time, by carefully filtered leakages, meet the increasing demands of journalists and public for information, it tended, by preventing full disclosure of government proceedings and policy-making, to prevent proper analysis, and encourage a trivial, personalized view of political activity. Secondly, it prevented the induction of MPs, as future ministers, into the real functions of high office, so that their first months (or year in the case of Crossman himself) in office might be spent in a powerless apprenticeship. Finally, quite apart from failing to keep pace with more open government in other countries, such as the United States, the conventions allowed no clear framework for debate about the nature and value of secrecy itself; and as the Crossman case was to show, the original constitutional formalities had been so modified that it was by no means certain what body of law, if any, sustained them.

It would have been surprising if the Attorney-General had not sought his injunction, even if Crossman had been alive. The conventions had been flouted both by the *Sunday Times* serialization and the proposed publication. But in 1975 the Official Secrets Act no longer served, partly because of the Home Secretary's pledge to amend Section 2, partly because of a change in public opinion and the courts since the days of Lansbury. In any case, the *Diaries* scarcely came under Section 2, and to use the Act would have meant waiting for publication to take place. To have reverted to pre-1914 practice, however, and insist on the binding nature of the Privy Councillor's oath, would have been to expose the Crown to some degree of political argument and, in the future, to an inordinate amount of paperwork, virtually duplicating the efforts of the Cabinet Office.

During the preliminary hearing, and in the main trial in July, the Attorney-General instead held to the doctrine set out in Sir John Hunt's correspondence with Crossman's executors and the *Sunday Times*, that the Crossman *Diary* contravened three principal categories (or parameters) of information which fell within Cabinet Office purview: A. Cabinet and Cabinet Committee discussions or papers; B. Discussion among ministers, and advice given to ministers by civil servants; C. Discussions of senior appointments in the civil service. It was stated that the submission of memoirs was a 'long-established rule', that 'it was the practice to warn ministers on taking office of their obligations'; and that ministers were personally free to publish their own versions of events, subject to clearance by the Cabinet Secretary.

Not all of this was in accordance with the development of the conventions; even if one excepts the inclusion of parameters B and C on a par with A, they represented, according to Lord Goodman, a tightening up on the procedure current in the 1960s. However, the prosecution case went further: in Sir John's words, 'the principle (of collective responsibility) necessarily imposes limits on what former ministers are free to publish. These limits do not spring primarily from the operation of the Official Secrets Act. Initially they arise from the requirements of good government, and the proper functioning of the public service, that Cabinet discussions and the formulations and execution of government policies should be conducted with complete candour, with ministers being able to rely on the mutual trust upon which their collective responsibility depends and with ministers and senior civil servants being able to communicate together frankly and freely, confident that when a minister leaves office the information and advice which he receives in office which was of a confidential nature will not be disclosed without proper authority.[2]

Here was the crux of the whole debate about secrecy; and despite all the arguments adduced in court, the issue came down first to the words, 'of a confidential nature', and second to the proposition that the Cabinet Office were the proper judges, in scope and time, of what was harmful to the public interest, or what had become of 'only historical interest'. The defence contested both these positions; and the assumption that it was for the court to decide. They therefore had no choice but to deny the existence of what the Attorney-General called 'a public right in the public interest' – although they accepted, without reserve, the need for some unspecified period of restraint. They attempted to widen the argument by defending the right of ministers to defend their actions in public, according to their own judgement: and by adducing another 'public right', in the free debate about policy and the criticism (chiefly by the press) of governmental and ministerial actions characteristic of a mature democracy.

Generally, the Attorney-General sought to narrow the issues: by insisting on his function, on behalf of the Crown, to guard the public interest, he almost abandoned the old 'constitutional' position, and concentrated on the conventions, above all on the doctrine of confidentiality. The public interest, he said, required that certain documents and information should not be disclosed, even in litigation between individuals, and a line of argument was traced beginning with Prince Albert *v.* Strange in 1849, continuing through various commercial cases, including Attorney-General *v.* Times Newspapers (the thalidomide case), and Reg. *v.* Lewes Justices (1973), and culminating in the strange case of Argyll *v.* Argyll (1967) – where the court granted the Duchess of Argyll an injunction restraining the Duke from publishing secrets relating to her private life and conduct.

On the legal issue, the defence contested that it was proper only to proceed by statute, since conventions, even of collective responsibility and confidentiality, had no force in law. As Professor Wade argued, the whole essence of a convention was that it was regarded as binding for non-legal reasons, so that if it were broken there were no legal sanctions. The cases cited by the Crown were not analogous, and as for Argyll, the defence argued, the judge, Mr Justice Ungoed-Thomas, had taken a great leap into the unknown by extending a limited doctrine to private and personal affairs – which was in itself no justification for applying his judgement to public matters.

The judgement and after

The Lord Chief Justice laid aside any revision of Argyll *v.* Argyll for the Appeal Court, if necessary, and accepted fully that, as it stood, it applied to Cabinet secrecy. 'The court must have power to deal with publication which threatens national secrecy, and the difference between such a case and the present is one of degree rather than kind. I conclude, therefore, that when a Cabinet minister receives information in confidence, the improper publication of such information can be restrained by the court. . . .' Of course, the court had to be satisfied that the public interest was indeed at stake, and should intervene only in the clearest of cases: since the LCJ found that the *Diary* did not endanger the public interest, after a lapse of ten years, it might be published. But, since the Attorney-General stated, when declining to appeal, his satisfaction that 'the major issue of principle' had been decided in his favour, the implications of the judgement merit further analysis.

Several points of substance were still unresolved. Lord Widgery restricted his ruling on the general issue of whether parameters B and C fell within the orbit of the public interest only to the Crossman *Diaries*. The question of the publication of discussions about the promotion of senior civil servants, and the advice which they give ministers, while being *prima facie* confidential matters, will presumably need to be considered by the Radcliffe Committee. Equally, it is not certain whether the new definition of power of the courts supersedes or is added to the functions performed by the Cabinet Secretary under existing conventions. A new document will pre-

sumably have to be drafted for ministers to read on their appointment – and it may well test the abilities of the Treasury Solicitor.
Again, the trial produced some confusion between the rights of
ministers, which have no time limits, and the right of the public to
access, which at present stands at thirty years.

More seriously, it is by no means certain what would be the
Attorney-General's criteria in a future case – say with volumes 2 and
3 of the *Diaries*. Under the old system, the Cabinet Secretary could
refer to precedents and to conventions with a certain logic. In this
first case, Mr Silkin took a very high line; but we know from the past
that Attorneys have at times been swayed by political motives.
(Apropos of a possible prosecution, after a Cabinet leak in 1926, the
then Attorney-General wrote to Hankey: 'I do not regard the *Daily
Telegraph* as in the same category as the other paper [the *Daily
Express,* which had been prosecuted earlier in the year]. I doubt
very much if it would be politic to embark on a criminal prosecution
of the *Daily Telegraph*.'[3]) Moreover, one may ask whether the right
of prosecution is limited to the Attorney-General – or may we see a
series of Raymond Blackburns conducting private prosecutions of
books of which they disapprove? Finally, while in no way suggesting
that the judiciary is not competent to rule in individual cases, it is
fair to say that judges differ greatly; that they inhabit a world some
distance from government and its preoccupations; and that such
cases, in the nature of political change, are unlikely to form suitable
ground for precedent.

On the credit side – and forgetting the longueurs, spleen, and
misunderstanding of the role of the civil service only too evident in
the 620 pages of Crossman's first volume – there is an enormous
gain. For the first time in the post-war years, we have a broad and
yet intricate picture of modern Cabinet government, impressive as
much for its accumulation of detail as for its critique of the political
process. During a vital time in the 1960s, when a relatively un-
broken period of harmony and qualified prosperity came to an end,
there is now considerable evidence of how policy was made, and in
response to what interests, stimuli, or arguments. An overall analysis must wait for the archives to be opened, but this permits
something more satisfactory than polemic – a means to test existing
accounts of the 1964–9 government, and an answer to the fashion-
ably trivial presentation of day-to-day political activity. In that
sense, the deficiencies of the conventional system, mentioned
above, can be partially remedied. No future minister need suffer
Crossman's disillusionment in his first year of office, nor learn the
hard way the virtues as well as the vices of the civil service.

But beyond this particular case, the new power of the courts may
prove a double-edged weapon. It is possible that judges may use it

further to limit the power of governments, so that future Attorneys-General will appeal to the law on confidentiality only with trepidation. Past experience, however, suggests otherwise. In indirect ways the power of government has certainly been increased. Contravention of the Official Secrets Act was a criminal offence, and it seems from earlier cases that governments in the past were reluctant to put ministers in the dock. (Apart from the Lansbury case, the sanction has only been threatened – *vide* Lloyd George's use of a 1921 Cabinet Paper, in the House of Commons, in December 1932.⁴) Paradoxically, since confidentiality is a civil action, prosecutions could multiply.

Secondly, an economic sanction has been introduced. Ex-ministers may dare to reveal more than before. But will their publishers? The Crossman case cost £70,000 – a sum which the joint publishers could never have found if the *Sunday Times* had not carried the brunt. In a routine case, as will be normal in the future, it is highly unlikely that the defendants will be as lucky, and win costs, even if they win judgement. Publishers' margins are desperately narrow, and few books of memoirs, unless remarkably sensational, would carry the costs of a five-day hearing. Publishers, therefore, will be cautious, whatever the autobiographer says, and go through the hoops, Cabinet Office and all, to avoid a possible prosecution. In this sense, the old censorship may be enhanced.

Finally, reverting to Sir John Hunt's parameters, there is a distinct danger that the scope of secrecy may be widened by the conflation of ministerial discussions and civil service advice with Cabinet matters. However necessary it may be to protect civil servants, at least in the short term, their interest is materially different from that of the Cabinet, as Lord Armstrong argued in his lecture to the British Academy in June 1970. For half a century after 1916, the conventions rested on a very simple assessment of what was, or was not, Cabinet and Cabinet Committee business. If this is now to be abandoned in favour of a vague category of 'governmental business', then Lord Radcliffe's Committee will have serious problems of definition, to forestall a rising tide of 'secret' and exempted categories.

Lord Widgery's judgement, far from settling the case, raises issues which almost certainly require legislation. Five years elapsed after Taff Vale, before the Trade Disputes Act of 1906; in a less complicated field, two or three may be enough for the present government. A Bill should also cover the access of the public, to meet modern conditions, preferably with a new limit of ten to fifteen years, with the usual reservations for files held back in the interest of national security. This should keep the historians quiet for a generation; and political scientists will be able to reflect not only on a mass of reasonably modern evidence but on the habit of secrecy itself as an analogue of Britain's social and political values.

REFERENCES

1. cf. *The Times*, 20–26 August 1952.
2. Sir John Hunt's affidavit, pp. 3 and 18.
3. CAB 21/443.
4. CAB 63/45. Memo of 15 December 1932 from Hankey.

PART FOUR

Stagnation?

The Thatcher style of government*

HUGO YOUNG

With the arrival in power of Mrs Margaret Thatcher's administration in May 1979, both the theory and the practice of secrecy in government took a new turn. In the run-up to the election, and in the Conservative election manifesto, no pretence was made that the party, if elected, would attach any importance to greater 'openness'. This was in contrast to the ritual utterances made by both main parties during the previous ten years. Little fundamentally changed in those years. But the air was heavy with rhetoric and promises. Even the Conservative Party, captivated by the reformist spirit of the sixties, lent itself to the belief that somewhat more open government – along with numerous other structural changes in Whitehall and Westminster – would lead to better government. Under Mrs Thatcher, the prevailing philosophy did not even admit of this as a modish platitude. Like most other presumptions of the Wilson–Heath–Callaghan era, open government started out thoroughly suspect in the eyes of all good Thatcherites.

In theory, therefore, the new Conservative government foreshadowed a new ice age, as far as information was concerned. But in practice things turned out rather differently.

If by 'openness' one means a conscious, systematic policy of exposing more governmental decisions to public knowledge at a time when public opinion can still be brought to bear on their outcome, then Mrs Thatcher and her ministers were and are adamantly opposed to greater openness. Still less have any of those who are sympathetic to it produced a convincing theory to justify it. All, moreover, are by temperament and history even more opposed to the informal processes – leaks, gossip and the like – by which openness is sometimes brought about *de facto* in a system which rigorously denies it *de jure*. Labour politicians are temperamentally different. Several of them, one suspects, enter office at least partly because they want to write about it when they leave. Conservative politicians tend to be uninterested in communication as a good in itself. Combined with the natural preference for secrecy among

---

*Paper prepared especially for this volume. Hugo Young is Political Editor of the *Sunday Times*.

almost all civil servants, this was always likely to ensure that openness, under a new Tory government, would be at a premium.

And this, in fact, duly became apparent. One of the most explicit manifestations of greater openness under the Labour government, however grudgingly granted, was the so-called Croham memorandum. In this Lord Croham, then Sir Douglas Allen and head of the civil service, composed guidelines for a Whitehall information policy, which authorized departments to give more information when asked and to initiate the publication of rather more documents. The memorandum was not quite what it seemed: not so much a charter for openness as an urgent attempt by the senior civil service to head off the Freedom of Information Act which Labour had talked about often in opposition, and which, if enacted on the American model, would have radically altered the balance of power inside the British political system. Minor though its effects were, however, the Croham memorandum fell quickly into disuse in 1979. No doubt this was partly the fault of the media which, with one honourable exception (*The Times*), stopped making use of the opportunities it provided to extract material from departments. Much more important was the fact that Conservatives, almost as a political type, attach little importance to the creation of a genuinely well informed electorate.

This propensity can be seen at its most extreme in the Prime Minister herself. For all her radicalism in other directions, Mrs Thatcher is a traditionalist as far as the process of government is concerned. On the whole she prefers decisions to be handed down from above, rather than rise up from below. Official information, in her judgement, is better seen as the property of the government than as ammunition for its critics, and should be dispensed only after critical decisions have been taken. Even within the government, the style of decision-making reflects this prejudice. Like many Prime Ministers Mrs Thatcher would like to stifle Cabinet argument and debate. Unlike most of her predecessors she has succeeded in doing so. This has been achieved by the simple expedient of ruthlessly organizing Cabinet business so as to minimize both the occasions for argument and the information with which argument is conducted. Well-known antagonists in the Cabinet are kept apart rather than let loose upon each other. The decline of the Cabinet has been accompanied by the rise of the Cabinet Committee to heights not reached before. Although the Cabinet Committee network remains one of Whitehall's better kept secrets, there are ministers who testify privately that no government has placed such dependence on it. The merit of this, of course, is that from the Prime Minister's point of view it greatly strengthens the hand of 10 Downing Street, where the membership, agenda and meeting-times of the Committees are set. The further merit is that open debate can be strictly curtailed. Nor is this visible merely in the most obvious field of economic policy, where for the first two years of the Thatcher government's life, decisions were effectively confined to half-a-dozen ministers. It can be seen at work in industrial-relations policy, energy policy and aspects of foreign policy – where differences within the Cabinet have been neutralized by the remarkably effective practice of acting as though they did not exist.

A further practice peculiar to this government is also revealing. All recent Prime Ministers – Harold Wilson, Edward Heath, Jim Callaghan – have been to a greater or lesser extent obsessed with the media and its management. Harold Wilson may be an extreme case: he became mesmerized not merely by the press he was getting but by such technicalities as edition-times and the length of television news bulletins. Mr Heath, towards the end of his time as Prime Minister, became quite outraged by the scurvy and uncomprehending treatment which, as he saw it, he got from the media. All this, while not evidence of an interest in more open government as such, at least showed that these Prime Ministers were deeply concerned by information policy and practice. It is both the strength and the weakness of Mrs Thatcher that she is not. To be as easily deflected from a course of action as Harold Wilson could be by the sight of yesterday's headlines cannot be good for government. To be as ready as Mr Heath was to blame the press for the failures of British industry is, likewise, not the stuff of strong government. But equally, to be as indifferent as Mrs Thatcher sometimes seems to be to the state of public knowledge is hardly likely to lead to the reduction of secrecy. On the whole, Mrs Thatcher would like openness to be as limited inside government as outside.

The real picture, however, is considerably less bleak than these theories and priorities suggest it ought to be. The theory of secrecy remains intact, but the practice of secrecy has suffered several blows, with dramatic effect. It is no exaggeration to say that we probably know more about how the country is governed under this government than under any previous Conservative administration.

The first forum where this is visible is Parliament. Once the House of Commons voted to appoint Select Committees to shadow the Whitehall departments, a whole edifice of lore and custom reached the point of collapse. These Select Committees are a specifically Tory creation, which came about without the Prime Minister's support but which, once in place, will be impossible to shift. They are, in fact, an enduring memorial to the name of the first Cabinet minister she sacked, Mr Norman St John Stevas. He had favoured such bodies for a long time. When he was made leader of the House of Commons, he saw his opportunity. Only a handful of the Cabinet were enthusiastic, and the Prime Minister was actually against him. But the decision proved to be a classic instance of how a tactically astute minister can sometimes smuggle a policy past Cabinet, provided his colleagues are sufficiently preoccupied by other matters. So it was with the new Select Committees. And, while civil servants are finding ways to avoid direct answers to awkward questions, there can be no doubt that the system now offers a legitimate and powerful channel by which secrecy can, if MPs are determined enough, be broken down. As far as openness is concerned, in fact, they raise new and quite different problems from those posed by taciturn ministers and officials. First, will MPs actually care enough to seize these opportunities and put them to maximum effect? Secondly, what will the media do? Newspapers are accustomed to a regime where information is scarce, and find no difficulty in erecting into news of sensational importance the discovery of one possibly minor fact which acquires interest out of all proportion to its weight simply by virtue of being secret. What newspapers and television are not good at is making real discoveries, and a proper contribution to public enlightenment, out of material published in massive quantities by Her Majesty's Stationery Office.

The second development is accidental but, in particular, of considerable relevance. It is that the very exclusion of debate inside the government tends to have precisely the opposite effect from the one the Prime Minister and others are seeking to achieve. Denied an opportunity to contribute centrally inside Cabinet, ministers resort to more public representations, which in turn often reveal significant detail about the state of an argument and the imminence of a policy decision. Whether through frustration or subtle calculation or an appetite for sheer mischief-making, the Thatcher government contains more ministers prepared to undercut their colleagues than any Tory administration in living memory. This means that the terms of a proposed decision, and the alternative options, may become clear long before the decision is taken. Leaks, of information and even documents, have become far commoner: a process which has been accelerated as much by dissident civil servants as by politicians, but which is all part of a climate induced by the Thatcher style of governing. Government is no longer monolithic, and nobody even pretends it is. Open disagreements openly arrived at are one way towards a kind of open government.

At the apex of these disagreements sits the Prime Minister herself. By an apt irony she is as much an emblem of this method of breaking secrecy down as she is an upholder of the virtues of keeping secrecy tight. It is largely due to her public utterances that the world knows of her disagreements with, for example, Mr James

Prior, her [then] employment secretary. It was because of her public performance over the re-negotiation of the European Community budget in 1980 that few secrets remained about the British negotiating position, or about the different tactical views taken by the Foreign Office and 10 Downing Street. This may not be so pleasing to reformers as would be a Freedom of Information Act. But if we are talking within the realm of practical politics, we can perhaps take some comfort from the fact that Mrs Thatcher is against open government – but is, by British standards, one of its more notable practitioners.

Index